SRA Imagine It!

Language Arts Handbook

Level 4

McGraw Hill **SRA**

Columbus, OH

Grade 4 Imagine It! Acknowledgements Language Arts Handbook

Grateful acknowledgement is given to the following publishers and copyright owners for permissions granted to reprint selections from their publications. All possible care has been taken to trace ownership and secure permission for each selection included. In case of any errors or omissions, the Publisher will be pleased to make suitable acknowledgements in future editions.

"Mrs. Frisby and the Crow" reprinted with the permission of Atheneum Books for Young Readers, an imprint of Simon & Schuster Children's Publishing Division from MRS. FRISBY AND THE RATS OF NIMH by Robert C. O'Brien. Copyright © 1971 Robert C. O'Brien; copyright renewed 1999 Christopher Conly, Jane Leslie Conly, Kate Conly and Sarah Conly.

Maxine Kumin, "The Microscope." from THE WONDERFUL BABIES OF 1809 (AND OTHER YEARS) G.P. Putnam, 1968. Copyright © 1968 by Maxine Kumin. Reprinted by permission of the author.

Carol Saller: The Bridge Dancers, by Carol Saller, text copyright 1991 by the author.

From LOUIS BRAILLE: THE BOY WHO INVENTED BOOKS FOR THE BLIND by Margaret Davidson. Copyright © 1971 by Margaret Davidson. Reprinted by permission of Scholastic Inc.

MAE JEMISON, SPACE SCIENTIST by Gail Sakurai. © 1995 BY Children's Press, Inc. All rights reserved. Reprinted by permission of Children's Press an imprint of Scholastic Library Publishing, Inc.

From Carole Charles' "Martha Helps the Rebel" © 1975 by The Child's World Inc./www.childsworld.com. Reprinted with permission of copyright holder.

Reprinted with permission of Atheneum Books for Young Readers, an imprint of Simon & Schuster Children's Publishing Division from EDDIE, INCORPORATED by Phyllis Reynolds Naylor. Copyright © 1980 Phyllis Reynolds Naylor.

"The Acrobats," from HOP, SKIP AND JUMP! By Dorothy Aldis, copyright 1934, renewed © 1961 by Dorothy Aldis. Used by permission of G.P. Putnam's Sons, A Division of Penguin Young Readers Group, A Member of Penguin Group (USA) Inc., 345 Hudson Street, New York NY 10014. All rights reserved.

"The Germ" from VERSES FROM 1929 by Ogden Nash. Copyright © 1933 by Ogden Nash, renewed. Reprinted by permission of Curtis Brown, Ltd.

"Escape" From CHARLOTTE'S WEB by E.B. WHITE. Copyright 1952 by E.B. White. Text copyright renewed 1980 by E.B. White. Used by permission of HarperCollins Publishers.

THE BIG WAVE by Pearl Buck COPYRIGHT © 1947 BY THE CURTIS PUBLISHING COMPANY; COPYRIGHT © 1948, 1976 BY PEARL S. BUCK. Used by permission of HarperCollins Publishers.

"Lemonade Stand" reprinted with the permission of Margaret K. McElderry Books, an imprint of Simon & Schuster Children's Publishing Division from WORLDS I KNOW AND OTHER POEMS by Myra Cohn Livingston. Text copyright © 1985 Myra Cohn Livingston. From WORLDS I KNOW AND OTHER POEMS by Myra Cohn Livingston. Copyright © 1985 by Myra Cohn Livingston. Used by permission of Marian Reiner.

ONE TV BLASTING AND A PIG OUTDOORS by Deborah Abbott and Henry Kisor. Text copyright © 1994 by Deborah Abbot and Henry Kisor. Excerpt reprinted by permission of Albert Whitman & Company.

"The Early Houses" from THE PILGRIMS OF PLYMOUTH by Barbara Beck. Copyright © 1972 by Barbara Beck. All rights reserved. Reprinted by permission of Franklin Watts an imprint of Scholastic Library Publishing, Inc.

SRAonline.com

Send all inquiries to this address:
SRA/McGraw-Hill
4400 Easton Commons
Columbus, OH 43219-6188

ISBN: 978-0-07-610992-0
MHID: 0-07-610992-5

3 4 5 6 7 8 9 RRC 13 12 11 10 09 08

Table of Contents

You Are a Writer

A Talent or a Skill?

Do you think writing takes talent or skill? Many people believe that only a few lucky ones have a talent for writing. They think good writers were born knowing how to write well.

Actually, writing is not a matter of talent. Writing is a skill. The more you practice writing, the better you will become at it. This book will help you understand who writers are and how they write. You will learn that you are a writer too!

Who Is a Writer?

Everyone is a writer, including you. Writers write many things, from letters and lists to reports and journals. Here are some things writers write:

▶ a letter to the director of a zoo requesting information on snakes
▶ a memo to members of the student council about a car wash to raise money for school supplies
▶ a report on classical music
▶ a list of things to do after school
▶ a story that takes place in a make-believe world

Many things you have written make you a writer. You may have written a note to a friend. At school, you may have written your ideas and have shared them with others. At home, you may have written a funny story to entertain a younger sister or brother. All of these things and more make you a writer.

What Do Writers Do?

Writers have power. They can change lives. For example, the writers of the Declaration of Independence helped change the course of history in the United States and England. Writers can persuade others to do things.

Writers also give information about many topics. They explain how to do things and how to fix problems. They entertain readers. They keep businesses running smoothly. You can make a difference with your writing.

Developing Your Skill as a Writer

Any practice in writing helps develop your skill as a writer. Writing e-mail messages to your friends that are clear and organized is good practice. Organizing information and writing good notes for reports for science, social studies, and other classes help, too. Writing in a journal or a diary every day is excellent practice, even if no one reads it but you.

This handbook will help you gain more skill as a writer. You will learn about and follow the stages in the writing process. Following the stages in the writing process will help you get from your first fuzzy idea to a finished piece of writing that will make you proud. Let's get started!

The Traits of Good Writing

Can you remember getting absorbed in a story? A writer who creates a story like that knows what the traits of good writing are. The traits are things in writing, such as word choice and ideas, that affect how the piece sounds and reads. These traits make writing enjoyable and even exciting to read. Here they are. Learn them and make them a part of your writing.

Organization

Writing that is well-organized

▶ has a structure, or pattern, such as time order, sequence of events, spatial order (on top, underneath), or order of importance, within each paragraph and in the entire composition

▶ uses signal words in sentences to help show how ideas and paragraphs are organized, such as *first, second, most important, before,* and *later*

▶ has a beginning that gives clues about what is to come and invites the audience to keep reading

▶ has ideas and paragraphs that flow smoothly from one to the other

Well-organized writing has a clear beginning, middle, and end. All the details relate closely to the main ideas and follow a specific order. For example, ideas in a paragraph can be organized by sequence. A paragraph organized this way would begin with the first thing that happens. The middle of the paragraph would tell what happens next. The last few sentences should tell what happens last. The paragraphs in your writing should follow a specific order, too. Each of the paragraphs should follow one another in a way that readers can follow easily.

Voice

Writing that has a strong voice
▶ is lively
▶ shows the personal touch of the writer
▶ shows that the writer is aware of his or her audience

Voice is the feeling that a real person is speaking to us through his or her writing. When a writer cares about his or her message, the voice is strong. A strong voice adds a personal touch to writing and encourages readers to care about the message, too.

Read the paragraph below. This paragraph, taken from the story "Elias Sifuentes, Restaurateur," vividly expresses Mr. Sifuentes' thoughts and mood.

> I used to work at a General Electric factory. I was a punch-press operator. I was making good money, but working there frustrated me because I like to work with people, talk to people. And there, there was nobody to talk to. The only time I got together with others was during lunch or during meetings. And I said to myself, "I like the money. I like the benefits. But this is not what I want to do all my life."

Mr. Sifuentes sounds like he is talking to the reader. The voice in this paragraph makes the reader care about what he has written.

Not all of your writing at school will allow you to express your personality in this way. Still, don't stand too far back from any topic you write. Allow your personality to color your writing.

Word Choice

Good writers choose the best words
▶ to make their ideas clear
▶ to provide accurate and colorful descriptions
▶ to help create a mood or scene

Good word choices are colorful and precise. They are fresh, not boring. To make good word choices, you do not have to have a huge vocabulary. Just think about what specific words mean. Choose words that mean exactly what you want to say.

This is another passage from the story "Elias Sifuentes, Restaurateur." Here Mr. Sifuentes talks about how he and his partner opened their first restaurant. Look at how Mr. Sifuentes talks about the hard times he and his partner experienced.

> We started from scratch. In the beginning, we didn't get a paycheck. The only money we got was to buy groceries. My partner was kind of *frustrated*. Whatever we were making was going to pay our bills.

Try It!

Carefully reread the passage above from "Elias Sifuentes, Restaurateur." Find the word *frustrated* in italics in the paragraph. Is this a good word choice? Why?

Sentence Fluency

Writing with sentences that flow well
▶ sounds pleasing to the ear
▶ is rhythmic

Sentence fluency means the sentences should sound good when you read your writing aloud. Writing that flows well also has some short, some medium, and some long sentences. Paragraphs with a variety of sentences add interest to writing.

As a young boy, Louis Braille knew about many people who tried to create books for the blind. Read this paragraph from Louis' story. Notice how the writer uses a variety of sentences.

Louis knew this was true. He knew that people had tried so many things—raised letters, lowered letters, letters of stone and letters of string, letters of wax and letters of wood. One man had even made an alphabet of pins. Louis tried to imagine how it would feel to read a page of pins. Ouch!

Conventions

The conventions of writing are
▶ spelling
▶ grammar
▶ punctuation
▶ capitalization
▶ usage

Good use of the conventions of writing makes whatever you write easy to understand. Spelling, grammar, punctuation, or capitalization mistakes distract readers from your writing.

Read this paragraph from "Whales: Songs from the Deep." Look at the author's use of capitalization and punctuation. Imagine how difficult it would be to read this paragraph if it were filled with mistakes.

The Paynes couldn't believe what they were hearing. If the tape proved the songs of the whales near Hawaii were the same as those of the Baja California whales, then their theory that whales don't sing during migration would be completely discredited. Whales must sing while migrating or other whales couldn't hear the songs and learn them.

Presentation

The way writing looks on a page is important. This is called **presentation.** It is the readers' first impression of your work. Your work should be neatly typed or handwritten. The format of the writing and illustrations should be appealing to the eye.

FUN FACT

Like humans, whales use sounds to communicate. You can read more about whales and how they communicate in *Animal Communication* by Jacci Cole.

Reading Your Writing

Writing that has these traits is clearer and more interesting than writing that does not. As you write, think about your ideas, organization, voice, word choice, sentence fluency, use of conventions, and choice for presentation. By making sure these traits are a part of your writing, you will become a more effective communicator.

The Writing Process

Writing is a process that is done in stages. Each stage is different and has its own characteristics. These stages are prewriting, drafting, revising, editing/proofreading, and publishing. You can go back and forth between the stages as often as you like until you are satisfied with what you have written. Using the writing process in this way will help you improve your writing.

The Writing Process

Let's say you are going to build a house. Would you begin by nailing boards together to make the walls and floors? No! Beginning this way would waste time and materials. Instead, you begin by drawing a plan. A plan helps you know how many boards you will need to build an entire house.

Some people start writing without a plan. They just put words together. In time, they might fill a page. However, they have not created a clear, interesting piece of writing. Without a plan, their words go in all directions.

Good writing, like building a house, starts with a plan. A good plan will help move you toward your goal: a piece of really good writing. The five stages of the writing process are prewriting, drafting, revising, editing and proofreading, and publishing. They will help you as you plan, write, and publish your writing.

Prewriting

Prewriting is the discovering and planning stage or phase. During this phase think about your writing task, your purpose, and your audience. Brainstorm topic ideas and choose one. Then brainstorm and organize ideas about your topic on paper. Write down your ideas and decide which ones you might use. Choose the ones that will support your topic and interest your audience. For example, if you write to persuade readers to do something, you should choose reasons that will most likely convince them. Organize your ideas in notes, lists, outlines, or graphic organizers. (A graphic organizer helps you see your ideas at a glance.) As you organize your ideas, think about the order in which you might present them. For example, you might choose to present your ideas in time order if you are writing a biography.

Drafting

Here's where you turn your ideas into sentences and paragraphs. During this phase, you write and write, following the plan you created in the prewriting step. You don't worry about punctuation or even spelling. You just keep writing. The goal is to get your ideas down in sentences and paragraphs. You will get a chance to make corrections later.

Revising

During this phase, you look for and fix problems. You might ask yourself and answer the following questions. Do too many sentences start the same way? Too many sentences that begin the same way are boring! Do you leave out important information? Make sure you include information your reader needs to know. Is your writing easy to follow? Look at how you organize your ideas in sentences and paragraphs. Do you use the best words to express your ideas? Take another look at the words you use to talk about your topic. Make sure they are clear and specific.

Editing/Proofreading

This is the time to check for errors in spelling, punctuation, capitalization, usage, and grammar. Correct misspelled words and sentences with incorrect punctuation. Make sure the first letter of all words that begin a sentence is a capital letter. Have a friend read your paper to help you look for problems with subject-verb agreement, irregular plurals, and other things in your writing that you may miss on your own.

Publishing

Share your best pieces of writing with others. During this final phase, you make your writing look good for public presentation. You might mail a letter you've written. You could bind the pages of your short story into a book. You might work with a group to act out a play you wrote together.

While it is best to follow the stages of the writing process in order, you may need to change the order based on your writing needs. For example, during the revising step, you might realize you need more information. You may need to go back and do some more prewriting to organize the new information and to figure out how it fits your topic. Using the writing process in this way can make planning, writing, and publishing your work easier.

Prewriting: How Do I Get Started?

Getting started is the hardest part. Some people think writers are able to just sit down with a blank sheet of paper and begin writing, starting with the first sentence. However, writers don't usually start that way. Most writers begin with the first stage in the writing process—prewriting.

During prewriting, you decide what you are going to write and how you are going to organize your ideas. Maybe you have already thought of a good writing topic. Maybe you have just half an idea. Either way, prewriting is the way to begin. Let's follow four fourth graders in Mr. Johnson's class—Kevin, David, Nazanin, and Rosa—as they begin to write.

Understanding Task, Audience, and Purpose

Task

Before you start, make sure you know what you are going to do. The task defines the type of writing you are going to do. Your task can be something you want to write on your own, such as a friendly letter to a relative. Sometimes a school assignment helps define your task.

For example, Mr. Johnson asked his fourth-grade class to write a research report on an endangered animal or an unusual animal kept as a pet. Kevin remembered reading an article in a magazine about manatees. He read that the manatee is an endangered species. Since Kevin's task—to write a research report —was already defined by the assignment, he just needed to choose a topic. Kevin decided to write a research report on manatees. He wrote his topic in his notebook.

Audience

The people who will read your writing are your audience. You need to know who your audience is before you begin to write. Think about what your audience needs to know about your topic. If your audience does not know much about your topic, you have to give them enough information and examples so that they can see the big picture. Often your task will help you figure out who your audience is. Sometimes you might have an audience in mind and choose a topic that interests them. Knowing your audience will help the organization and presentation of ideas in your writing. Keep your audience in mind as you write.

For example, Kevin's teacher would be his audience based on his task. He thought Mr. Johnson was pretty smart. However, Kevin did not know how much Mr. Johnson knew about manatees. So he decided to write his essay as if Mr. Johnson knew nothing about his topic. Writing his report that way, Kevin thought he'd be sure to include all the important facts.

Purpose

Choosing your purpose for writing is something that you should do before you begin to write. Your purpose tells why you are writing. Your purpose might be to inform, to persuade, to entertain, or to explain something to your audience. Most of the time, your task will make your purpose clear.

For example, Kevin decided that his purpose would be to inform his audience. Kevin's friends, David, Nazanin, and Rosa, had other ideas. David's report would be about bald eagles. He would write to persuade his audience that it was worth saving these birds from going extinct. Nazanin was writing about Florida panthers. She wanted to explain why there weren't many panthers left. Rosa wanted to write about ferrets. She wanted to write to persuade her audience not to keep ferrets as pets.

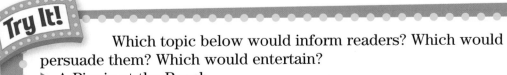

Try It!

Which topic below would inform readers? Which would persuade them? Which would entertain?
- ▶ A Picnic at the Beach
- ▶ How to Write a Report
- ▶ Why We Need to Stop Polluting Our Rivers

Organizing Ideas

You have chosen your topic. You sit and stare at your notes. You have plenty of ideas to start writing, but you don't know where to begin. You ask yourself, "Now what do I do?" Does this sound familiar? Before you begin writing, think about what you want to say about your topic. One way to help you think is to organize your ideas. You can organize your ideas using a **graphic organizer.** A graphic organizer is a type of diagram that helps a writer put his or her ideas in an order that makes sense.

There are different ways of organizing ideas. Some common ways of organizing ideas are time order, sequential order, spatial order, and order of importance. Specific types of graphic organizers go with specific ways of organizing ideas. Also, keep in mind your audience and purpose. Remembering these things will help you choose the graphic organizer that works best. Let's look at some examples from Mr. Johnson's fourth-grade class.

Using Time Order to Organize Ideas

Time order is also called **chronological order.** This means events are put in order starting with the earliest and ending with the most recent. Use time order to explain events in the order they happened in time. For example, you might use time order in an essay on the history of the space program. You could also use time order to tell an entertaining story about a person's life. Time order is often used to organize writing that informs or entertains readers.

David planned to write a paper that would persuade his audience. However, he wanted to present information about eagles to make his case more convincing. He drew a time line to help him organize his ideas.

Subject of Time Line: Eagles

1940	1950	1970	1990
1940-Eagles became an endangered species.	1950s-DDT used as a pesticide. It nearly wiped out the eagle population.	1972-DDT was not used as a pesticide anymore.	1999-Eagles were taken off the Endangered Species List.

Using Sequential Order to Organize Ideas

Sequential order is used to explain how to do something or when something occurs. When you put things in order by sequence, you begin with the first thing that happens. Then you list the next thing that happens. You list the final thing that happens last. You could use sequential order in instructions on how to play baseball. You could use it to explain how plants use sunshine to grow. Sequential order is usually used to organize writing that informs or explains something to readers.

Nazanin thought her readers needed to know something about how panthers are born and grow. She used a chain-of-events chart to help her organize her information in sequential order.

How Florida Panthers Grow

Female panther fixes den for the birth of her kittens.

Female panther gives birth to 1-4 kittens. They are born with dark spots. Their eyes are closed. Their mom feeds them.

After 10 days, the kittens open their eyes. Mom panther still takes care of her kittens.

In $1\frac{1}{2}$-2 years, the kittens are large enough to survive on their own.

Using Spatial Order to Organize Ideas

Use spatial order to describe a space or an object. The word *spatial* is from the word *space.* Using spatial order, you can organize your ideas from top to bottom or from left to right. Ordering your ideas from top to bottom works best when you are describing something that is vertical. For example, if you want to describe yourself to someone, think about how you look from head to toe! Start with a description of your face and end with a description of your feet. Your readers would be able to follow this easily—and know what you look like! Ordering your ideas from left to right works well if your purpose is to describe something to your audience that is horizontal. For example, you might describe the objects in your bedroom. Start describing the objects you see on the left side of the room. Turn your head slowly towards the right. As you turn your head, describe the things you see in the middle and then on the right side of the room.

Kevin decided to include a description of a manatee in his report. Since the manatee is long, Kevin thought that describing it from left to right, starting at its head, would be easiest. Here's Kevin's graphic organizer.

What a manatee looks like

Head	Middle	Tail
• big, round muzzle with whiskers • dark, round eyes–kind of small	• has two flippers • thick, round and long	• big, flat, and round

Using Order of Importance to Organize Ideas

Usually, when you organize your ideas by their order of importance, you put the most important information first. That way, your busy readers will be likely to see it. You might use this order to write a newspaper article.

However, if you are writing to persuade, build your case by putting the most important reason last. Your writing will be more convincing that way. Order of importance is usually used to organize writing that informs readers or persuades them to act or think a certain way.

Rosa decided to write about ferrets as pets. She thought people should think carefully before they get one. Rosa created this graphic organizer to organize her ideas.

Statement: Ferrets should not be kept as pets.

> Important reason
> They chew and destroy everything.

> Next important reason
> They are expensive to buy and keep.

> Most important reason
> They often run away and get lost.

Conclusion: Because they are more trouble than they're worth, ferrets do not make good pets.

Reading Your Writing

Prewriting takes time. However, it saves much more time than it takes. You must have a clear idea of where you're going before you start writing. Otherwise, you're likely to get lost!

Drafting: How Do I Begin to Write?

You have organized your ideas. Now it's time to turn them into real writing. This step is called **drafting.** Drafting means putting your ideas into sentences and paragraphs. The goal is to get all your thoughts down on paper. There is no such thing as a perfect draft. Don't worry about mistakes. You can fix them later.

Here are some tips to help you write your draft quickly.

▶ As you write, don't forget your purpose and your audience.

▶ If you are writing on paper, use only one side of the page. Then you will be able to spread out the pages and see all of your draft at the same time. Write on every other line to leave room for changes.

▶ If you can't think of a word, leave a space. You can add the word later.

▶ Cross out words instead of erasing them. Erasing takes too much time. It also interrupts your thinking. If you're using a computer, you can delete the word later.

▶ If you're not sure how to spell a word, you might write the first few letters of the word and leave room for the rest. You can look up the word in a dictionary later.

Here is part of Rosa's draft. She wrote about her first idea for her report on ferrets. Rosa thinks ferrets should not be kept as pets. Notice how she used the drafting tips.

> Ferrets do not make good pets. Ferrets can be very destr_____. They will chew your mother's plants. Ferrets will tear open plastic garbage bags and spread the mess all over everything.

Turning Your Ideas into Paragraphs

Although your goal is to get all your ideas on paper, your draft should be in sentences. Your sentences should be grouped into paragraphs. A way to figure out how to group sentences into paragraphs is to use your graphic organizer. As you are writing your draft, look at your graphic organizer to help you figure out where to begin a new paragraph. Also, use your graphic organizer to help you write the supporting details in your paragraphs as sentences.

Here's Rosa's graphic organizer again. She created this during the prewriting phase of the writing process. Remember that she is trying to convince readers not to keep ferrets as pets. Rosa put her ideas in order of importance. She decided that each box in her graphic organizer would be a paragraph.

Statement: Ferrets should not be kept as pets.

Important reason
 They chew and destroy everything.

↓

Next important reason
 They are expensive to buy and keep.

↓

Most important reason
 They often run away and get lost.

Conclusion: Because they are more trouble than they're worth, ferrets do not make good pets.

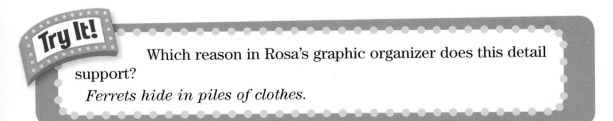

Try It!

Which reason in Rosa's graphic organizer does this detail support?

Ferrets hide in piles of clothes.

Here's the rest of Rosa's draft. She used the drafting tips so she could write quickly. She did not worry about spelling or other mistakes. She also used her graphic organizer to help her write her draft in sentences and paragraphs.

Ferrets do not make good pets. Ferrets can be very destr____. They will chew your mother's plants. Ferrets will tear open plastic garbage bags and spread the mess all over everything.

Ferrets are not cheap. They cost about $130 each. A cage can cost from $90 to $150 Ferrets can also be kept in a ferret-proof room. A yearly trip to the vet can be as much as $150. That includes ~~an examination~~ a checkup and shots.

It's easy to lose a ferrets It can ____ into openings that only are 2 in. wide. Ferrets can hide in cupboards cabinets and drawers. When you put clothes in your mashine, your ferret might be sleeping in the clothes. he could end up in the washer and drawn. You won't even know he is in their. You can never turn your back on a Ferret.

Ferrets are not good pets. They are too expansive. They cause too much trouble. They might be cute. Cuteness isn't everything. Dogs and cats are better. Don't you agree?

Since she had to write quickly, Rosa was glad that she organized her ideas into sentences and paragraphs before writing her draft. Rosa remembered to use topic sentences in her draft. Look at the topic sentences underlined in her draft. Her graphic organizer helped her come up with topic sentences easily for her paragraphs.

Try It!

Look at Rosa's draft. How might you write it differently?

Reading Your Writing

Drafting is the phase where you get everything down on paper. You turn your ideas into sentences and paragraphs. You will be amazed at how quickly your writing starts to take shape. Drafting is an important step in creating a piece of writing that will make you proud.

Revising: How Can I Improve My Writing?

Your first draft is probably not your best work. It's not supposed to be! Now is the time to improve it. The next phase is **revising.** During this phase, you will make changes to your writing to make it better. You might revise your writing by yourself, with a partner, or with a small group of your classmates.

The purpose of revising is to make sure you say exactly what you want to say in your writing. Read your draft—or have a partner read it—to see if your ideas are clear and complete. Check your draft to see if it matches your task, your audience, and your purpose. Look at the order of your paragraphs. Think about whether the way you have organized your ideas is the best way. Also, read each paragraph carefully and make sure all of them that need a topic sentence have one. Check to see if all the sentences in each paragraph are on the same topic. Pay attention to your use of different types of sentences, your choice of words, and how you express your ideas as you revise your paper.

The students in Mr. Johnson's class were ready to revise their papers. Mr. Johnson helped his students come up with questions they could use in a revising checklist. (You can read about a revising checklist on page 40.) Here are some of the questions.

Ideas
► Is my main idea clear and supported by details?
Organization
► Are my ideas well-organized?
Word Choice
► Do I use the best words to talk about my ideas?
Sentence Fluency
► Do I use a variety of sentences? Do they flow well?
Voice
► Does my interest or concern for my topic show in my writing?

Revising means making changes to improve your writing. Read on to learn what you can do to make a difference in your writing.

Keep Your Audience Reading

Readers stop reading for many different reasons. For example, they may give up if they become confused. In addition to adding variety to your writing by using different types of sentences, you may need to reorganize your ideas to make your writing clearer. Paying attention to your word choice and voice will also help make your writing sing! Here are four ways to help make the ideas in your writing clear.

Presenting Your Ideas in a Clear Order

During prewriting, if you used a graphic organizer to organize your ideas, then you will probably use it to write your draft. When you revise your draft, chances are you will make changes. For example, you might want to add new ideas to your paper. However, be sure these new ideas fit the type of organization you planned to use in your prewriting. You don't want to end up with good ideas presented in a mixed-up way. If you find your organization does not work with your new ideas, you may need to create another graphic organizer to reorganize your ideas.

Word Choice and Organization

Did you know certain words can help make the organization of your ideas clear to readers? **Signal words** can help show readers how your writing is organized. Here are some things signal words show.

▶ They show time and order: *first, second, next, later, tomorrow.*
▶ They show place and location: *overhead, across, behind, under, downward.*
▶ They show that more information is coming: *in addition, also.*
▶ They show that a conflicting idea is coming: *however, on the other hand, instead, but, although.*
▶ They show cause and effect: *because, so, therefore.*

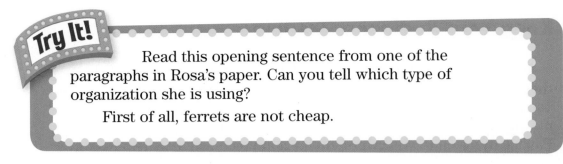

Try It!

Read this opening sentence from one of the paragraphs in Rosa's paper. Can you tell which type of organization she is using?

First of all, ferrets are not cheap.

Including Enough Details

To keep readers interested, include enough details so they can picture what you mean. You have several choices when it comes to adding details. Here are four of them.

▶ Add descriptions.
▶ Add specific examples.
▶ Add facts.
▶ Add definitions.

As Rosa read her draft for revision, she thought about how she might add more details to her report.

▶ **Add descriptions.** In her report, Rosa might describe a ferret so readers could picture this animal. She might compare a ferret to another animal.
▶ **Add specific examples.** Rosa's audience would probably like to read about places where her family's ferret hid.
▶ **Add facts.** Rosa might tell her audience how many ferrets are kept as pets. She might also explain how long ferrets live.
▶ **Add definitions.** Rosa might need to define any unfamiliar words to her readers.

Using the Right Words

If you are describing specific things or ideas, choose specific words instead of general ones. For example, use *collie* in place of *dog*. Use *chocolate pudding* instead of *dessert*. Use words that provide your readers with a clear and vivid picture of things and ideas in your writing.

The way you organize your ideas and choose your words helps the reader hear your voice in your writing. If your voice is strong and clear, your audience will pay attention to what you are expressing.

Peer Conferencing

Working with a partner (a peer) or with two or more people in a group can be very helpful during the writing process. It is especially valuable during the revision phase. After you work on a piece of writing for a while, it becomes difficult to see it clearly. It's hard to separate the words on the page from the words in your mind.

However, a partner can read your work with a fresh eye. Partners can find confusing words and sentences. They can ask questions to help you fill in missing information. They can even tell you what they like about your writing. You can do the same for them!

Understanding the Process

During a peer conference, you will play two roles—writer and listener. As a writer, you will read your work to your partner or group members. As a listener, you will listen and respond to your partner's or group members' writing. Here are some steps to follow.

As a writer, you will
- read your work aloud to your partner or group members
- write down the comments of others
- ask questions
- decide which comments to use to help you revise your work
- mark your paper for revision

Remember,
- others can help you improve your writing
- all writing can be improved

As a listener, you will
- listen carefully
- repeat the main idea and details of the piece to the writer
- describe something you like about the writer's work such as, "I like the part where …" or "I like your example of …"
- answer the writer's questions
- point out places in the writer's work that are unclear and difficult to understand

Remember,
- respect the writer's hard work
- be polite

Using a Revising Checklist

Use a checklist to help you revise your paper. A checklist will remind you of things you should look for in your writing, such as sentence variety and paragraph organization. You can also use it to keep track of the changes you will make in your work. Here's a checklist you can use when you revise your work.

Ideas

- ▶ Are my task and purpose clear in my writing?
- ▶ Is my main idea clear?
- ▶ Do I include enough details to support my main idea?
- ▶ Do I include details that will interest my audience?

Organization

- ▶ Do I arrange my paragraphs in an order that fits my purpose (such as time order, sequential order, spatial order, or order of importance)?
- ▶ Do all of my paragraphs have topic sentences?
- ▶ Do I support the topic sentence in each paragraph with details (such as descriptions, examples, facts, or definitions)?
- ▶ Do all of my paragraphs have closing sentences?

Word Choice

- ▶ Do I repeat the same words too often?
- ▶ Do I use the best words to express my ideas clearly?
- ▶ Do I use signal words to show the order of my ideas in paragraphs?

Sentence Fluency

- ▶ Do my sentences read smoothly?
- ▶ Do I have some variety in my sentence beginnings?
- ▶ Do I use some short, some medium, and some long sentences?

Voice

- ▶ Does my interest in my topic show in my writing?

Rosa used the checklist to revise the opening paragraph of her report. She thought that a different beginning would make her writing more appealing to her audience. While she thought the organization of her draft was okay, some of her sentences were dull and boring. Rosa also found new information that she wanted to add to her report. Here's her revised paragraph.

Ferrets are cute furry, animals that are kept as pets. They look a lot like otters but they live on land. People who are allergec to dogs and cats are usually not allergec to ferrets. To many families these little animals seem like ideal pets. In fact, our family had a ferret for nearly a year. However, these relatives of weasels cause so many problems that no one should keep them as pets.

Try It!

Look at Rosa's revised opening paragraph. How does she use sentence variety and word choice to capture the reader's attention?

Reading Your Writing

Revising means making changes to the organization of paragraphs, sentences, and words to improve your writing. When you write, you want your readers to "hear" your voice. Revising your paper will help make your ideas clear and help you connect with your audience.

How Do I Edit/Proofread My Writing?

The next step is **editing/proofreading.** In this step, you check how you used the conventions of writing. The conventions of writing are spelling, grammar, usage and mechanics. Read each and every word to make sure you have no misspelled words. Look over your sentences carefully to make sure they are complete. Also, make sure you use the different parts of speech (such as nouns, verbs, and adjectives) in your sentences correctly. Editing/proofreading is another way to polish your writing. As in revising, you can edit/proofread your work by yourself, with a partner, or with others in a group.

Using Proofreading Marks

Writers and editors use a set of marks, called **proofreading marks,** to show changes that should be made in a written work. Learning how to use them will make editing easier and faster. You can also use these marks to edit others' work. Here are the proofreading marks you will use most often.

¶	Indent.	¶	This is the first sentence in a paragraph.
∧	Add something.		The dog ran.
✗	Take out something.		The dog dog ran.
∽	Transpose.		Bobs
≡	Make a capital letter.		ohio
/	Make a small letter.		Sister
○ SP	Check spelling.		dawg
⊏	Close up space.		go ing
∧#	Add space.		Weate
⊙	Add a period.		The dog ran ⊙

Rosa and her friends edited/proofread her report. Rosa marked the corrections she needed to make. She will make these changes in her final draft. Here's how one of Rosa's paragraphs looks.

> Also, it's easy to lose a ferret. It can slip into openings that only are two inches wide. A ferret can hide in cabinets and drawers in your kitchen, bathroom, or bedroom. When you pick up a pille of clothes and put them in your *washing* machine, your ferret might be sleeping in the clothes. he could end up in the washer and drown. You can never turn your back on a Ferret.

Try It!

How would you correct the following sentences?

1. I would like have a ferret for a pett.
2. When you get a Pet you must take care of it

Using an Editing/Proofreading Checklist

Use a checklist to help you edit/proofread your work. An editing/proofreading checklist will remind you of things you should check in your paper, such as spelling, grammar, usage, capitalization, and punctuation. You can also use a checklist to keep track of the changes you will make in your work. Here's a checklist you can use when you edit and proofread your work.

Conventions

▶ Do I have any fragments in my paper?

▶ Does my paper contain any run-on sentences?

▶ Do I use commas to separate a series of three or more words, phrases, or clauses?

▶ Do I use commas correctly in the compound and complex sentences in my paper?

▶ Do all my sentences begin with capital letters and have the correct end punctuation?

▶ Do all the proper nouns begin with capital letters?

▶ Are there any misspelled words in my paper?

▶ Is each paragraph in my paper indented?

Editing/Proofreading on a Computer

If you write your paper on a computer, use the spelling and grammar tools to edit/proofread your work. Editing/proofreading on a computer allows you to make changes quickly. However, the computer cannot decide what you should change in your paper. It is a good idea to read a printed copy of your work to check for errors.

Here are some tasks you might perform as you edit your work on a computer. These tasks might be different on certain computers.

▶ **Adding Punctuation, Letters or Words** Move the cursor to where you want to add the letter, word, or punctuation. Then type the new character.

▶ **Deleting, or Taking Out, Punctuation, Letters, or Words** Place the cursor after the punctuation, letter, or word. Then press **backspace** until the character is erased.

▶ **Moving Text Using the Mouse** Select the text to be moved by highlighting it. Click the **cut** icon ✂ . Move the cursor to where you want to place the text. Then click the **paste** icon 📋 .

▶ **Inserting Paragraphs** Place the cursor in front of the first word in the paragraph. Press **tab**.

▶ **Checking Spelling** Using the mouse, click the **spelling** icon ✓ .

> **FUN FACT**
> Some spell-checkers have dictionaries with more than 100,000 words. You can add new words too.

Reading Your Writing

If your writing contains spelling and grammar mistakes, readers are not likely to notice how well organized it is. Let your work shine by getting rid of these kinds of errors during the editing/proofreading phase. Take time to edit/proofread your writing carefully. If you use the conventions of writing correctly, your audience can read your text with ease.

Publishing: How Can I Share My Writing?

You've just finished your piece of writing. Now it's time to publish your work. Of course, your writing doesn't have to be published as a book. There are many other ways to share your work with your readers. You can read a story you wrote aloud to a group of classmates. You can also perform a script you wrote for a puppet show for kindergartners.

Of course, the way you publish depends on your purpose for writing and your audience. You will probably decide to publish your best pieces of writing. Read on to learn about some great ideas for publishing. You might find one that fits a piece you have written. Keep the other ideas in mind for future projects.

Ways to Publish

Here are ways to publish by mailing.

> ▶ Send a thank-you note to a friend or relative, thanking them for a gift or a special favor.
> ▶ Write a letter to the editor of your local newspaper. Share your views on an issue. Explain what *should* be done about it!
> ▶ Write and mail a letter to the president of a company that manufactures something you really like. Ask for information about the company's product.
> ▶ Write and mail a friendly letter to a pen pal on the other side of the country or the world. You could send a neatly handwritten letter or an e-mail.

Find the automatic letter-formatting program on the computer using the **Help** function. Try writing a business letter using this program.

To publish your work by performing or presenting it, you can

- ▶ find people to act in a play you have written and videotape the performance
- ▶ write announcements for school events and have them read over the school public address system
- ▶ read aloud poetry you have written
- ▶ give a speech at a school assembly based on a persuasive report you've written
- ▶ write and give an introduction for a speaker at a neighborhood meeting
- ▶ audiotape yourself reading a story you've written, then share it with visually impaired children in your community

You can publish your work by binding it into a book. You can put a collection of your stories, poems, and essays in the reading resource room (if your school has one) or lend it to other classes. You might want to bind your poems or short stories together with the work of your classmates.

Follow these simple steps to bind a book of your work:

Step 1   Stack the pages to be included in order. (Make sure the pages are numbered at the bottom.)

Step 2   Staple the pages together along the left edge of the stack.

Step 3   For the cover, cut two pieces of cardboard a little larger than the pages. Use tape to join the covers together.

Step 4   Open the cover and place it on contact paper. Fold the edges of the paper around the cardboard to attach the contact paper to the cover.

Step 5   Use tape to fasten the pages into the cover.

Step 6   Make your own drawings or use magazine pictures to decorate the cover.

Preparing to Publish

Chances are you will not publish everything you write. Before you publish your writing, think about your purpose and audience. Then ask yourself the following questions:

▶ Should I publish this type of writing?

▶ Is this work one of my best pieces of writing?

▶ Have I carefully revised, edited, and proofread my work?

▶ Who will read or listen to my work?

Presentation

Once you've decided to publish your writing, think about ways to present your work. Adding illustrations, photographs, and other graphics (such as charts, tables, and diagrams) can help your audience "see" what you are saying. The format, or layout, of your writing on a page can also tell the reader what he or she is reading. For example, a newspaper or newsletter page is printed in columns, but the page of a business letter is not. To publish your work, you might

▶ illustrate a short story or poem you've written and bind it into a book

▶ include charts or diagrams in an informative report

▶ present news stories written by you and your classmates in a newsletter, using headlines, bylines, and a column format

Charts, Tables, and Diagrams

If you are making an oral presentation or writing a report with lots of information, you may want to use charts, tables, or diagrams in your finished work. Charts, tables, and diagrams can present a lot of information in a small space.

Using Charts and Tables

Charts and tables organize information into rows and columns. They are usually labeled with a title that tells what the information represents. Readers can read the title and then look across a row or down a column to quickly understand the information. They can also easily compare information, such as the strength of several earthquakes or the cost of several kinds of cereal.

Take a Look

Compare the paragraph below with the table on the next page. Both contain the same information. Notice how much easier it is to read the information when it is presented in a table.

Many different modes of transportation were invented in the 1800s. In 1829, George Stephenson of England invented the steam locomotive. In 1885, James Starley of England invented the bicycle. The same year, Gottlieb Daimler of Germany invented the motorcycle. In 1892, Charles and Frank Duryea of the United States invented the automobile.

Transportation Inventions			
Year	Invention	Inventor	Country
1829	Steam locomotive	George Stephenson	England
1885	Bicycle	James Starley	England
1885	Motorcycle	Gottlieb Daimler	Germany
1892	Automobile	Charles and Frank Duryea	United States

Follow these steps to create a chart or table.

▶ Decide how many categories of information to include. Draw that many columns.

▶ Write the categories at the top of each column.

▶ Decide how many items to include under each category. Draw that many rows.

▶ Give your chart or table a title and fill in the information.

Using Diagrams

Diagrams can also be used to show different kinds of information. A diagram can show

▶ how something works, such as the gears on a bicycle

▶ how something is arranged, such as the rooms in a house

▶ how to do or make something, such as a model airplane

▶ what stages make up a cycle, such as the life cycle of a butterfly

▶ what steps make up a process, such as photosynthesis

A solar eclipse happens when the moon moves between the sun and Earth. The diagram below shows what causes a solar eclipse. All the elements in the diagram are clearly labeled. Notice the diagram has a title that lets the reader know what is being shown.

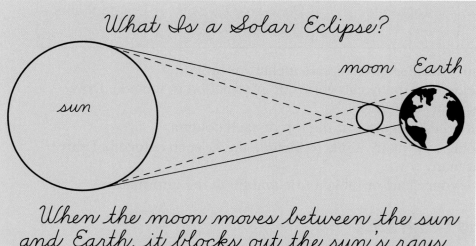

What Is a Solar Eclipse?

sun   moon   Earth

When the moon moves between the sun and Earth, it blocks out the sun's rays. This is called a solar eclipse.

Keeping a Writing Portfolio

A writing portfolio is the place where you can keep your ideas, prewriting, drafts, works in progress, lists of words, and finished writing. What does your writing portfolio look like? It might be a file folder, a large envelope, or a three-ring binder. Whatever form it takes, it should be easy for you to add to it.

Organizing Your Portfolio

You might divide your portfolio into sections. One way is to use a three-ring binder and pocket dividers.

▶ **Ideas for Writing** File all your ideas here, even if they're written on tiny scraps of paper. Include topics or questions you are thinking about. You can look here for ideas whenever you get a new assignment—or when you just feel like writing.

▶ **Prewriting** This section might include graphic organizers you've used or might use. Some of your graphic organizers might already have ideas written on them. That's okay. Old ideas can often lead to new ideas.

▶ **Work in Progress** Save your old drafts here. Then you can check them as you improve your work by revising and editing/proofreading it. You might use paper clips to keep all the drafts from a project together. You can also leave a draft of a current project here for a day or two. When you look at it again, you will have a fresh eye. You will see new ways to improve it.

▶ **Finished Writing** Of course, not everything you write will reach this section. Carefully choose your best work to show what a skillful writer you're becoming. Be sure to include everything you've published.

▶ **Challenging Spelling Words** We all have certain words that give us problems. If you have to look up a word more than once, list it in this section of your portfolio. Just writing it there will help you remember how to spell it. Every week or so, ask a friend or family member to give you a quiz on these words. Soon, you won't have to look them up again.

Reading Your Writing

The word *publish* is based on the Latin word for "public." Publishing means making your work public—sharing it with people. The main goal of writing is communicating with others. Don't hide your thoughts and skills. Share them!

How Does It All Work Together?

The students in Mr. Johnson's class have all completed their assignments. Rosa's paper on ferrets was a success! Now she is ready for her next assignment. Let's follow her to see how she used the writing process to create a report for her new assignment.

Prewriting

Task, Audience, and Purpose

Mr. Johnson asked the class to write an informative essay about pollution. He also asked them to think about how they might publish their work so that people in their communities could read it.

Rosa knew what her task would be. She would write an informative essay about pollution. Rosa's **audience** will be people in her community. She hasn't decided yet how she will publish her work. She will think about that later. Rosa decided that her **purpose** will be to convince her readers to do something about pollution.

Getting and Narrowing Ideas

Rosa decided to brainstorm ideas about pollution with her classmates Kevin, David, and Nazanin. She and her classmates

tried using different types of graphic organizers, including a word web, to find a specific topic. She wrote *environment* in the center circle and added other circles. As she wrote *trash* in one of the smaller circles, Rosa remembered some problems in her own neighborhood. A trash-burning power plant was releasing pollution into the air. It had to be shut down. She decided to write about ways to get rid of trash. She will persuade her audience that one way is better than another. To organize her report, Rosa chose a problem-solution chart, which can be used to organize persuasive writing. After doing some research, she filled in her graphic organizer.

Organizing Ideas

Here's the graphic organizer Rosa used to organize her ideas and information.

> Problem: We are creating too much trash. We have no place to put it, so it is polluting the environment.

↓

> Possible solutions:
>
> 1. Landfills
>   Filling up
>   Include hazardous waste
>
> 2. Incinerators
>   Get rid of trash
>   Cause air pollution
>
> 3. Recycling

↓

> Things that can be recycled
> Uses for recycled materials

↓

> Recommended Solution: Recycling is the best choice.

Drafting

Next Rosa created a draft of her report using her graphic organizer. To write quickly, she used abbreviations and left spaces for words she couldn't think of right away. She spelled difficult words as best she could. Rosa did not want to stop to look them up in a dictionary. She might forget what she was going to write next.

Rosa reminded herself to write her draft using sentences and paragraphs. Here is the first part of Rosa's draft.

Every day each Amer. throws out four pnds of trash! We throw out newspaper and kitchen gar_____. We also get rid of broken refrijerators, old toasters, and worn-out ~~chairs~~ furnature. We are running out of places to put this trash. We are polluting the envt. We have to find a good way get rid of it!

We get rid of some stuff in landfills. A landfill is sometims called a dump. It is a low area that we fill with gar_____. Most landfills today are lined with plastic. Some are lined with clay. Some of the rotting gar___ turns into water. The plastic or clay is supposed to keep it from sooking into the grnd. Putting gar_____ in landfills won't work much longer. In less then ten years the landfills in more than half of the States will be filled! The stuff already in landfills is poisoning the air and land. Like batteries and paint. It is polluting the air and land.

Try It!

Read Rosa's second paragraph carefully. She should divide it into two paragraphs. Which sentence begins a new topic?

Revising

During the revising step, Rosa tried to better organize her paragraphs. She changed some of her sentences for variety and for clarity.

Here is Rosa's revision of this part of her draft.

How much stuff did you throw away today?

Every day each Amer. throws out four pnds of trash! We throw out newspaper ~~and~~ kitchen gar_____. ~~We also get rid of~~ broken refrigerators, old toasters, and worn-out ~~chairs~~ furnature. *However,* We are running out of places to put this trash. *The trash is piling up and* We are polluting the envt. *soon*

We have to find a good way get rid of it!

One way *trash is by putting it*

We get rid of ~~some stuff~~ in landfills. A landfill ~~is sometims called~~ *or* a dump. It is a low area that we fill with gar_____. Most landfills today are lined with plastic. ~~Some are lined~~ with clay. ~~Some of the~~ *or* *as the* *rots, some of it* ~~rotting~~ gar_____ turns into water. The plastic or clay is supposed *and causing pollution* to keep it from sooking into the grnd. Putting gar_____ in landfills won't work much longer. In less then ten years the landfills in more than half of the States will be filled! *some of the trash* ~~The stuff~~ already in landfills *such as batteries and paint is leeking out and* is poisoning the air and land. ~~Like batteries and paint. It is polluting the air and land.~~

The Writing Process • How Does It All Work Together?   51

Editing/Proofreading

Rosa knew the changes she'd made had already greatly improved her report. Then her writing partner helped her edit/proofread. Rosa and her partner checked for spelling, usage, grammar, capitalization, and punctuation errors. They also looked for places to improve Rosa's word choices. She wanted her voice to be strong and clear in her paper.

Here is Rosa's edited/proofread version of the first part of her report.

How much stuff did you throw away today? Every day each American throws out four pounds of trash! We throw out newspapers, kitchen uneaten food, broken refrigerators, old toasters, and worn-out furniture. However, we are running out of places to put this trash. The trash is piling up and polluting the environment. We have to find a better way to get rid of this trash soon!

One way we get rid of trash is by putting it in landfills. A landfill, or a dump, is a low area that we fill with garbage. Most landfills today are lined with plastic or clay. As the garbage rots, some of it turns into water. The plastic or clay is supposed to keep it from soaking into the ground.

Putting garbage in landfills won't work much longer. In less than ten years, the landfills in more than half of the States will be filled! Some of the trash already in landfills, such as batteries and paint, is leaking out and poisoning the air and land.

Publishing

After she made all her corrections, Rosa decided to submit her report for publication in the community newspaper. She mailed a letter addressed to the editor of the newspaper along with her report. Rosa wanted the editor to know why she was mailing her report to him. She wanted to encourage more people to recycle unwanted things instead of tossing them in their trash cans. Rosa was pleased with her work and hoped it would get published in the community paper.

Reading Your Writing

Communicating your ideas to others in writing is not easy, but you can do it. The stages in the writing process can guide you from your first fuzzy idea to a finished product that will make you proud!

Forms of Writing

The purpose of writing is to communicate a message. When you write, it's important to choose a form of writing that fits the message you want to convey.

Sometimes the message is very simple. For example, you want to thank a friend for a gift. You write a thank-you note.

At other times, the message is more complex. You want to communicate to your classmates your concern about the need for more recycling. You have some choices about how to communicate that message. You might write a poem. You might write a story in which the events of the plot and the actions of the characters reflect your message. You might prepare an informational report. These are just a few of your choices. There are many others.

In this unit you will learn about the different forms of writing: personal, expository, narrative, descriptive, persuasive, and poetry. Think about how and when to use them when you write.

Forms of Writing

Personal Writing

Do you write notes to your friends? Do you make lists to remind yourself to do things? Do you write in a journal?

These are all examples of personal writing. In these kinds of writing, you can express yourself in a more personal, or individual, way.

Some kinds of personal writing, such as lists and notes, are very practical. Others, such as journals, are more reflective. Think about how you can use each of them.

Writing in a Journal

Think of a special event you'd like to remember. It could be going to the zoo with your best friend or winning a soccer game. A good way to remember all the details of an event is to write them down in a **journal.** A journal is a place to write about happy moments and other experiences. You can also use a journal to write about things you've learned or read. Let's look at different kinds of journals.

Personal Journal

A **personal journal** can be a place to write about yourself and your world. You can write about any new and interesting experiences you've had. If you're curious about anything, you can write down your questions and thoughts in your journal. You can use your journal to be creative. Write ideas you might use in other work, such as essays, poems, or stories.

Here's what writing in a personal journal looks like. This is a page from Brian's personal journal.

Tuesday, October 14

Today we got off the school bus. Like we always do, my sister Kira and I were racing to see who could get home first. As we went around the corner, my arm brushed against her and she fell. She skinned her knees. I helped her get up. She was crying hard. It didn't look bad. I thought she was just being a baby. I was sorry.

Learning Log

A **learning log** is a type of journal you might write in as part of science or math class. In a science learning log, you might predict the results of or explain what happened during an experiment. In a math learning log, you might describe ways that people use percentages or fractions in everyday life.

Here is a page from Kayla's math learning log.

Tuesday, December 12

When I went to the store with my mom today, I saw a sign that said 50% off everything. We learned about figuring out problems with percentages in Mrs. Kane's class. The shirt I wanted was $15.00 × .50 = $7.50.

Literature Response Journal

You might write in a response journal before, while, or after you read a piece of literature. Before you read, you could describe what you expect to happen in the story. You might write a make-believe conversation with one of the characters while you are reading. After you've finished, you might write a summary or a different ending to the story.

Below is a page from Roberto's literature response journal.

Wednesday, January 10

The thing that surprised me most about the story "Eddie, Incorporated" was how much Eddie and his friends used math.

Dialogue Journal

In a dialogue journal, you and a partner take turns "talking" about a topic.

Here is part of Sarah's dialogue with her language arts teacher.

October 23

Dear Ms. Perry,

When I read Sallie Hester's diary, I thought about my grandparents. I wonder if they would be able to tell me whether my ancestors traveled West like Sallie and her family. I wonder whether they went though the same trials and whether they were homesick.

Sarah

October 25

Dear Sarah,

I think you should ask your grandparents about your ancestors, if that is possible. Maybe your mother and father remember hearing about your ancestors too. You might want to read parts of Sallie Hester's diary to them to see whether her experience was anything like theirs.

Ms. Perry

Tips for Writing in a Journal

To write in a journal, all you need is a notebook or a computer. These tips will help you get the most out of your journal writing.

▶ Choose a regular time to write. Many people write just before they go to bed. If you write at a certain time, it will become part of your routine.
▶ Write every day if you can. Don't forget to put the date on every page.
▶ Write freely. Don't worry too much about grammar or spelling.
▶ Give details. Think about and explain what your ideas, thoughts, observations, and experiences mean to you.

Reading Your Writing

Recording your experiences, ideas, and questions in a personal journal creates a great source of writing ideas. Writing in other kinds of journals is an excellent way to share your responses and ideas with others.

FUN FACT

Amelia Earhart sent pages of her diary to her husband while on her famous flight around the world. After Earhart and her plane disappeared, her husband published her diary in a book titled *Last Flight.*

Writing Notes and Cards

Do you like to get notes and cards from friends and relatives? Whether it's paper mail or e-mail, it's great to know that someone's thinking about you. Many people buy blank cards and write their own personal and special messages in them. You can also make your own notes and cards with paper, markers, and rubber stamps and write your own greetings. Writing your own notes and cards is a good way to show your friends and family members that you care about them.

Invitations

Think you might want to invite your whole class to a party to celebrate a successful project? When you want to invite people to a special event, it's best to send invitations. An invitation gives your guests information they need to know about a party or another type of event. Your invitation should include this information.

▶ **What you're planning** (a party, a dinner, or a game night)
▶ **Who's giving the event** (yourself or another person)
▶ **Who will be honored** (yourself, another guest, or no one)
▶ **When the event will take place** (include the day of the week, month, date, year, and time)
▶ **Where the event will take place** (include the address)
▶ **Why you are having a event** (to celebrate a birthday or to welcome someone back)

Here's what the inside of a printed invitation usually looks like.

You're Invited to a Birthday Party

For: _Tasha Jones_

Given by: _Tasha's mom_

When: _October 24, 2007_

Where: _117 Rose Avenue_

Rochester, NY

Time: _2:00 p.m._

RSVP: _Call Ms. Jones by October 22 at
437-5842 if you plan to attend_

Write how and when you want your guests to respond in the space after the letters *RSVP*, which stand for French words that mean "Respond, if you please."

If you don't want to use a printed invitation, you can use a sheet of paper or a blank note card to write your own.

You're invited to Serena's birthday party on Saturday, November 12. Meet at Serena's house on 123 Center Road at 4:00 p.m. Then Serena's dad will drive everyone to the Game Place for the party. Hope you can come. It will be lots of fun! Call Serena's mom at 523-4564 if you cannot come.

Thank-You Notes

People always like getting thank-you notes. If they sent a present through the mail, the note lets them know that the person received it. More importantly, the note tells them that their gift or their kindness was appreciated.

When you write a thank-you note, be specific. If the person did something for you, say what it was and why you appreciate it. If you received a gift, tell what you like about it and when or where you will use it.

What if the gift was the wrong size or style? What if you already have one just like it? In this case, think of something positive to say without being untruthful. For example: "The sweater you sent is my favorite color!"

Try It!

Which pair of sentences is best to use in a thank-you note?

▶ Thanks. We had fun.
▶ Thanks for getting the tickets for us. We really enjoyed the game.

Here is a thank-you note that Henry sent to a neighbor.

Dear Mr. Walker,

Thanks so much for telling me about your experiences during your trip to Paris in 1950. In my social studies report, I wrote about some of the famous artists and writers you met. My teacher thought it was so interesting that she asked me to read it aloud to the class. Thank you again for your time and your stories!

Sincerely,

Henry

Get-Well Cards

Writing a get-well card to someone who is ill is a way of showing the person you care. When you write a get-well card, pay attention to your audience. For example, if a person has a cold or a stomach ache, you can wish him or her a speedy recovery!

Dear Hal,

I am sorry you are not feeling well. A cold can really make you feel awful. Eat plenty of soup. My mom says it's good for your cold. Get well soon!

Your friend,

Guy

Birthday Cards

Everyone enjoys getting birthday cards. When you write a birthday greeting, keep your audience in mind. For example, a greeting for a close relative or friend would be different from one for your teacher. Your friend might appreciate a humorous greeting, but your teacher might not. Also, if you've missed the date of someone's birthday, you can send a "belated" greeting. Make sure you apologize for missing the birthday. Here's a birthday greeting Megan wrote to her younger sister, Rachel.

Happy Birthday to the best little sister in the whole world! I hope you have lots of fun on your birthday!

Love,

Megan

Telephone Messages

When you take a telephone message, write all the information the person receiving the message needs to know. Keep a pad of paper and a pencil near the phone to make taking messages easier.

Here are some things that should be included in a telephone message.

▶ The person being called
▶ The name and phone number of the caller
▶ The day and time of the call
▶ What the person being called is expected to do (such as return the call or meet at a certain place)
▶ Your name at the bottom of the message

Be polite to the caller as you write down his or her message. Ask questions if you need more information, such as a telephone number. Also, if you don't understand the caller, politely ask him or her to repeat the information.

Take a Look

Tomas,

Nick called about 2:30 today (Monday). He said to meet him at the school at 6:30 tonight. Call him at 759-3427 if you can't make it.

Isabel

Writing Notes and Cards on the Computer

Isn't it exciting to get mail when you turn on your computer? Writing notes and cards on the computer and sending them as e-mail is a quick and easy way to send personal messages and greetings. You can write an e-mail message, design and write a card on the computer, or select a free card from the Internet and write your greeting.

When you write an e-mail message, you can follow the same guidelines for writing paper notes and cards. Here's a get-well message Omara wrote as an e-mail to her friend Barbara.

Send Now · Send Later · Save as Draft · Add Attachments · Signature ▼ · Options ▼ · Rewrap

From:

To:

Cc:

Bcc:

Subject:

Attachments: *none*

Verdana · Medium · **B** *I* <u>U</u> T

Dear Barbara,

I heard that you are not feeling well. I will miss you at camp this weekend. I will bring back pictures and a surprise for you! I will visit you when I get back. Get well soon!

Your pal, Omara

There are many computer software programs that allow you to make your own notes and cards. You can illustrate your cards using the paste, draw, and paint tools on your computer. Then you can write your own message and send the card as e-mail.

Reading Your Writing

Short notes and cards are meaningful ways to communicate with people. Make sure your messages are clear, considerate, and complete.

Writing a Friendly Letter

What can you do to receive more letters in the mail? The answer is simple: write more letters. A **friendly letter** is the type of letter you would write to a friend or a family member. In a friendly letter, you can let others know what is happening in your life. You can also ask the person receiving the letter how she or he is. Writing friendly letters is a great way to stay in touch with friends and family.

Here are some things you might write about in a friendly letter.

- ▶ a recent trip—or a trip you're planning
- ▶ a special accomplishment, such as making the softball team
- ▶ something you're learning, such as how to play the guitar
- ▶ neighborhood or school news that would interest a friend or family member
- ▶ a poem or short story you've written or read

Parts of a Friendly Letter

Below are the five parts of a friendly letter.

Heading

The **heading** is your address and the date. Put it in the upper right-hand corner of the page.

Salutation

The **salutation** is sometimes called the **greeting.** It begins with the word *Dear* followed by the name of the person you are writing. A comma is placed after the person's name.

Body

The **body** of the letter is your message to the reader. Because you are writing to someone you know well, the body of your letter should have a friendly tone.

Closing

The **closing** comes just before your signature. Here are some closings you might use in a friendly letter. Notice that only the first word is capitalized. The closing ends with a comma.

Love,

Your friend,

Sincerely,

Signature

Your **signature** is last. Sign your name below the closing.

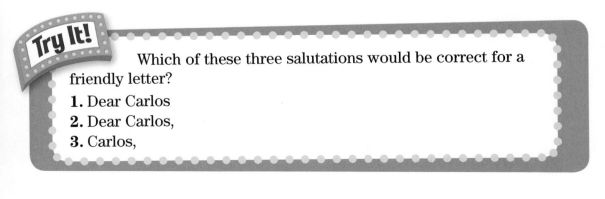

Try It!

Which of these three salutations would be correct for a friendly letter?

1. Dear Carlos
2. Dear Carlos,
3. Carlos,

Here is a friendly letter that Sam wrote to his cousin Karen.

82 North Fork Avenue
Denver, CO 80987
September 12, 2007

Dear Karen,

We just got back from our trip to New York City. Have you ever been there? It was great! The part I liked best was the boat ride around New York Harbor. We went at night, and all the lights in the buildings and bridges came on while we were on the boat. The buildings are right on the edge of the water. They looked amazing! We got to see the Statue of Liberty, too.

The other part I liked was Greenwich Village. We ate lunch on tables outside a little restaurant and watched the people walk by. I could tell I wasn't back in Denver!

We took lots of pictures. I'll show them to you at Thanksgiving at Grandma Turner's house. See you then. Don't forget to write back.

Your cousin,
Sam

Reading Your Writing

To get letters, write letters. Writing letters can help you build strong friendships. It can also help you feel closer to family members who live far away.

Tips for Writing a Friendly Letter

Prewriting   Make a Plan

▶ Get the full name and address of the person you are writing. Write it down and keep it where you can find it easily.

▶ Think about the person who will read your friendly letter. Write down all the things you might tell this person. For example, you might want to tell about a specific event or write about a trip you took recently.

Drafting   Get Your Thoughts on Paper

▶ Include the heading, salutation and closing in your draft. Write the parts of the letter in the correct places in your draft.

▶ Write a draft of the body of your letter. Don't worry about misspelled words or poorly constructed sentences. You can fix these before you mail your letter.

Revising   Be Sure Your Letter Makes Sense

▶ **Sentence Fluency** Include questions in your letter. For example, you can ask your friend or family about a new pet. Questions will add variety to your letter and encourage a friend or relative to write back.

▶ **Voice** Think about how your message will affect the person receiving your letter. Show yourself as interested, kind, and friendly through your writing.

Editing/Proofreading   Look Closely at the Details

▶ **Conventions** Check the spelling of people's names and addresses in your letter. Also, make sure you use commas after the salutation and the closing of your letter.

Publishing   Get Your Letter Ready to Mail

▶ Write or type your final copy on clean paper.

▶ Fold your letter and address the envelope. See page 76 for how to do this.

Writing a Business Letter

Writing a business letter is the best way to contact a company, an organization, or a person whom you do not know. Here are three types of business letters and the reasons for writing each one.

If you want something from a company or business, you would write a **letter of request.** In this type of letter,

- ▶ tell who you are and why you are writing
- ▶ describe what you want
- ▶ thank the reader for helping you

To show that you care about something, you would write a **letter of concern.** In this type of letter,

- ▶ describe the situation, including what you think about it
- ▶ explain how you would change or improve the situation
- ▶ ask that the situation be changed

You would write a **letter of complaint** if you believe a policy, product, or service should be changed or improved. In this type of letter,

- ▶ explain the problem and tell what caused it
- ▶ describe what you would like the reader to do
- ▶ thank the reader for helping you

Business letters should be neat and well organized. Your goal is to convince the reader that your request deserves a response or that your opinion is important. Your business letters should be polite and to the point.

Try It!

Is the following statement the topic of a letter of concern or a letter of complaint?

- ▶ You write a letter to the manager of a bicycle shop about the bicycle you bought recently that has broken pedals.

Parts of a Business Letter

A business letter is like a friendly letter in some ways—and different in other ways. All business letters have the same six parts.

Heading

The **heading** is your own address and the date. In a business letter, it goes in the upper left-hand corner of the page.

Inside Address

The **inside address** should be two lines below the heading. It includes the name and address of the reader. If the person has a title, add it after his or her name, with a comma between them.

Salutation

The **salutation** or greeting is followed by a colon in a business letter.

Body

The **body** of the letter is your request, concern, or complaint. Start the body two lines below the salutation.

Closing

The **closing** is placed at the left-hand margin in a business letter. Put it two lines below the body of the letter. As in a friendly letter, only the first word is capitalized. End the closing with a comma. As with the rest of a business letter, the closing is more formal than that of a friendly letter. Here are two closings you might use.

Yours truly,

Sincerely,

Signature

Your **signature** is last. If you are typing your letter, type your full name four lines below the closing. Then sign your name between the closing and your typed name.

Take a Look

Here is Maria's letter of request. Notice how she tells why she is writing and what she wants. Then she thanks the reader, Dr. Healy, for helping her.

Heading ▶

14B South Pico Street
Aurora, IL 60387
October 2, 2007

Inside Address ▶

Mark W. Everson, President
American Red Cross National Headquarters
2025 E Street, NW
Washington, D.C. 20006

Salutation ▶ Dear Mr. Everson:

Body ▶

Our class is studying many of the problems that bad weather causes. I have to find out what happens to people after a flood, hurricane, or tornado hits a town or city. I have seen commercials on television about the Red Cross that show how you help people. Please send me information about how the Red Cross helps people after bad weather hits their town or city.

My report is due November 15. Thank you very much for your help.

Closing ▶ Sincerely,

Signature ▶ *Maria Hernandez*

Maria Hernandez

Below is part of a letter of complaint. How would you revise the salutation and the body of this letter?

Dear Super CD Services:

I want my money back! The CD player I bought just doesn't work. Thank you for your help.

Folding a Letter

For a long (#10) envelope

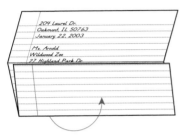

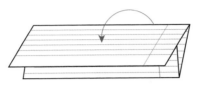

Fold the bottom of the letter one third up.

Then, fold the top of the letter one third down.

For a smaller envelope

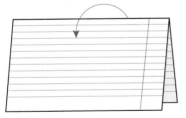

Fold the letter in half, short sides together.

Next, fold the left one third in toward the center.

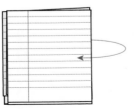

Finally, fold the right one third in.

Addressing the Envelope

For all kinds of letters, follow these steps.

▶ Put your name and address in the upper-left corner of the envelope.

▶ Write or type the name and address of the person receiving the letter a little left of the middle of the envelope.

▶ Put a stamp in the upper-right corner.

Maria Hernandez
14B South Pico Street
Aurora, IL 60387

Mark W. Everson, President
American Red Cross National Headquarters
2025 E Street, NW
Washington, D.C. 20006

Reading Your Writing

The purpose of business letters is to get results. They must be clear, short, and polite. If you use the guidelines in this lesson to organize your business letters, you are more likely to get the results you want.

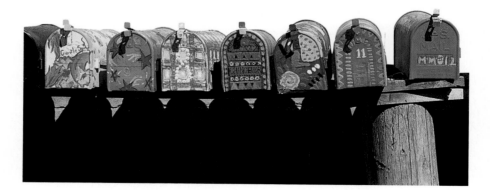

Tips for Writing a Business Letter

Prewriting Make a Plan

▶ Brainstorm about people in businesses or organizations you could contact with a request, concern, or complaint.
▶ Use a phone book, the Internet, or another source to find the address of the business or organization you choose. Look for the name of a specific person to contact.
▶ Plan and organize your letter based on the type you are writing, your audience, and purpose.

Drafting Get Your Thoughts on Paper

▶ Keep in mind the type of letter you are writing. Write your draft in sentences and paragraphs.
▶ Include the heading, inside address, salutation, closing, and signature in your draft.

Revising Be Sure Your Letter Makes Sense

▶ **Ideas** Take out any sentences that move away from your purpose. Your sentences should clearly state and support the main idea of your letter.
▶ **Organization** Make sure your purpose for writing appears in the first paragraph in a business letter.
▶ **Sentence Fluency** Use a variety of sentences in your letter.
▶ **Voice** Check your tone. It should be polite and formal.

Editing/Proofreading Look Closely at the Details

▶ **Conventions** Make sure you include in your letter all six parts of the business letter in the correct places. Look at the sample letter on page 74 to remind yourself of the parts of a business letter.
▶ Make sure you have capitalized the names of businesses, people, and titles. Check the spelling and capitalization in addresses, too.

Publishing Get Your Letter Ready to Mail

▶ Type or neatly handwrite your letter on a clean sheet of paper.
▶ Fold your letter and address the envelope. Add a stamp.

Forms of Writing

Expository Writing

Expository writing does two things. It explains how to do something, or it presents information about something. The steps in the explanation are arranged in a logical way so that the reader can follow the procedure or repeat the activity. When information is presented, it is clear, correct, complete, and well organized.

Much of the writing you do for school is expository. Some of the following lessons can help you improve your reports and book reviews. You can use the others to try types of expository writing that may be new to you.

Writing a Summary

Do you sometimes have trouble remembering the important ideas in a piece of writing you've read? Everybody does. Summarizing can help. When you write a summary, you identify the main idea and the main points. Then you rewrite them in your own words. For example, you might summarize the main events in a story or the main ideas in a newspaper article. You might also summarize a whole book for a book report. Summarizing can help you understand and remember the important ideas in a piece of writing.

Steps in Summarizing

These steps will help you write a summary:

1. Read the material once to get the general idea.
2. Find the topic sentences and other main points.
3. Begin your summary with the main idea of the material you've read.
4. Add the main points in your own words. Include any **boldface** or *italicized* words that are in the material. These words will be important to remember.
5. Revise your summary so it reads smoothly.
6. Reread the material you've chosen to summarize and your summary. Check to see if you missed any important points.

These paragraphs are taken from "Food from the 'Hood: A Garden of Hope," an informational article by Marlene Targ Brill. Compare them to Tony's summary of the passage.

Sometimes horrible events turn into the most hopeful dreams. That's what happened to students at Crenshaw High School in South Central Los Angeles, California. In May 1992, riots destroyed the neighborhood surrounding their school. Businesses went up in flames. Hundreds of shopkeepers were left with nothing but ashes. Families, some too poor to afford gas money, were forced to travel from the city to the suburbs just to buy food.

Students in Tammy Bird's biology class felt awful. "This is where we all grew up," said Carlos Lopez. "The corner store in my neighborhood burned down. That was where we hung out."

Carlos and his classmates refused to let riots wreck their lives. They talked about different ways to help rebuild their community. Nothing seemed quite right. Then Ms. Bird remembered the weed-infested patch behind the football field. Perhaps the school would give them the quarter-acre plot of land for a garden. As a bonus, Ms. Bird offered extra credit to attract student gardeners.

Tony's Summary

Students at Crenshaw High School in South Central Los Angeles had hopeful dreams after the riots destroyed their neighborhood in May 1992. At first the students in Tammy Bird's class felt bad about what the riots did to the neighborhood. Then they talked about different ways to rebuild their community. Ms. Bird remembered a weedy patch behind the football field. She thought the school might give them some of the land for a garden. Ms. Bird suggested that the students should take care of the garden. This could be their way to grow food for the people in the neighborhood.

Putting the Steps to Work

After Tony read the entire passage, he looked for topic sentences and other main points. Let's take a closer look.

> **The first two sentences say something about the main idea of this article.**

> **The sentences in this paragraph add details. The need to buy food seems to be an important detail because growing a garden is mentioned later.**

> **The teacher's name appears in this paragraph.**

Sometimes horrible events turn into the most hopeful dreams. That's what happened to students at Crenshaw High School in South Central Los Angeles, California. In May 1992, riots destroyed the neighborhood surrounding their school. Businesses went up in flames. Hundreds of shopkeepers were left with nothing but ashes. Families, some too poor to afford gas money, were forced to travel from the city to the suburbs just to buy food.

Students in Tammy Bird's biology class felt awful. "This is where we all grew up," said Carlos Lopez. "The corner store in my neighborhood burned down. That was where we hung out."

Carlos and his classmates refused to let riots wreck their lives. They talked about different ways to help rebuild their community. Nothing seemed quite right. Then Ms. Bird remembered the weed-infested patch behind the football field. Perhaps the school would give them the quarter-acre plot of land for a garden. As a bonus, Ms. Bird offered extra credit to attract student gardeners.

> **This sentence is the main point of this paragraph.**

> **In this paragraph, the second sentence is the topic of the paragraph.**

> **The information about the patch of land and how it might be used as a garden are connected to the main point of this passage.**

Tony's Notes

While looking for the main points of the passage, Tony wrote down his ideas for his summary. Here are his notes.

"Food from the 'Hood" notes

1. Bad things happened in South Central Los Angeles, California.

2. The students of Crenshaw High School turned these bad things into hopeful dreams.

3. The May 1992 riots destroyed the neighborhood around the high school.

4. Poor people had a hard time getting food.

5. Tammy Bird was a teacher at the high school.

6. The students wanted to rebuild the community.

7. Ms. Bird knew about a patch of land. The students could turn it into a garden.

Try It! Look at Tony's notes on this page and his summary on page 81. Does he use the main points he writes in his notes in the summary? What does he add to the summary?

Responding to Fiction

How can you tell what you like or dislike about a story? How can you show that you understand a story you have read? One way is to analyze a character or the plot.

Analyzing a character helps you understand why he or she acts a certain way. When you analyze a character, look for words and actions in the story that make him or her seem real. Also, look at what the other people in the story say and how they act toward the character you are analyzing.

Analyzing the plot shows you how the author draws readers into the action and makes the story seem believable. It also helps you understand how the author makes the story move forward.

Analyzing Character

When you write about people in stories, you usually analyze their characteristics. These characteristics can be physical features, such as hair and eye color, but more often they are the ways people behave. When you analyze a character's behavior, you write about the reasons they act in particular ways. In addition, you would include any changes in the character's behavior that are the result of events in the story.

Bridget read Paul Robert Walker's story "John Henry Races the Steam Drill." The story takes place at the Big Bend Tunnel on a West Virginia mountain railroad. John Henry is a worker on this stretch of railroad that is under construction. John Henry is a very fast and hard-working man. Bridget decided to analyze the main character of the story, John Henry. She created a character web to show John Henry's traits. On the next page is the character web Bridget created.

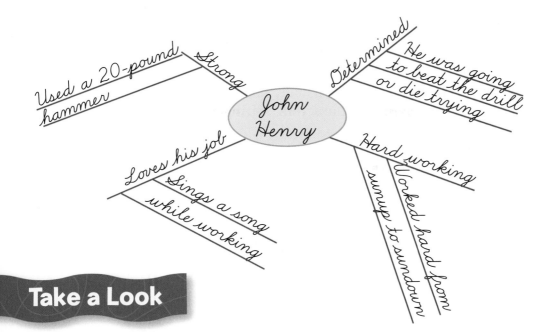

Character web:

- **Strong** — Used a 20-pound hammer
- **Determined** — He was going to beat the drill or die trying
- **Hard working** — Worked hard from sunup to sundown
- **Loves his job** — Sings a song while working

Center: John Henry

Using the information in her character web, Bridget wrote this analysis of John Henry. Notice how Bridget included all four character traits. She also used examples from the story to give reasons why she thought John Henry had those traits.

John Henry is the main character in "John Henry Races the Steam Drill." At the beginning of the story, John Henry is described as a strong man with lots of muscles. He hammers into solid rock with a nine-pound hammer. John Henry then asks for a twenty-pound hammer for his competition. John Henry is a hard-working man. He drives his hammer without complaint from morning until sunset.

In fact, John Henry loves his job so much that he sings a song while he works. He even sings while he is in the competition against the steam drill. John Henry's determination is present when he begins talking about competing against the drill. He tells everyone, including his wife, that he is going to beat the steam drill or he will die while trying to beat the steam drill. All of these traits make John Henry seem perfect, but these traits lead to his downfall.

Analyzing the Plot

It helps to know how writers organize the plot before you begin analyzing it. The plot in a story usually has four parts.

1. a beginning (where the characters, setting, and the problem are introduced)
2. a middle (where the characters deal with the problem)
3. a climax, or the high point of the story (where the characters begin to resolve the problem)
4. a conclusion (where the problem is resolved)

When you write a plot analysis, use time order to organize your writing. Tell what happens in the order the events appear in the story. Bridget also decided to analyze the plot of "John Henry Races the Steam Drill." She chose a different graphic organizer for this analysis: a plot line.

Here is how Bridget filled in her graphic organizer for the story.

> **Climax**
> John Henry and the steam drill compete, and John Henry beats the drill.

> **Middle**
> John Henry talks about how he will beat the drill in the competition.

> **Beginning**
> Characters: John Henry, other railroad workers
> Setting: Big Bend Tunnel
> Problem: John Henry wants to prove he is better at drilling than a steam drill.

> **End**
> John Henry lays down his hammer and dies.

Here is Bridget's analysis of the plot of "John Henry Races the Steam Drill."

The setting of "John Henry Races the Steam Drill" is the Big Bend Tunnel on a West Virginia mountain railroad. The main character is a man named John Henry. The problem of the plot is that John Henry wants to prove he can drill faster than a steam drill.

John Henry is a strong and confident railroad worker. His boss and the other workers believe he can beat the drill. John Henry talks about how he is only a man, but he will beat the steam drill or die trying.

The day of the competition arrives. John Henry and the steam drill begin drilling. John Henry continues at his regular pace as the steam drill works along side him. When time is called, John Henry has drilled deeper than the steam drill. John Henry wins the competition.

After the competition is over, everyone cheers for John Henry. John Henry slumps to the ground and dies. He won the competition like he said he would, but he also died while trying to win.

Tips for Writing a Character Analysis

Prewriting Make a Plan

- ▶ Read the story and select one character to analyze.
- ▶ Look for words about the character that show his or her character traits. Pay attention to how the character changes the story.
- ▶ Use a character web to organize your ideas.

Drafting Get Your Thoughts on Paper

- ▶ Use your graphic organizer to write a draft of your analysis.
- ▶ Include details and examples from the story that show the character's traits and actions.
- ▶ Don't worry about making mistakes. You will fix them later.

Revising Be Sure Your Analysis Makes Sense

- ▶ **Organization** See if you described the traits in a logical way. You might use time order to organize your analysis. If you use time order, describe each trait in the order in which it appears in the story.
- ▶ **Sentence Fluency** Read your analysis aloud to see if the sentences flow smoothly together. If necessary, add words and combine some simple sentences.

Editing/Proofreading Look Closely at the Details

- ▶ **Conventions** Check the punctuation of your sentences.
- ▶ Look at your spelling, even if you already used a spell-checker. Make sure you spelled the characters' names correctly.

Publishing Get Ready to Share Your Analysis

- ▶ **Presentation** Write or type your final copy.
- ▶ Read it again so you are ready to share it with your class or a small group.

Tips for Writing a Plot Analysis

Prewriting   Make a Plan

▶ Read the story and identify the beginning, middle, climax, and end.
▶ Write down the setting, the characters, and the problem.
▶ List the ways the characters deal with the problem, the high point of the story, and how the problem is solved.
▶ Use a plot line to organize your writing. Fill in the organizer. Remember that the climax is the place where the action is the most exciting.

Drafting   Get Your Thoughts on Paper

▶ Use your graphic organizer to write a draft of your analysis.
▶ Describe the beginning, middle, climax, and end of the story. Add other details to make your analysis complete.
▶ Don't stop to check for spelling or punctuation. You'll do that later.

Revising   Be Sure Your Analysis Makes Sense

▶ **Organization** Make sure you described the story events in the order in which they occurred.
▶ **Ideas** Include enough information to clearly describe the beginning, middle, climax, and end of the plot.
▶ **Word Choice** Use specific words instead of general ones. Choose the clearest and most descriptive words to make your plot analysis clear.
▶ **Sentence Fluency** Check to see if you use a variety of sentences. You might want to begin some sentences with adverbs or prepositional phrases.

Editing/Proofreading   Look Closely at the Details

▶ **Conventions** Check the subject-verb agreement in your sentences.
▶ Make sure the names of your characters are capitalized in your plot analysis.

Publishing   Get Ready to Share Your Analysis

▶ **Presentation** Write or type the final version of your analysis.
▶ Read it aloud to your class or a small group.

Responding to Nonfiction

Some of what you read—at school and on your own—is nonfiction. Nonfiction books and articles are based on facts. They help you learn about the real world. Some nonfiction contains so many facts that it can be hard to identify the main message. Identifying the main idea and supporting details in nonfiction can help you understand what you read.

When you respond to and write about nonfiction, you explain why a certain point is the main idea and present the details that support your explanation. These can be examples from the book or article. You can also use examples from your own experience.

Identifying the Main Idea

Nina read Stephen Krensky's nonfiction text "Striking It Rich: The Story of the California Gold Rush." She learned about the how the Gold Rush changed California and America. The author described the many changes that resulted from people heading west to find gold.

Nina used a main-idea web to organize her ideas for this article. First, Nina identified the main idea of the article. Then she found details and examples from the text that support the main idea.

Effected western towns

People in the East and Midwest headed West to find gold.

Easterners traveled by ship.

Midwesterners traveled by land.

Some went by way of Central America.

People quit their jobs.

Soldiers abandoned their posts.

Schoolhouses closed after teachers left.

The discovery of gold in the West changed America.

The Gold Rush helped populate the West.

Mining paid better

People settled and hoped to get rich

Many people faced danger and even died on the trip.

Cholera

Rattlesnakes and grizzly bears.

Indians

Take a Look

Following the web she created, here is what Nina wrote about the article.

In "*Striking It Rich: The Story of the California Gold Rush,*" the author talks about how the discovery of gold in 1848 put California on the map and changed America. Before 1848, people in the Midwest and the East did not know much about the West or California. California was a new region with a small, spread out population. ◀ **Main Idea**

After gold was discovered, San Francisco was practically abandoned as people headed for the hills to find gold. ◀ **Details from the Article**

When word of the discovery finally reached the East, newspapers began printing stories about an abundance of gold, making people want to travel west. Travelers took one of three routes. Easterners went by sea. Midwesterners traveled by land. Some people traveled by way of boat to Central America and then walked across Panama to take another boat to California.

No matter which way travelers went, they always faced danger. Some travelers got sick from cholera. Those who traveled across land had to watch out for dangerous animals and attacks by Indians.

Those who made it all the way to California were relieved and ready to settle down. They wanted to make more money as miners than they did back home as farmers and store clerks. Many of them hoped to find a lot of gold and strike it rich. ◀ **Details from Nina's Experience**

Try It!

Nina needs to add a conclusion to her paper. Create a sentence to conclude Nina's thoughts.

Analyzing the Model

Did you notice that Nina did not copy sentences from her graphic organizer into her report? She combined some sentences. She put other sentences in different order. She also added more details and explanations. Nina thought about how the author of "Striking It Rich: The Story of the California Gold Rush" used time order to organize his article. Organization helped Nina easily see how California and America changed because of the Gold Rush.

The Main Idea

The author's descriptions of what happened before and after the Gold Rush helped Nina locate the main idea—she wrote the main idea in her own words.

The Supporting Details

To support her main idea, Nina used details and examples from the article. For each paragraph, she chooses one supporting detail to focus on. In paragraph two, Nina uses the example of abandoned towns to show how California changed. In paragraph three, she uses details from the story to show how the rest of America got involved in the Gold Rush. She describes the different ways people traveled to California. In paragraph four, she describes the dangers faced by travelers going west, using specific examples from the story.

Reading Your Writing

Identifying the main idea is an important part of understanding nonfiction. Once you've identified the main idea in a piece of nonfiction, write a response. Writing about nonfiction will help you explain the main idea and the supporting details and examples in a clear and logical way. Being able to write about nonfiction helps you learn more and share information with others.

Tips for Responding to Nonfiction

Prewriting   Make a Plan

▶ Read the article or book and look for the main idea that ties it all together. In a book, you might figure out the topic of each chapter. The chapters can offer clues to the main idea.

▶ Use a graphic organizer, such as a web, to organize your information.

▶ Fill in your organizer with your main idea and details that support it. Use examples from the book or article as well as examples from your own experience.

Drafting   Get Your Thoughts on Paper

▶ Follow your graphic organizer to write a draft of your response.

▶ Start with your main idea. Writing paragraphs for each of the supporting details is a good idea.

Revising   Be Sure Your Response Makes Sense

▶ **Organization** Think about the best way to organize your information. You might organize the supporting details by order of importance or by time order.

▶ **Ideas** Make sure the details you include support the main idea.

▶ **Word Choice** See if you have repeated any words too often. If so, think of synonyms you could use.

▶ **Sentence Fluency** Ask a partner to read your report aloud. Listen for sentences that sound choppy. You may need to combine simple sentences or add transition words.

Editing/Proofreading   Look Closely at the Details

▶ **Conventions** Check the punctuation of any compound and complex sentences.

Publishing   Get Ready to Share Your Response

▶ Write or type your final copy.

▶ **Presentation** Read your response to your class or a small group. You may want to create a chart, diagram, or table (such as a time line) to use during your oral presentation.

FUN FACT

The first printing presses operated by pressing ink-covered metal letters against paper. Now computers do most of the work.

Writing a Book Review

In a book review, you summarize the book and tell your opinion of it. This section will help you write reviews for both fiction and nonfiction books.

Reviewing a Fiction Book

Here's how Eric organized his ideas for a review of the book, "Island of the Blue Dolphins" by Scott O'Dell.

Summary of Plot

Beginning (problem): Karana is alone on her island because all her people ran away to escape an enemy tribe. She is overwhelmed with loneliness.

Middle (events):

1. She decides to take off in a canoe hoping she will find another island where there are people.

2. The canoe gets a leak, and she tries repeatedly to repair it.

3. Eventually she realizes the safest thing to do is to return to the island from where she came.

Ending (How the problem was solved): The dolphins help Karana return safely to the island.

Opinion: I liked the book. I liked the way Karana fought to survive no matter how lonely she was or how difficult and dangerous it was to survive. She was a strong and courageous character.

Here is Eric's book review, based on his graphic organizer.

"Island of the Blue Dolphins" by Scott O'Dell begins on an island where Karana has been left behind and is alone. Her people have ran away to escape an enemy tribe. She hopes her people will return for her, but eventually she gives up hope. She is overwhelmed with loneliness and must decide what to do.

She decides to take off in a canoe to find another island where there are people. After the first day of her journey, the canoe gets a leak. She tries to repair it with scraps of cloth from her skirt. Eventually she realizes the safest thing to do is to return to the deserted island from where she came. On her way back, dolphins appear and escort her back to the island, easing her loneliness and giving her the strength to make the journey safely to shore.

I really liked this story because the author shows how strong and courageous Karana is. She fought to survive no matter how lonely she was or how difficult and dangerous it was to survive.

Reviewing a Nonfiction Book

When you review a nonfiction book, you should summarize the main ideas and the details that support the main ideas. Like a review of a fiction book, the title and the name of the author should be included in your nonfiction book review. The title of the book and name of the author should be in your first sentence. Also, tell the reader what you think about the book.

Samantha chose to review the biography of *Mae Jemison, Space Scientist*. Here is the graphic organizer she used for her nonfiction book review.

Title: Mae Jemison, Space Scientist

↓

Author: Gail Sakurai

↓

Summary: Before being an astronaut
1. born in 1956 in Alabama
2. teachers discouraged dreams of traveling in space
3. became a doctor
4. served in Peace Corps

Astronaut experience
1. began training in 1987
2. 1992, served on Endeavour
3. did experiments in space

Since retiring
1. formed a company
2. encourages others

↓

My opinion and reasons for it: good story! She's a good role model. She worked hard and followed her dreams.

Take a Look

Samantha wrote her book review based on the notes in her graphic organizer.

Mae Jemison, Space Scientist, was written by Gail Sakurai. It is the biography of the first African American woman in space. Jemison was born in Alabama and moved to Chicago. She always wanted to travel in space, but some of her teachers discouraged her. She became a doctor and served in the Peace Corps.

She was accepted as an astronaut in 1987. She flew on the space shuttle Endeavour in 1992, where she performed experiments.

After she retired, she formed her own company. The people who work in her company are scientists. They think about ways to use science to improve our lives. Mae still teaches young people to follow their dreams.

This book is good. It wasn't easy for Dr. Jemison to do the great things she did. Her hard work paid off. Her story shows that dreams do come true.

Reading Your Writing

When you write book reviews for others you can help them choose books that they might enjoy reading.

Tips for Reviewing a Fiction Book

Prewriting Make a Plan

▶ Use a story map to organize your writing.

Drafting Get Your Thoughts on Paper

▶ Follow your story map to write a draft of your review.
▶ Include the title of the book, the author, and the setting at the beginning of your opening paragraph.
▶ Summarize the important events in the plot. Don't forget to talk about the main characters of the story in your plot summary. Be brief.
▶ Explain why you liked or disliked the book. Give examples of what you liked or disliked, such as certain events in the story, the characters, or the problem they solved.

Revising Be Sure Your Book Review Makes Sense

▶ **Organization** Make sure the story events are in the correct order.
▶ **Ideas** Check to see that you have chosen the most important events for your summary.
▶ **Voice** Let your readers know what you think about the story. If you really liked it, make that clear. If you didn't, explain why.
▶ **Word Choice** Make sure you used words that will create a clear picture in the reader's mind.

Editing/Proofreading Look Closely at the Details

▶ **Conventions** Check your sentence structure, spelling, and punctuation.

Publishing Get Ready to Share Your Review

▶ Write or type your final copy.
▶ **Presentation** Consider drawing a picture of a story event to go with your review.
▶ Share your review with your class or a small group. If possible, display the cover of the book.

Tips for Reviewing a Nonfiction Book

Prewriting Make a Plan

- ▶ Read the book. Look for the main idea and supporting details.
- ▶ Choose a graphic organizer to help you organize your ideas for writing the summary.
- ▶ Fill in your organizer with details and examples from the book.

Drafting Get Your Thoughts on Paper

- ▶ Follow your graphic organizer to write a draft of your review.
- ▶ Mention the title and the author in the opening sentence.
- ▶ Include the main ideas of the book in your summary. Choose the most important details and examples from the book that support the main ideas. Include these in your summary, too.
- ▶ Give your opinion of the book at the end of your review. Explain why you think others should (or should not) read the book.

Revising Be Sure Your Book Review Makes Sense

- ▶ **Ideas** Make sure the main idea and details of the book are clear in your review.
- ▶ **Organization** Make sure you describe the details that support the main ideas in the order they appear in the book.
- ▶ **Word Choice** Look for words that the reader might not understand without first reading the book. You may need to define these words or choose more familiar words.
- ▶ **Sentence Fluency** Read your review aloud to check for awkward sentences. If you hear any, revise them.

Editing/Proofreading Look Closely at the Details

- ▶ **Conventions** Check your sentences and make sure they have subjects and predicates.
- ▶ Check the punctuation of your sentences.

Publishing Get Ready to Share Your Review

- ▶ **Presentation** Neatly write or type the final version of your review.
- ▶ Read your review again. Think of any questions the class or group might ask and make sure you know the answers.

Explaining a Process and Giving Directions

Have you ever explained how something happens? For example, in science class, you might have been asked to tell how rain clouds form. By telling how something happens, you are explaining a process.

Have you ever given someone directions? Maybe you have told a friend how to get to your home. By telling someone how to do something, you are giving directions.

When you explain a process, you tell the reader how something happens step by step. When you give directions, you tell the reader how to do something, in sequence order, from beginning to end. To make sure the steps of a process or the directions are clear to your reader, ask yourself these questions.

▶ What does my audience already know?

▶ What are the steps of the process or directions?

▶ What is the sequence or order of the steps in the process or directions?

Often a picture or diagram will make the process or instructions clearer. This section will help you with both kinds of writing.

Explaining a Process

When you describe a process, you tell what happens in the order it happens. To help the reader understand the order of the steps in a process, use words that show order. Here are some words you can use.

first	second	third
next	then	before
after	last	finally

Take a Look

Below, Alicia explains how bats find insects. Notice the words that tell what happens first, next, and so on. (They are underlined here for you.)

How Bats Find Their Food

Most bats eat insects. The brown bat can eat up to 600 mosquitoes an hour. Bats feed at night. How can they find mosquitoes and other insects in the dark?

First, bats send out sound waves that we cannot hear. Next, sound waves hit an object, such as an insect. Then, they bounce back to the bat like an echo. Finally, the sound waves tell the bat where the object is. The bat swoops in and catches the insect. The bat does not need to see the insect to catch it!

Giving Directions

When you give directions, you tell the reader how to do something, step by step. You can write the directions in a paragraph, or list them and number the steps.

To make your directions clear to the reader, you can use some of the words used to explain a process. However, because giving directions is different from explaining a process, you will also need words that tell direction. Here are some place and location words you can use when giving directions.

behind	bottom	across	top	left, right
under	near	beside	between	through

As you begin writing, think about the steps in the directions. Then, organize your information based on the order of the steps.

Oscar's teacher asked him to write directions for his classmates. They need to know how to change the name of a computer file. Oscar thought about the steps, chose a graphic organizer, and filled it in. Here is his graphic organizer.

Step 1: Open old file.

↓

Step 2: Click "File" on toolbar.

↓

Step 3: Click "Save as."

↓

Step 4: Type new file name in the space after the words "File name."

↓

Step 5: Click "Save."

Take a Look

Below are Oscar's directions for his classmates. Notice how he uses words that tell time order and direction. He also adds a title.

How to Rename a Computer File

Do you want to change the name of a computer file? If your answer is yes, here's how to do it. First, open the old file so that it is on your screen. Then, click "File" on the toolbar at the top of your screen. You will see a menu on the left side of your screen. Now click "Save As."

The computer will place another screen on top of your file. Look toward the bottom for the window that says "File Name." Type in the new name of your file. The old name will disappear.

Look on the right side of this screen for "Save." Click it. This screen will disappear. Next, look at the file name at the top of your screen. It should be the new name.

Now you have a copy of the old file with the new name. You also have a copy of the old file with the old name.

Try It!

Which of these is a process? Which is a set of directions? What are the steps in each process or set of directions?

- How seeds sprout
- How to address an envelope
- How food spoils

Reading Your Writing

Being able to clearly explain a process or write directions is a valuable skill. Unclear explanations or directions can cause mistakes and make your readers confused.

Tips for Explaining a Process

Prewriting   Make a Plan

▶ Think about the steps in the process and what your audience already knows about it.

Drafting   Get Your Thoughts on Paper

▶ Explain each step in order by sequence.
▶ Add a short conclusion.
▶ Add a short introduction that tells the process you are explaining.

Revising   Be Sure Your Explanation Makes Sense

▶ **Organization** Make sure you described the steps in the correct order. Do not leave out a step. Have a partner read your writing to see if the sequence of steps makes sense.
▶ **Ideas** Provide enough details so the reader can understand the process. See if your partner can explain the process to you.
▶ **Word Choice** Do you use order words such as *first*, *next*, and *last*, that show the sequence of steps in the process? If necessary, add these words.

Editing/Proofreading   Look Closely at the Details

▶ **Conventions** Check your spelling, punctuation, and sentence structure.

Publishing   Get Ready to Share Your Explanation

▶ Make a clean copy with all your edits.
▶ **Presentation** Create a diagram to illustrate the process.
▶ Read it again before you share it with your class or a small group. Have your diagram ready to show them.

Tips for Giving Directions

Prewriting   Make a Plan

▶ Think about what you need to tell your readers and what you can leave out.

Drafting   Get Your Thoughts on Paper

▶ Decide whether to write the directions as a paragraph or numbered steps.
▶ Explain each step in the order it must be completed.
▶ Add a title, an introduction, and a conclusion.

Revising   Be Sure Your Directions Make Sense

▶ **Organization** Ask a partner to carry out the steps (or at least read them) to make sure that your directions can be followed.
▶ **Sentence Fluency** Make sure that each sentence telling the reader to do something starts with a verb. For example, write "Type in the file name," not "The file name should be typed in."
▶ **Word Choice** Have you used order and direction words?

Editing/Proofreading   Look Closely at the Details

▶ **Conventions** Check your sentence structure, spelling, and punctuation.

Publishing   Get Ready to Share Your Directions

▶ Write or type the final version.
▶ **Presentation** Create a diagram to illustrate your directions.
▶ Present your directions to your class or a small group. Have them follow your directions.

Writing a News Story

News stories are printed in newspapers. Some are posted on the Internet. How is a news story different from other stories?

▶ A **news story** tells about something important that just happened.

▶ In the first paragraph, a news story must answer these questions: *What? When? Where? Who? Why?* Less important information goes at the end of the story. Then, if the story must be shortened to fit on the page, the most important information will still be there.

▶ A news story contains facts and not the reporter's opinions. All facts are carefully checked.

Try It!

Read the headline and first paragraph of this news story. Based on what you just read above and the headline, what would you add to the paragraph? What would you take out?

Fire in Cafeteria at Roberts School

by Rebecca Oats

Roberts School, at 310 Oakhill Street, has 360 students in kindergarten through grade six. It also has 24 teachers and other staff. Karla Winters has been the principal for the past three years.

The Parts of a News Story

A news story includes some or all of the parts listed below.

Headline

The **headline** is the title of the story. It tells what the story is about in a way that gets the reader's attention.

Byline

The **byline** tells the name of the reporter who wrote the story.

Lead

The **lead** should "lead" readers into the story. It tells *what, when, where,* and *who.* The next sentences usually explain *why.* Many people will read only the lead of a news story, so the most important information must be there. (Editors often have to cut, or shorten, stories too. They cut from the end of the stories, not the beginning.)

Body

The **body** of the story provides more facts and gives background information.

Quotation

The story might have a **quotation** from people involved in the event.

Caption

If the story includes a photograph, a **caption** will tell about the picture. Often the caption adds more information to the story.

Close

The **close,** or ending, wraps up the story. The reporter can end his or her story with a brief summary of the events and his or her own observations.

This news story includes some of the parts described on page 107.

Group Wants Dam Removed ◀ **Headline**

by Robert Martin ◀ **Byline**

Yesterday, Timothy Brandon, president of the Friends of Mud ◀ **Lead**
River, contacted state and federal officials to request the removal of
a dam recently built on the river. Brandon feels that Bob and Shirley
Harris, who built the dam to stop erosion on their land, had no right ◀ **Body**
to build it. Brandon was surprised when a new dam interrupted his
canoe trip. He was paddling down Mud River just south of Eastonia.
Brandon later learned that Bob and Shirley Harris, who own property
along the river, constructed the dam.

"I couldn't believe my eyes," said Brandon. "Then I got angry. No ◀ **Quotation**
one has the right to stop the flow of the river!"

For several years, the Friends of Mud River have been
working on protecting the land around the river. Brandon
insists a new dam will threaten area wildlife.

Now the U.S. Army Corps of Engineering is trying
to determine whether the Harrises acted properly in
building the dam. Peter Sales, Corps spokesperson, says,
"People must have a permit before adding soil or rocks
to the riverbed. If they don't get one, we can require
them to remove the material."

The Mud River flows for 95 miles. It begins in
Cairo County and enters the Snake River south of
Eastonia. The new dam stretches almost across the Mud River,
which is about 40 feet wide at that point.

The Harrises say they have a right to protect their land, but ◀ **Close**
Brandon points out that the habitat for many animals will be lost.
Officials agree that balancing the two viewpoints will not be easy.

Try It!

Read the news story again. Can you locate two
quotations in the news story?

Tips for Writing a News Story

Prewriting Make a Plan

▶ Look for a school event that would make a good news story.
▶ Answer these questions: *What? Where? When? Who?* and *Why?*
▶ Observe the scene, if possible, and interview the people involved. Make some notes so you can write these details in your story.

Drafting Get Your Thoughts on Paper

▶ Use your notes to write a draft of your story.
▶ Answer the "W" questions in the first paragraph. Put the less important information later in the story.

Revising Be Sure Your Story Makes Sense

▶ **Organization** After you answer the "W" questions in the first paragraph, organize the rest of the information by order of importance or time order.
▶ **Voice** Show the excitement you feel about the story. For the lead, capture the readers' interest by asking a question or offering information that will grab their attention.
▶ **Word Choice** Check to see if you used the best words to explain the events in your news story.
▶ **Sentence Fluency** Read your story aloud to see if the sentences help readers move easily from one thought to the next. If necessary, add words to show transitions.

Editing/Proofreading Look Closely at the Details

▶ **Conventions** Check the punctuation of sentences that contain quotations. Make sure you use commas and quotation marks correctly.

Publishing Get Ready to Share Your News Story

▶ Write or type your final copy.
▶ **Presentation** You may wish to format your news story to look like a page in a newspaper.

Writing an Informative Report

An informative report helps you form a question that interests you, gather information about it, and answer that question.

Select Key Words to Locate Information

Sarah has to find information for her report. She thought of these key words to help in her search.

Peregrine falcons	Falcons	Birds
Endangered species	Bird breeding	Zoos

Choose a Structure for the Report

Sarah chose a problem-resolution chart to organize her report. She adds some topics she wants to include to her chart. She will select other headings as she learns more about this topic.

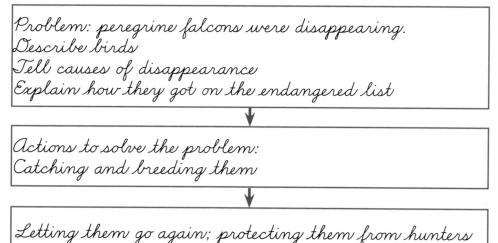

Problem: peregrine falcons were disappearing.
Describe birds
Tell causes of disappearance
Explain how they got on the endangered list

↓

Actions to solve the problem:
Catching and breeding them

↓

Letting them go again; protecting them from hunters

Writing the Report

Now Sarah organizes her note cards according to her problem-resolution chart. Then she writes a draft of her report. It is supposed to be 400 words.

Next, Sarah carefully revises and edits her report. She hopes it will be published in the school newspaper. That way, she can help other students and staff learn more about the peregrine falcons that are nesting in their city.

Take a Look

Here is Sarah's revised, edited version of her report.

Sarah's introduction offers some surprising facts about peregrine falcons.

The middle of her report contains facts Sarah collected from many sources. She used her chart to group them. She describes the falcons, explains the problem, and tells how the problem was resolved.

How Peregrine Falcons Were Saved from Extinction

Peregrine falcons are the fastest birds on Earth. They can fly 70 to 150 miles per hour. They used to live on every continent except Antarctica. However, about 50 years ago, they almost disappeared. This report tells why we almost lost the peregrine falcons and how we saved them.

Peregrine falcons are 15 to 21 inches long from the head to the end of the tail. Their wings are from 37 to 43 inches from tip to tip. Falcons are predators. They catch their food in the air. They eat small birds and bats. The photo shows what colors they are.

Sarah uses headings to show how her report is organized.

The word *birds* at the end of this paragraph is repeated in the first sentence of the next paragraph. Repeating a word helps link the end of one paragraph to the beginning of the next one.

How We Almost Lost These Birds

After World War II, many farmers used a chemical called DDT to kill insects on their crops. Small birds ate seeds that had been sprayed with DDT. Falcons ate these birds.

DDT from the birds started to build up in the falcons' bodies. It caused them to lay eggs with thin shells. The shells broke before the baby birds were ready to hatch. After a while, few baby falcons hatched. Peregrine falcons began to disappear.

In 1972, the use of DDT was outlawed. In 1973, the U.S. Fish and Wildlife Service put peregrine falcons on the list of endangered species.

How These Birds Were Saved

Stopping the use of DDT helped save the peregrine falcons and other birds, such as bald eagles. People also started to protect the places where falcons live, such as high cliffs.

Falcons were also captured and given safe places to breed. By 1975, about 200 young falcons were being bred every year. After the young birds learned to fly, most of them were taken to the wilderness. Then they were let go. Some were released in cities with tall buildings and lots of pigeons to eat.

Some of the young birds died, but many of them made homes in cliffs or on rooftops. They had more babies. By 1999, there were more than 1,650 pairs of peregrines.

In August 1999, the Fish and Wildlife Service took falcons off the list of endangered species. This agency will check on the falcons for the next five years. If their numbers drop again, they will be put back on the list.

The Fish and Wildlife Service and many others are making sure that peregrine falcons continue to soar through our skies.

In her short conclusion, Sarah summarizes her report.

Tips for Writing an Informative Report

Prewriting   Make a Plan

▶ Choose a general topic and narrow it down.
▶ Form a question about the topic.
▶ Select keywords for locating information.
▶ Identify possible sources.
▶ Choose a structure, such as problem resolution, to organize your information.
▶ Take notes on note cards. Add a heading to each card, such as *Description* or *History*. Write down the source and page number for each fact.
▶ Make your bibliography cards.

Drafting   Get Your Thoughts on Paper

▶ Put your note cards in order to match the organization you chose.
▶ Use your notes to write a draft of your report. Include an interesting introduction and a middle section full of facts. Add an ending that ties everything together.
▶ Consider using illustrations or a chart in your report.

Revising   Be Sure Your Report Makes Sense

▶ **Organization** Make sure the main points in your report are presented in a logical order, such as order of importance or time order.
▶ **Ideas** See if your introduction grabs readers' attention. You might start with a surprising fact or an interesting quotation.
▶ **Voice** Show the interest and curiosity you feel about the topic.
▶ **Sentence Fluency** Read your entire report aloud. If necessary, add transitions between sentences and between paragraphs.

Editing/Proofreading   Look Closely at the Details

▶ **Conventions** Check your sentence structure, spelling, and punctuation.

Publishing   Get Ready to Share Your Report

▶ **Presentation** Write neatly or type your final copy.
▶ Consider publishing your report in the school newspaper or the newsletter that goes home to parents.

Forms of Writing

Narrative Writing

Narrative writing tells a story. The story can be true, such as a biography or autobiography. These contain real people and real events. The story can be fictional, or make-believe. Some fiction stories can be realistic, with characters and events that could really happen. Others, such as fantasy and science fiction stories, contain characters and events that could never really happen.

When you do narrative writing, you are telling your readers what happened. Narrative writing has a beginning, a middle, and an end. It also needs a setting, a problem and solution, and characters. It may also need dialogue. Look on the next page for some of the different kinds of narrative writing.

Personal Narrative

Maybe you've read a story written by an athlete about competing in a sport. Perhaps you've read stories written by other kids who have done amazing things, such as start their own businesses. In these stories, called **personal narratives,** the writers shared their own experiences. A personal narrative is a true story from the writer's own life.

Not all personal narratives are about record-setting or life-changing events, though. Many are about very simple events. American author E. B. White wrote a personal narrative about catching sight of twin fawns at the Bronx Zoo.

The fact is, most of us are pretty ordinary. We don't start businesses or set Olympic records at age 11. We go to school, we eat meals with our families, and we get along with the people around us. Even these activities and events, simple as they are, can provide topics for personal narratives. What matters is that the subject of a personal narrative is important to you because of what you learned from the experience. When you share that with your readers, they may learn something as well.

Try It!

Here are some idea starters for a personal narrative. Think about how you might complete the following sentences.

I was so proud when . . .

I don't know how I did it, but . . .

Looking back, I wish . . .

Exploring a Topic

To make a personal narrative interesting for readers, it needs details. Writers must dig into their memories for details, answering questions such as these:

▶ What sounds, smells, or tastes are connected with my topic?
▶ What did things look or feel like?
▶ How did *I* feel?
▶ What did other people do or say?

Once you have a topic and ideas about details you want to include, use a web to help you organize your ideas.

A student named Megan remembers an event that changed her life quite a bit. It was the birth of her sister, Allison. Here's how she organized her ideas for her personal narrative.

Megan wrote her personal narrative using her plan.

Allison

Three days had gone by since I got the news. I kept saying it over and over. My mother was going to have a baby. I couldn't believe it. Lots of people have babies, but they're younger than my mom. She's not really old, but it's been nine years since she had a baby. Why did she need another baby? She had me, didn't she? I was not ready for this.

I did not think things would happen so soon. Mom wanted me to move into the other bedroom. She said it would be best for the baby. My old room was closer to the bathroom, and that would make it easier to dump the baby's dirty diapers. Already it was my old room. She didn't ask me. Everything had to be best for the baby. Even the crib, the blankets, the clothes, the toys were the best. Nothing was best for me.

Already, everyone forgot all about me. I spent two days making a big, bright sign for my new bedroom door. It said, "Megan's Room, I LIVE HERE." Nobody noticed.

I could tell Grandma cared about the new baby more than me. Grandma picked me up from school one Friday. She said Mom and Dad were at the hospital. It seemed scary to have Mom in the hospital. Grandma wanted to go straight home to be by the phone. She was so excited about the new baby. I was upset.

The next morning, Grandma asked if I wanted to know if Mom had a boy or a girl. I said I'd wait and see. While I ate breakfast, Grandma told me anyway. It was a girl. She said, "I just can't wait to hold my latest granddaughter."

I rolled that idea around in my head while I was eating my jelly toast. So I have a sister. I imagined how I would introduce her to my friends. I wondered if she had a name.

At the hospital, Dad was sitting on the edge of Mom's bed. I walked up to the bed and looked around for the baby. Then I saw her there in Mom's arms. She was so small! Mom pushed back the soft pink blanket so I could see.

"Megan, this is your baby sister Allison." That's all she said. I looked down into her bright eyes. She looked right back up at me as if she knew I was her sister. All of a sudden I realized I liked her.

While I waited for Mom and Allison to come home from the hospital, I made a sign for my sister's bedroom door. It said, "Allison's Room, I LIVE HERE TOO."

Parts of Personal Narratives

A personal narrative has an **introduction,** a **body,** and a **conclusion.**

Introduction

In Megan's narrative, her first paragraph is her introduction. She tells what's going to happen, and she hints at her feelings about it. Her first sentence makes readers want to find out what the news is.

Three days had gone by since I got the news.

Body

The next seven paragraphs of Megan's narrative make up the body.

▶ Megan shares some events that happened. She tells them in the order they happened so her readers can stay with the story.

▶ She also includes her own thoughts and feelings. Remember that this is a *personal* narrative, so thoughts and feelings may be the most important part of it.
It seemed scary to have Mom in the hospital.

▶ Megan uses sensory details.
Mom pushed back the soft pink blanket so I could see.

▶ Megan includes just a little bit of dialogue. It helps make the story seem personal.

▶ She used a good variety of sentence types, and she mixes longer sentences and shorter sentences. Her writing doesn't sound too formal, but it doesn't sound too informal either. The tone is warm and personal.

Conclusion

The final paragraph is Megan's conclusion. She doesn't exactly say that her attitude about the baby changed completely, does she? It's clear, though, from what she does in the last paragraph that Megan loves her little sister. Megan's change in feelings—from being upset to being glad—is what makes this a good topic for a personal narrative.

Reading Your Writing

In Megan's narrative, visual details, such as the color and texture of the blanket, are important. In your narrative, sounds, smells, tastes, or textures might be important too. Don't forget to include them.

Tips for Writing a Personal Narrative

Prewriting Make a Plan

▶ Think about important people, events, and activities in your life.
▶ The topic you choose may be a large or small event, but it must be important to you.
▶ Use a web to organize your ideas.

Drafting Get Your Thoughts on Paper

▶ Do I tell the events as they happened?
▶ Do I add details and my thoughts and feelings so readers can get the whole picture?
▶ Does my opening sentence make the reader want to read on?
▶ Is the meaning of the event in my conclusion?

Revising Be Sure It Makes Sense

▶ **Ideas** Is it clear to readers what I learned from the experience?
▶ **Organization** Do I tell the events in time order? Will my readers be able to follow?
▶ **Voice** Do my thoughts and feelings show in my writing?
▶ **Word Choice** Do I choose words that show my feelings?
▶ **Sentence Fluency** Do I use a variety of sentences?

Editing/Proofreading Look Closely at the Details

▶ **Conventions** Does each sentence begin with a capital letter and have the correct end punctuation?
▶ Read your narrative aloud slowly to catch missing words, spelling errors, fragments, or run-on sentences.

Publishing Get Your Personal Narrative Ready to Share

▶ Neatly write or type a final copy.

Writing a Biography

A **biography** is a book or article about a real person that is written by another person. This is different from an autobiography, which is something a person writes about his or her own life. A biography is full of true information about the person, who is the subject.

Some biographies cover the subject's entire life. Other biographies focus on a certain period of time that was important in the subject's life. For example, a biography of a president might cover only the years he was in office. A biography of an artist might cover only the years of his or her painting career.

Biographies are different from stories because biographies contain real people and real events. A biography may not contain any made-up information. Usually, the truth of a biography of a famous subject can be checked by looking in a reference book, such as an encyclopedia.

Because a biography is about the events in a person's life, information is usually organized in **chronological,** or time, **order.** For example, a writer would talk about Shel Silverstein's boyhood before talking about his career as a writer.

Try It!

Think about a biography you have read. Did it talk about the person's whole life, or just a specific period of time? What kinds of information did the biographies include?

Gathering and Organizing Information for a Biography

It is best to organize a biography in chronological order. A student named Eleanor wanted to know more about another Eleanor. She chose to write about Eleanor Roosevelt. After she gathered information from books, encyclopedias, and the Internet, she used a time line to organize her information. Here's how she organized her information.

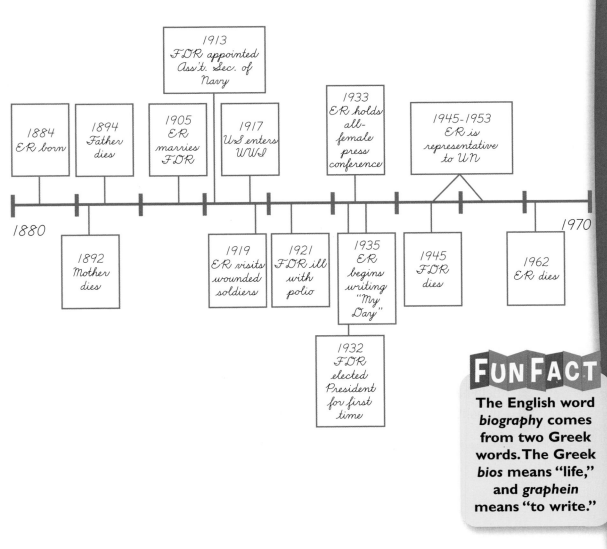

Eleanor Roosevelt

1913
FDR appointed Ass't. Sec. of Navy

1884 ER born

1894 Father dies

1905 ER marries FDR

1917 US enters WWI

1933 ER holds all-female press conference

1945-1953 ER is representative to UN

1880

1970

1892 Mother dies

1919 ER visits wounded soldiers

1921 FDR ill with polio

1935 ER begins writing "My Day"

1945 FDR dies

1962 ER dies

1932 FDR elected President for first time

FUN FACT

The English word *biography* comes from two Greek words. The Greek *bios* means "life," and *graphein* means "to write."

Using her notes, Eleanor wrote this biography.

Eleanor Roosevelt

She was more than just a smiling face beside the president. She did more than raise five children and look after her husband. Eleanor Roosevelt created a new role for the first lady. She had her own interests and goals. She spoke out on issues that mattered to her. Some people called her outspoken. Many people loved her.

Eleanor Roosevelt was born on October 11, 1884. Eleanor was very young when her parents died. She was only 8 when her mother died, and two years later her father died. Some people think that this sadness in her life is what helped her become such a strong woman.

Eleanor married Franklin Delano Roosevelt in 1905. She spent the next ten years caring for her growing family. During this time, her husband's career changed. First, he was a law student and then he became a lawyer. Next, he was a New York State Senator and then Assistant Secretary of the Navy in 1913.

When the United States entered World War I in 1917, Eleanor volunteered in a hospital, visiting wounded soldiers. This is just one example of the many things she did for people who needed help. In 1921 when her husband became ill with polio, Eleanor took care of him. After his illness, Eleanor wanted Franklin to stay interested in his dreams. She increased her own activities to help her husband stay in touch with the world. She became active in politics at a time when most women did not.

Eleanor became First Lady after her husband won the 1932 presidential election. Once she became First Lady, Eleanor played a big role in the nation. She traveled all over the country so that she could tell her husband what was happening. She paid special attention to people's working and living conditions. During World War II, she even traveled to the South Pacific to cheer up the soldiers. She worked for the rights of blacks and other minorities. Eleanor was the first first lady to hold her own press conferences. Only female reporters were invited. In 1935, she began writing a daily newspaper article.

"My Day" was the title of Eleanor's newspaper article. It appeared in U.S. newspapers six days a week until 1962, the year of Eleanor's death. Eleanor shared news of her life as first lady and later as a representative to the United Nations. She also expressed her opinions about topics such as Pearl Harbor, Native Americans, Hollywood, space exploration, and the rights of black people. By reading Eleanor's columns, Americans felt as if they knew Eleanor personally.

Eleanor lived through some of the most important events of the twentieth century. She didn't sit back and watch, though. She reached out and helped people all over the world.

Try It!

Like other forms of writing, a biography has an introduction, a body, and a conclusion. Can you find each of those parts in the biography of Eleanor Roosevelt?

Writing a Good Biography

A good biographer writes only facts supported by details and examples. If a biographer wants to draw conclusions, she must give evidence to support her conclusions. In this biography, the writer concludes that Eleanor Roosevelt "reached out and helped people all over the world." The body of her paper supports that conclusion.

Getting Readers Interested

Some people might think that reading about a president's wife—or about anyone else—isn't interesting. It's up to the writer to let readers know that what they're reading *is* interesting. If this biography had begun with "Eleanor Roosevelt was born on October 11, 1884," some readers probably would have stopped right there. Instead, the writer made the First Lady sound like a very interesting person.

Keeping Readers Interested

Think of your biography as a story, not as a time line written in paragraph form. Don't include too many sentences that sound like this: "In 1921, he did this. In 1922, this happened. In 1924, he did this." One way to get around this is to use different sentence styles. Another way is to use other kinds of time expressions. Here are some of the different expressions Eleanor used in her paper:

She was only 8 . . .	*. . . in 1905.*
. . . two years later . . .	*. . . the next ten years . . .*

Preparing a Bibliography

As Eleanor was doing her research, she kept track of where she found the information about her subject. When she completed her biography, she created a bibliography listing the books, encyclopedias, and Web sites where she got the information. For more about creating a bibliography, see page 316.

Tips for Writing a Biography

Prewriting Make a Plan

▶ Think of things that interest you—a period in history, an invention, a place. Then identify people connected with your interest.

▶ Research your topic. Read at least two sources such as an article in an encyclopedia or on the Internet. Take notes. Also remember to write down the necessary information about each source you use.

▶ Organize your notes in chronological order by using a time line.

Drafting Get Your Thoughts on Paper

▶ Follow your notes as you draft your biography carefully.

▶ Remember to use signal words that show time or order.

Revising Be Sure It Makes Sense

▶ **Ideas** Are the events and details of my subject's life clear?

▶ **Organization** Are the events organized in time order? Will my readers be able to follow the events I've written about easily?

▶ **Voice** Does my writing sound like me, or does it sound like my sources?

▶ **Sentence Fluency** Do I vary the beginnings of some of my sentences?

Editing/Proofreading Look Closely at the Details

▶ **Conventions** Begin each sentence with a capital letter and end with an end mark. Remember to capitalize all proper nouns.

▶ Indent each paragraph.

Publishing Get Your Biography Ready to Share

▶ Neatly type or handwrite your final copy.

▶ If possible, include a picture of your subject.

▶ Include a bibliography listing the sources you used to write your biography.

Realistic Fiction

In **realistic fiction,** the characters, places, and events are all made up, but they *seem* real.

A made-up story about an astronaut on a mission to the moon would be realistic fiction. If that astronaut grows wings and flies on his own power, instead of using a spaceship, the story would *not* be realistic—it would be a fantasy. A story about an astronaut who visits the citizens of a country on Venus would not be realistic either—it would be science fiction.

Try It!

Which of the following details could you use in realistic fiction?

- ▶ a talking butterfly
- ▶ a dog gets lost
- ▶ a boy builds a go-cart
- ▶ a duck stops a farm from being sold

Characters, Setting, and Plot

Like all stories realistic fiction has one or more characters. The characters are regular people or animals. They don't have special powers, nor are they from any planet other than Earth. If a story has animals for characters, they act as they would in real life. They don't think in words. They don't talk or wear clothes.

The setting, or where the action takes place, might be common or unusual, but it must be an actual place. For example, it can't be a rain forest in Kansas or a city under the ocean.

The plot, or series of events, in realistic fiction *could* happen. For example, a boy could meet an elephant walking down the street in Denver, but only if there has been an escape from a nearby circus or zoo.

Planning Realistic Fiction

Once you come up with your basic story idea, use a story map to plan your characters, setting, and plot. Here's a realistic fiction plan created by a fourth-grade student.

Title
Mississippi Lesson

Character(s)
Maria—smart, quiet kid in class
Mrs. Hoff—teacher with calm voice
Scott—another smart kid in class

Setting
classroom with a large pull-down map in front

Plot
Beginning: Maria knows certain things about her creek and about how things are at school.

Middle:
1. Mrs. Hoff asks a question about Mississippi River. Maria is sure she knows the answer.
2. Maria waits for classmates to give the answer. She wonders if they know what she knows about her creek.
3. Scott gives his answer. Maria is pleased. It seems only she knows the correct answer.
End: Maria is shocked. She learns more than one lesson that day.

Here's realistic fiction about what a girl learns in school based on the story map.

Mississippi Lesson

My dad had said it more than once. "The creek behind our barn flows into the Little Rib River. The Little Rib River flows into the Big Rib River. The Big Rib River flows into the Wisconsin River. Then the Wisconsin River flows into the Mississippi." Everyone in my family knew this. Of course, everyone knew the Mississippi River was very important.

There were other things everyone knew, too—things at school in Mrs. Hoff's class. I was the smallest and the quietest kid in the class. I was pretty smart, and the teacher liked me best. Everyone knew these things.

In November, Mrs. Hoff pulled down a big map of the United States and asked the class, "Who can tell me where the Mississippi River starts? Does anyone know?"

"Oh," I thought, "I wonder if they all know." I didn't raise my hand, though. I didn't want the other kids to think I was being a show-off because I knew the answer. Anyway, Mrs. Hoff knew I always knew the answer, even though I didn't raise my hand very often. After a couple of other kids answered wrong, I thought Mrs. Hoff would look at me and say, in her calm voice, "Maria, do you know?"

Scott and Donny, the two smartest boys in the class, were waving their arms back and forth like they usually did. "Well," I thought, "maybe they know. But maybe they don't." I tried not to smile. I knew the answer. Pretty soon, everyone would look over at me and admire me because the Mississippi River started behind <u>my</u> barn.

Mrs. Hoff picked Scott. He knew answers most of the time. "In Minnesota," he said, out of breath. He said it in the same way that I would have said "behind my barn."

"Minnesota?" I thought to myself. "HE GOT IT WRONG! HE DOESN'T KNOW! Oh, this is great." I felt warm all over. Any second now, Mrs. Hoff would look my way. I wondered how she would let Scott down. Would she just call on me, or would she smile at him nicely and tell him he was wrong?

"You're right, Scott."

My stomach flipped. If I had been warm before, I was roasting now. There she stood, actually pointing to a spot in Minnesota. I would have looked like such a fool if Mrs. Hoff had called on me. I had been so sure of myself. I learned more than one thing in school that day.

Real Story Ideas Come from Real Experiences

The story "Mississippi Lesson" could have happened in real life. Ideas for realistic stories may come from things that happen to the people around you, either at school or at home. Another great place to get ideas is from newspapers or magazines. Sometimes, just looking at a picture may give you a story idea.

Point of View

When you write a realistic story, you can use first-person point of view, like the writer of "Mississippi Lesson" did. She chose first person because she wanted to tell both the actions and the thoughts of her main character. In first person, a writer uses the pronouns *I*, *my*, *me*, *we*, and *our*.

In third-person point of view, the story is told by someone who sees and hears all the action but does not take part in the action. The pronouns *he*, *she*, *him*, *her*, *they*, and *them* are used to refer to characters.

Plot and Action

The plot of a story must have a problem or conflict. The action of the story is what the character does to solve the problem. In "Mississippi Lesson," the action takes place mostly in the main character's mind. The problem in this story is what Maria thinks she knows about the Mississippi River. Maria's problem is solved when she learns the answer to Mrs. Hoff's question.

Reading Your Writing

Remember, a realistic story has characters and events that could exist and happen in the real world. Writing about your experiences and things around you is a good way to create a realistic story.

Tips for Writing Realistic Fiction

Prewriting   Make a Plan

▶ Look around you, in magazines, newspapers, or at photographs to get ideas.
▶ Decide whether you want to use first-person or third-person point of view.
▶ Use a story map to organize your ideas.

Drafting   Get Your Thoughts on Paper

▶ Write your story, following your story map.
▶ Make sure you include the problem and how the problem is solved in your story.

Revising   Be Sure It Makes Sense

▶ **Ideas** Does my character act like a real person or animal?
▶ Is my setting a real place?
▶ Could the action really have taken place?
▶ **Organization** Does the action in the story move forward?
▶ **Voice** Do I make my characters sound real?
▶ **Word Choice** Do all my words describe people, places, and things in the real world?
▶ **Sentence Fluency** Do my sentences flow well?

Editing/Proofreading   Look Closely at the Details

▶ **Conventions** Make sure quotation marks and end punctuation are used correctly in dialogue.
▶ Read your story aloud to catch spelling errors, missing words, or sentence fragments.

Publishing   Get Your Realistic Story Ready to Share

▶ Type or write a final copy that is neat and error-free.
▶ Illustrate your story.

Historical Fiction

Historical fiction is a story set in a specific time and place in the past. Characters are fictional, but they act the way people of that time would have acted. The setting, characters, and plot are more than a figment of your imagination. They must fit in seamlessly with history itself. There is still plenty of room for creativity, but you will also have to do careful research to get your historical facts straight.

Elements

- ▶ The **setting** is a certain time and place in the past.
- ▶ **Characters'** decisions and actions involve actual historical events.
- ▶ The **plot** includes events/problems from the time period.
- ▶ **Details** (clothing, transportation, etc.) are true to the setting.
- ▶ With careful research, actual **historical figures** can be included in the story.

Gathering Ideas

Your teacher might give you a specific time and place in history to use as the setting of your story. Or you might be asked to choose one on your own. Either way, you will have to brainstorm ideas for your story.

- ▶ Who will be my main character?
- ▶ What problems will my main character face?
- ▶ What historical figures will my character meet?
- ▶ How will he feel about certain historical events?
- ▶ What will the general mood of my story be?

Point of View

You will have to decide whether to write your story from the first-person point of view or the third person. Some historical fiction is written as though the main character were keeping a journal. This point of view is more personal and makes it easier for the reader to identify with the character. The third-person point of view is written by a narrator who knows everything about the action but is not part of the story.

A *story map* is a good way to organize your setting, characters, and plot. The more information you include in your story map, the easier it will be to write your story. You could also draw up a time line (not shown) of historical events you want to include in your story.

Title: A Family Divided

Characters: Sally, a 10-year-old girl (narrator/main character)
Charles, her 16-year-old brother
John, their 10-year-old cousin
Sally's parents

Setting: a small town in Ohio, 1861
Abraham Lincoln is President
The Civil War is about to begin.

Plot:
John is sent from his home in South Carolina to stay with Sally's family in Ohio because of the fighting going on in his home state. With the country dividing into North and South, John feels out of place and misunderstood by his Ohio relatives. He tries to run away home by himself and almost gets badly hurt.

Here is the first part of Lindsey's historical fiction story set in Ohio in 1861.

A Family Divided
by: Lindsey Johnson

My cousin John isn't too excited about Abe Lincoln being our new president, but I couldn't be happier. I saw him give a speech once, and he's very smart and nice.

I live in Ohio with my parents and my brother Charles. Our cousin John lives down in South Carolina, but he's staying with us for a while on account of the war.

"Sally, we're going to have ourselves a war," he says, with a big grin on his face. Like war is something to smile about. He thinks war is all fun and games, but I know better. I've been reading about wars since I was four years old. That's not something I want any of my loved ones to be a part of, but there's no convincing Charles.

John's excited about the war, too. At least he was when he got here a couple weeks ago. I think it's starting to sink in with him though. At first, he just ate up everything Charles said. Of course a 10-year-old boy is going to look up to his 16-year-old cousin.

Last night, I caught him crying out in the barn. He wiped away his tears furiously and was mad at me for catching him. He ran down past the outhouse to the tire swing. He didn't come back to the house for over an hour.

Then today I saw him sneak back out to the barn with one of Pa's maps. I'm debating whether or not to tell Pa. I don't know what John thinks he's doing. Surely, he's not going to run off and try to fight in the war or something foolish like that.

Tips for Writing Historical Fiction

Prewriting   Make a Plan

▶ Who do you want to read your story?
▶ What do you want them to think about your story?
▶ Use a graphic organizer to plan your story.
▶ Research your historical time period, so your story will be accurate.

Drafting   Get Your Thoughts on Paper

▶ Write the first draft of your story.
▶ Remember that your story's setting, characters, plot, and details must seem real.

Revising   Be Sure It Makes Sense

▶ Do your words clearly describe the time and place?
▶ Does your plot deal with problems or events from that time and place?
▶ Does your story sound like it really could have happened?

Editing/Proofreading   Look Closely at the Details

▶ Does each sentence and proper noun start with a capital letter?
▶ Did you check your spelling, even if you used a computer spell-checker?

Publishing   Get Your Realistic Story Ready to Share

▶ Check your story for any final errors.
▶ Write or type a neat final copy.

Folktale

A **folktale** is an old story. Most folktales teach a lesson about life. Usually, a folktale is passed around from storyteller to storyteller before it is ever written down. Today, many of these old folktales have been written down.

Character, Setting, and Plot

The characters in folktales may be people or animals. The people may be very common or very special. They sometimes have special powers. Animal characters in folktales may act like normal animals, or they may speak.

The setting of a folktale is usually "long ago" and "far away." In a modern retelling of a folktale, a writer may choose to set the tale in the modern world instead of "long ago." The setting of a folktale is usually a certain place, such as a kingdom, town, or village.

Just as other stories do, a folktale has a plot. There are many different folktale plots. In many folktales, goodness wins out over evil, ignorance, and stupidity. In some folktales, love changes something ugly into something beautiful. In others, a reluctant hero goes off on a quest to an impossible place and brings back a wonderful object or treasure. In still other folktales, a selfish person is taught a lesson. No matter what the plot of the folktale is, the sequence of events usually leads to a surprise at the end.

Try It!

Rumpelstiltskin is one well-known folktale. What is the surprise at the end of this story?

Retelling a Folktale

Many writers retell folktales. For example, they may change the setting and the characters, but the plot of the story usually remains unchanged. Most folktales often depend on repetition, or a repeated series of actions. For example, a character trying to solve a problem may go to several different people and ask the same question. Keep this in mind as you plan your retelling of a folktale.

Here's how one writer organized her ideas, using a chain-of-events chart for her retelling of the folktale "Arella's Answers."

King sees peasant girl, Arella; he greets her.

King calls for Arella.

King asks girl why people like her.

Arella answers.

King passes out corn and grain.

Again, king asks Arella why people like her.

Arella answers.

King delivers cloth to people in kingdom.

Again, king asks Arella why people like her.

Arella answers.

King smiles and waves at people.

People wave back.

Here is the retelling of the folktale shown in the chain-of-events chart. It is about a clever peasant girl who outsmarts a rich, powerful king.

Arella's Answers

Once there was a king who lived in a beautiful palace. He had lots of servants. He told lots of people what to do. He had lots of money, too. The trouble was that the king was lonely.

No one in the kingdom really liked the king because he wasn't very nice. He made the people give him much of their corn and grain. This left the people with very little to eat. The king also demanded half of the wool from the kingdom's sheep. Because of this, the people had very little wool left to make clothing for themselves.

One day the king watched a peasant girl enter the marketplace. Everyone waved and said "hello" to her. The king wondered why people liked this plain peasant girl. He ordered two servants to bring her to him.

As the girl, whose name was Arella, slowly approached the throne, the king spoke in a loud voice, "Why do people like you so much? What did you do to make people like you?"

Arella thought that the king's question was silly, but she quickly answered. "They smile and greet me so because I give them corn and grain."

The very next day the king was seen handing out baskets of corn and grain to the people in the marketplace. The people went straight home to make bread in case the king changed his mind. But the king was disappointed. Still no one waved or greeted him with a smile. The king ordered his servants to bring the peasant girl to him again.

As Arella quietly approached, the king tapped his fingers on the arm of his throne. "What else did you do to make people like you?"

Arella thought this question was silly, but she quickly answered. "They smile and greet me because I bring warm woolen cloth to their homes."

The very next day the king was seen delivering warm woolen cloth to people's homes. The people began making blankets and pants and coats right away, in case the king changed his mind. Later that day, he stood in the marketplace, waiting for people to greet him. No one did. Again he called for the peasant girl.

As Arella calmly approached, the king said to her, "What else?"

Arella thought that the question was silly, but she quickly answered. "They smile and greet me because in addition to giving them corn and grain and warm woolen cloth, I smile and greet them."

The very next day the king was seen smiling and waving to the people in the marketplace. The people's bellies were full of the king's corn and grain. Wearing their new warm woolen coats and pants, the people cheerfully waved back to the king.

Try It!

Selfish, greedy kings or rulers are common characters in folktales, just as clever peasant girls are. The kings almost always learn that being selfish and greedy leads to unhappiness. Can you think of another way to teach this king the same lesson?

Keeping Folktales Interesting

All folktales should include repetition. However, repeating the action of a character too many times can make the story boring. If you retell a folktale, don't include too many repetitions in your plot. Here are some ways to avoid repeating actions too much and to keep your folktale interesting.

▶ Within each repeated action, include a little variety or twist. For example the main character might ask the same question throughout the story but get a different answer each time he or she asks it.

▶ Vary the way in which the repeated action takes place. In "Arella's Answers," note that she approaches the throne in a slightly different way each time. And the king asks the question in a slightly different mood each time.

Sometimes it's tricky to include the lesson in a folktale without making it really obvious. The story should tell itself clearly enough that readers can figure out what the lesson is without being told.

Reading Your Writing

A folktale that includes too many repeated actions will make your readers lose interest. As you write, keep in mind the lesson about life that is in the story. The plot should move from one step to the next towards the point, or lesson, of the story. Two or three repeated actions is probably enough.

Tips for Writing a Folktale

Prewriting   Make a Plan

▶ Think about folktales that you have read and the lessons about life in them.

▶ Plan and organize the plot using a chain-of-events chart.

Drafting   Get Your Thoughts on Paper

▶ Write your story, following your chain-of-events chart.

▶ Stick to the plot. Don't stray from the main point of the folktale.

Revising   Be Sure It Makes Sense

▶ **Ideas** Is the lesson about life clear in the telling of my folktale?

▶ Does my plot include enough repeated actions? Is there too much repetition?

▶ **Organization** Do I include only those details that help show the folktale's lesson?

▶ **Voice** Do I make my characters speak in a way that makes sense in the tale?

▶ **Word Choice** Do my words describe the moods and feelings of my characters well?

▶ **Sentence Fluency** Do my sentences help readers move from one point to the next?

Editing/Proofreading   Look Closely at the Details

▶ **Conventions** Make sure quotation marks and end marks are used correctly in dialogue.

▶ Read your folktale aloud to catch spelling errors, missing words, or sentence fragments.

Publishing   Get Your Folktale Ready to Share

▶ Make a final, neat copy, either handwritten or typed.

▶ Decide whether you want to illustrate your folktale.

Fable

Like a folktale, a **fable** is a tale that teaches a lesson about life. However, a fable is shorter than a folktale and has a sentence or

two at the end that tells exactly what the **moral,** or lesson, of the story is. The moral is a statement such as "Don't count your chickens before they're hatched" or "Honesty is the best policy." Most fables are very old. People are still writing new fables, though. Two of the most well-known fables are "The Hare and the Tortoise" and "The City Mouse and the Country Mouse." Characters in a fable are sometimes animals that talk and act like humans.

Characters, Setting, and Plot

Though fables are short, they still contain the usual story elements—characters, setting, and plot. "The City Mouse and the Country Mouse" is a good example. The characters are two mice, sometimes described as friends or cousins. The setting consists of the city mouse's home and the country mouse's home. The plot is below.

> A city mouse visiting his country cousin finds his home rough and unpleasant. He persuades the country mouse to come to his fancy city house. The country mouse willingly agrees. In the city mouse's house, however, is a cat that nearly catches the mice while they dine on fine leftovers. The country mouse decides he prefers the peace and safety of the country to the luxurious, but dangerous, life of the city.

Unlike other stories, fables usually do not include detailed descriptions of the characters and setting. For example, the setting may be mentioned only briefly. The whole story moves toward telling the fable's moral, which is stated at the end of the tale.

Try It!

Reread the plot of "The City Mouse and the Country Mouse" above. Which of the following statements might be the moral of the fable?

▶ Cats are dangerous.　　　▶ There's no place like home.

Planning a Fable

Because a fable includes the story elements of characters, setting, and plot, you can use a story map to plan and organize your fable. You may choose to write your own fable or write a retelling of an old fable. Here's one writer's plan for the retelling of a fable.

Title
The Ant and the Grasshopper

Characters
ant-busy, hardworking
grasshopper-lazy

Setting
in field, near homes of ant and grasshopper

Plot
Beginning: Ant is busy collecting food for winter.

Middle:
1. Grasshopper wants to sit around and do nothing with ant.
2. Ant warns grasshopper about winter.
3. Grasshopper tries to get ant to stop working.
4. Winter comes.

End: Ant has food, goes into tunnels, and is safe; grasshopper starves.

The Ant and the Grasshopper

A very busy ant hurried back and forth, collecting food for the winter. He carried everything he could find back to his nest. He knew his nest must be full of food by winter.

A passing grasshopper remarked on how hard the ant was working. "It's a lovely summer day. Why don't you rest under this maple tree with me. We can watch the leaves flutter in the breeze."

"Oh, no, no, I couldn't," replied the ant breathlessly. "I'm much too busy. I must store up food for winter."

"Bah!" laughed the grasshopper. "Winter is far away. There's time for storing food later."

"Oh, no, no, there's not," warned the ant. "Winter will come sooner than you think."

The grasshopper moved on to the maple tree and watched the leaves on the trees blow in the wind. Many times that summer he watched the busy ant. He thought the ant was silly for working so hard in the middle of summer. Many times the grasshopper tried to get the ant to stop and watch the leaves blow in the wind or listen to the frogs or play with the crickets. But the ant's answer was always the same.

"Oh, no, no, I couldn't. I'm much too busy. I must store up food for winter."

Summer turned to autumn, and the days grew shorter. Still the busy ant went on, dragging food into his tunnels. Still the grasshopper couldn't be bothered. He was more interested in looking at the colorful leaves on the trees.

Autumn turned to winter, and snow fell at last. The ant crawled deep and safe into his tunnels and ate the food he had stored. The grasshopper, who had stored no food, starved.

Moral: <u>He who plans ahead, lives ahead.</u>

Writing or Retelling a Fable

The best way to write or retell a fable is to start with the moral. Don't try to write the entire story then come up with a moral. The moral might be too difficult to write in a sentence.

Suppose you've chosen a moral that goes something like this: "Greedy people never win." This fable will need a greedy character, of course. Then there is almost always another character who is the *opposite* of the first. So this fable will need an unselfish character. Starting a fable with the moral can help you decide which characters to use and organize the plot of your fable.

Adding Dialogue

Using dialogue is a way to give your version of a fable a new twist. Having characters talk in certain ways adds interest. In "The Ant and the Grasshopper," the busy ant talks "breathlessly." He also talks in a way that a very busy person might talk.

Reading Your Writing

Does your fable sound new and fresh, or does it sound a lot like other versions of the fable? Think of how you can make your characters stand out by giving them certain qualities or by having them act or speak in certain ways. Make the moral of your story carry a lesson by which your readers can learn.

Tips for Writing a Fable

Prewriting   Make a Plan

▶ Think about the morals of fables you have read. Start with the moral and decide whether to retell a fable or write your own.
▶ Plan your fable using a story map.

Drafting   Get Your Thoughts on Paper

▶ Write your fable following your story map.
▶ Include the moral at the end of your fable.

Revising   Be Sure It Makes Sense

▶ **Ideas** Did I choose the best characters for this fable?
▶ Does my plot stay focused on my moral?
▶ **Organization** Does the organization of the plot move toward the moral of the story?
▶ **Voice** Do I make each character "sound" unique?
▶ **Word Choice** Have I chosen words that clearly express the moral of the story?
▶ **Sentence Fluency** Do I use some compound and complex sentences to combine ideas in my story?

Editing/Proofreading   Look Closely at the Details

▶ **Conventions** Place quotation marks and end marks correctly in dialogue.
▶ Read your fable aloud to catch missing words and spelling errors.

Publishing   Get Your Fable Ready to Share

▶ Make a final, neat copy, either handwritten or typed.
▶ Decide whether you want to make a cover or illustrate your fable.

A **tall tale** is an entertaining story that has made-up characters and uses humor and exaggeration to tell the events in the story. Usually, a tall tale includes a series of unusual events that the character handles with cleverness, quick-thinking, and, sometimes, luck. The writer of a tall tale often states that his or her story is true!

Paul Bunyan and Pecos Bill are perhaps the two most well-known tall tale characters. Paul Bunyan's tales tell of how Minnesota's 10,000 lakes were formed from Paul's footprints. He used a pine tree for a comb and had a huge blue ox named Babe for a pet.

Exaggeration Is the Key

Writers of tall tales exaggerate things, people, places, or events in a story to make it entertaining and funny. When a writer exaggerates something, he or she makes it much larger, smaller, or different from how it appears in real life. For example, the size of Paul Bunyan and his ox is an exaggeration. Here are some more examples.

▶ Paul was so big when he was born, it took five storks working overtime to deliver him.

▶ His clothes were so big, his mother sewed on wagon wheels for buttons.

▶ One winter it was so cold, the loggers' words froze right out of their mouths. In the spring when they thawed, there was a chattering in the woods for weeks.

Try It!

Make sentences that finish each of the following as though you were writing a tall tale.

One day it was so cold that . . .

My brother is so tall that . . .

My dog can jump as high as . . .

The other day it rained so hard that . . .

Planning a Tall Tale

One way to plan a tall tale is to make an idea web. Write the main idea or character in the center. Then write the details that support the main idea or the character's qualities, physical appearance, activities, and so forth on the "arms" of the web.

In the tall tale, "My Three Amazing Pets," on the next page, the writer included several pets as characters, so in the center of his web is the word *pets*. Then each arm covers one of the pets.

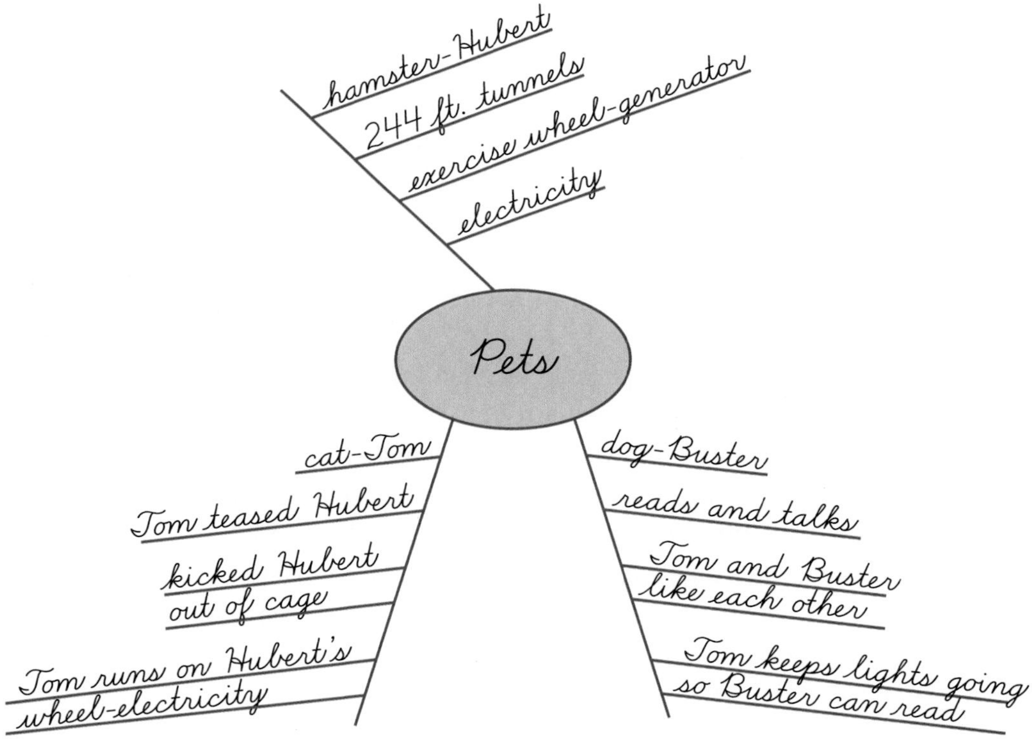

hamster-Hubert
244 ft. tunnels
exercise wheel-generator
electricity

Pets

cat-Tom
Tom teased Hubert
kicked Hubert out of cage
Tom runs on Hubert's wheel-electricity

dog-Buster
reads and talks
Tom and Buster like each other
Tom keeps lights going so Buster can read

My Three Amazing Pets

When I was six, my parents decided I was ready for a pet. I got a hamster and named it Hubert. I knew from the start that Hubert was not just any old hamster. He was very strong and ran around in his cage day and night. I don't think Hubert ever slept. He ran so much we had to buy 244 feet of tunnels to attach to his cage. One day we clocked him at 62 miles per hour. He kept at it all night. That gave my dad an idea.

He hooked a generator to Hubert's wheel. Hubert created so much electricity from running on his wheel that every light bulb in our house blew up. We got new light bulbs. Then Dad got a couple of the neighbors to hook up. Hubert supplied all the electricity for us and three of our neighbors. The electric company hasn't found out yet.

When I was seven, my parents decided I was ready for another pet. I got a cat. I named him Tom. Tom didn't seem to like Hubert very much. Tom would push his dishes over next to Hubert's cage and tease him with the food. Then he started sticking his paw into the cage and blocking the wheel so it wouldn't turn. We caught on to this because our electricity starting running out at about noon each day. I think Tom was jealous of Hubert.

One night, Tom kicked Hubert out of his cage. The lights went out suddenly. Soon, they came on again and burned brighter than ever. Then we walked in the room and saw Tom running on the wheel. We looked all around for Hubert, but there was no sign of him anywhere. We figured Hubert got tired of being pushed around by Tom. I was sad, but at least we were getting plenty of electricity. Two more neighbors were added to our electricity pool. The electric company hasn't found out yet.

Last year, when I was nine, my parents decided I was ready for another pet. I got a dog. Buster was the most amazing pet of the three I had. He could read and talk. He didn't talk around us, but one day, I caught him talking to Tom. He was telling Tom about a book he'd read that he thought was very good. Buster liked Tom a lot. He really liked the way Tom produced all this free electricity for us and our neighbors. Tom really liked Buster, too. Tom liked Buster so much that he would sometimes keep the lights burning all night so that Buster could finish a book.

I've told many people about my pets. No one seems to believe me, but my story is true! My dad, mom and our neighbors will tell anyone that they have never had to pay another electric bill.

Stretching Your Tall Tale

It's pretty easy to exaggerate. You probably do it every day. Have you ever said anything like this?

> I'm so hungry I could eat a horse!

That is a perfect example of exaggeration. For exaggeration to be funny in a tall tale, a writer needs to exaggerate and then exaggerate again. For example, the author of "My Three Amazing Pets" exaggerates by saying that the hamster was going 62 miles per hour on the exercise wheel. Then he goes a big step further and adds the part about hooking up the generator. Then he goes another step by having the light bulbs blow out.

Weaving a Tale

A tall tale has characters, setting, and plot, like other stories. A tall tale will be most effective if all of these elements are exaggerated in one way or another. For example, in "My Three Amazing Pets," the characters' behaviors are certainly exaggerated. The setting is exaggerated in the detail about the hamster's tunnels, for example. Imagine a room with 244 feet of hamster tunnels in it. And the plot is exaggerated in the events that occur, especially the events connected with the electric generator.

Reading Your Writing

Remember to think BIG when you write a tall tale. Ordinary ideas just won't do. Take the details in your tall tale all the way to the ridiculous.

Tips for Writing a Tall Tale

Prewriting Make a Plan

▶ Read a tall tale written by another writer. Look at how he or she uses exaggeration in the story.
▶ Develop your character or characters and plot.
▶ Use your main-idea web to plan and organize your ideas.

Drafting Get Your Thoughts on Paper

▶ Write your tall tale, using the details from your main-idea web.
▶ Remember to exaggerate the things, people, places, and events in your tale.

Revising Be Sure It Makes Sense

▶ **Ideas** Have I used enough exaggeration so that my tale is really funny?
▶ **Voice** Does the style of my writing fit the way my characters act and talk?
▶ **Word Choice** Are my words as descriptive and exact as they can be?

Editing/Proofreading Look Closely at the Details

▶ **Conventions** End each sentence with a period, question mark, or exclamation mark.
▶ Read your fable aloud to catch missing words and spelling errors.

Publishing Get Your Tall Tale Ready to Share

▶ Make a final, neat copy, either handwritten or typed.
▶ Create illustrations to go with your tall tale.

A **play** is a story written so that actors can perform it for an audience. Because a play is acted out, its story is told mostly through dialogue, or talk, between the characters.

One of the most important things to remember when you write a play is to include sensory details, such as how an object or a person looks, feels, or sounds. Although some people will only read your play, more people will see and hear it. A play contains elements, such as characters, scenes, dialogue, and stage directions. These are written a certain way so that actors can follow and perform the play. They will help the actors perform your play on stage the way you've imagined and written it.

Characters and Scenes

Like any other story, a play has characters and a setting. However, the setting and characters in a play have a different purpose. The setting of a play is called a **scene.** In most plays, there is usually more than one scene. The scene gives the time and place of a particular set of events in a play. The action is not described by a character. Instead, the characters' actions are *seen* by the audience.

Dialogue

Dialogue, the conversations the characters have, is the heart of a play. The audience depends on dialogue to learn about characters. The dialogue also moves the action of the play along. Almost everything about the story and the characters is shown through dialogue.

Stage Directions

The information about the characters' movements, facial expressions, emotions, or the use of props on stage are written in the stage directions. The stage directions usually appear in parentheses ( ) or brackets [ ]. Sometimes these directions appear in italic type or are underlined, so that readers and performers won't think the directions are part of the dialogue. Stage directions that apply to several actors may appear between speakers. Stage directions that give information about one actor usually appear right after the speaker's name.

Take a Look

A group of students is planning to write and perform a play for a school assembly. They decided to put a new twist on an old story. They made a play out of the story "The Three Little Pigs." Before they began writing the story as a play, they created a plot line diagram to organize their ideas for each scene. Here's the diagram for the first scene.

Pigs split up.

Pigs argue.

Pigs stop to rest along the way.

Each pig decides to build his or her own home.

Pigs leave home; they need to decide what type of home they will share together.

Take a Look

Using their diagram, the students wrote the first scene of the play. They underlined the information about the setting and all the stage directions.

<u>The Three Little Pigs: Scene 1</u>

Characters

Mr. Pig   His sons, Mason and Strawberry

His daughter, Wiggy   Mr. Wolf

<u>(Setting: In the country with woods and a few houses. A dirt road leads to the city. The road goes by the home of Mr. Pig. He stands in the doorway of his home. Mr. Pig's daughter and sons, Wiggy, Mason, and Strawberry, set off down the road. Each is carrying a backpack. They are planning to build and share a house together. They are moving closer to the city, where they will attend college.)</u>

Mr. Pig: <u>(waving)</u> Good-bye, dears! Remember everything I've told you, and please stay together.

Mason, Wiggy, and Strawberry: We will, Dad! We promise!

<u>(All continue waving. Right side of stage darkens; lights on Wiggy, Mason, and Strawberry walking down the dirt road. They begin to get tired and stop to rest.)</u>

Wiggy: Whew, I'm ready for a snack. Who's got the food?

Strawberry: Dad gave it to Mason because he said Mason is the most responsible.

Mason: That's right. One of you would have left it on a stump an hour ago.

Wiggy: Not me! I'd have eaten it an hour ago.

Mason: Yeah, and that's why Dad gave the food to me.

Strawberry: Well, anyway, what do we have? I'm hungry too.

Mason: <u>(opening backpack)</u> Let's see. One apple for you, one for you, and two for me.

Wiggy: Hey, that's not fair! Why do you get two?

Mason: Because I'm the responsible one.

<u>(Wiggy frowns at Mason and takes a bite out of her apple.)</u>

Strawberry: Well, anyway, what are we going to do next?

158   Play • Narrative Writing

Mason: Once we get to the spot where we'll build the house, we have to gather materials and get to work. We don't have too much farther to go.

Wiggy: I can't wait to have our own house! I'll start collecting sticks right after I finish my apple.

Mason: That would be just like you to use sticks to build a house.

Wiggy: (angrily) Dad said you were responsible, but he didn't say you were the boss! I know all about houses.

Strawberry: You tell him, Wiggy!

Mason: (acting superior, to Strawberry) And what would you build a house out of, Strawberry?

Strawberry: (not prepared for the question) Well, . . . uh . . . I'd build it out of straw.

Mason and Wiggy: (suddenly united against Strawberry, laughing) Ha! That would be great—a house of straw! Good for you, Strawberry!

Strawberry: (surprised and hurt) Well, fine then. I'll just go and build my house and you'll see! (stalks off)

Wiggy: Gee, Dad told us to stay together. You suppose Strawberry will be all right?

Mason: He'll be back soon enough.

Wiggy: I hope so. Anyway, I'll go get some sticks.

Mason: (rolling his eyes) You still want to use sticks? I can't believe you! We are going to use bricks!

Wiggy: Oh, yeah, Mr. Boss? I'm not going to haul bricks all over the woods just for you. I'll go get sticks and build my own house. You can haul your own bricks! (runs off)

(Mason slowly packs up the food in the backpack and heads in another direction.)

Mr. Wolf: (to audience) And that, folks, is how the whole thing started. (Licks his chops in a sneaky way, then exits the stage)

(End Scene I)

The Script

The written text of a play is called a **script.** Scripts are prepared so that actors can find their lines easily. Each speaker's name is printed in bold type. That speaker's words, or lines, then immediately follow. Unlike dialogue in a story, dialogue in a script is not enclosed in quotation marks. Stage directions appear in italic type or are underlined so actors can clearly see the difference between their lines and stage directions. A script also includes two other elements—the list of characters and scene description.

List of Characters

A list at the beginning of the script includes all the characters in the play. Notice how the list for "The Three Little Pigs" gives more than just the characters' names. It tells the relationships between the characters, as well.

Scene Description

Each scene of a play usually begins with a brief statement that tells where the action takes place. The statement might be as brief as "in the living room." Sometimes, though, a scene description is very long if the stage includes many props and if the exact position of those props is important. Readers use this information to help them "see" the action. People who produce plays use the information to design the stage properly.

Reading Your Writing

The best way to check the voice of a play you've written is to read it aloud. Deliver the lines just as you want the actors to do so. Do they "feel" right? Might the actors need more stage directions to help them? Remember that dialogue and the characters' actions will tell the story of the play.

Tips for Writing a Play

Prewriting Make a Plan

▶ Look through stories you have written or read to see if one would make a good play.

▶ Plan and organize the action in your play using a plot line diagram. For more about plot line diagrams, see page 250.

Drafting Get Your Thoughts on Paper

▶ Write your play, following your plot line diagram.

▶ First write the dialogue. Then add the stage directions.

Revising Be Sure It Makes Sense

▶ **Ideas** Does the flow of your dialogue help move the plot along?

▶ **Organization** Have you included any statements or actions that seem out of sequence?

▶ **Voice** Does the dialogue between your characters seem natural, or does it seem stiff or awkward?

▶ **Word Choice** Do you use words your characters would use?

Editing/Proofreading Look Closely at the Details

▶ **Conventions** Check to see if each speaker's name is in bold type. Be sure that all stage directions are in italic type or are underlined.

▶ Read your play to a classmate to catch missing words and spelling errors.

Publishing Get Your Play Ready to Share

▶ Make a final, neat copy, either handwritten or typed.

▶ Invite classmates to take part in your play. Plan some time to practice.

▶ Perform your play before an audience.

Forms of Writing

Descriptive Writing

Descriptive writing provides the reader with a clear, vivid picture of something or someone. Think about the best place you ever visited. What do you remember about the way it looked, sounded, and smelled? When you use those kinds of details in your writing, you help your readers see what you see, hear what you hear, and feel what you feel. The following lessons will give you tips on writing good descriptions.

Writing a Description

When you write a description, your task is to create a picture for readers. You can let your readers know how something looks, sounds, smells, tastes, and/or feels by using **sensory details.** Using sensory details will make the object or place you describe seem more real.

Both nonfiction and fiction writers include descriptions in their writing. A nonfiction writer might describe a historic event such as a famous battle. A fiction writer might describe the characters or the setting of the story.

A fiction writer might include a detailed description of a character. He or she might use sensory details, such as the color of the character's hair and eyes, to make the reader pay attention to these specific characteristics. A fiction writer often uses vivid details to describe settings and events so that readers can experience what is happening.

Take a Look

Here is an example of a description from the book *Toto*, by Marietta D. Moskin. Look for the words that tell you how something looks, sounds, or feels.

Clutching his sharp reed knife, Suku followed the winding path down the hill to the riverbank, searching for a good stand of feathery papyrus.

Suddenly the silence at the river was broken by a loud rustling sound. The sound came again—not just a rustling this time, but a snapping of twigs and a swishing of the tall grasses. Carefully, and a little fearfully, Suku moved around the next curve in the path. And then he stopped again.

Sensory Details

What kinds of words can help your readers see, hear, smell, taste, or feel what you are describing? Adjectives, adverbs, verbs, and nouns can be used to draw vivid pictures of persons, places, or objects.

Adjectives

Describing an apple as "red" will give your readers a picture, but will it be a vivid picture? Does the apple have green spots on it? You can look closely at the apple and think of more ways to describe it, such as "deep red." Maybe the apple just fell off a tree and is "bruised." Try to make your readers feel as if they are actually looking at the exact apple you are describing.

Adverbs

Different adverbs can change the tone and feeling in a sentence. Notice how the adverbs make the following sentences different.

I closed the door **gently** and spoke to him **quietly.**

I closed the door **loudly** and spoke to him **impatiently.**

I **always** closed the door and spoke to him **politely.**

Verbs

Most verbs tell what someone or something is doing. However, choosing a verb that really describes an action takes practice. Notice how the verbs create pictures in these sentences.

I **shut** the door.	I **slammed** the door.	I **fastened** the door.
I **spoke** to him.	I **whispered** to him.	I **pleaded** with him.

Nouns

Some nouns are very general—*shoes, people.* Other nouns are more specific. These nouns do a better job of creating pictures for your readers. Here are some sentences with precise nouns in place of general nouns.

As I ran, my **sneakers** felt as heavy as lead.

The **office workers** poured out of the building at noon.

Organizing a Description

Writers can help readers see the person, place, or object being described by organizing sensory details and ideas in a logical way. There are different ways to organize the details and ideas in your description. The person, place, or thing being described helps a writer decide which type of organization to use.

Organizing from Top to Bottom

Imagine yourself looking at a totem pole. Your eyes would probably start at the top and follow the pole all the way to the bottom. If you were to describe that totem pole, that would be a way you could organize the description—from top to bottom.

Take a Look

Here is a paragraph with the description of a house. Notice how the paragraph follows the top to bottom organization.

> One particular seaside house rose up and up so that it looked like a three-layer birthday cake. The candles at the top were, of course, the cast iron railings around the widow's walk. Below the widow's walk, the attic windows were arched like eyebrows. They often glowed at night and people wondered what went on in those rooms. On this particular night, it was the second-floor windows that were lit. The eight long narrow windows across the front of the house stood open to the balcony. Below, the first-floor windows were covered with dark, heavy curtains. The neighbors wondered what old Mrs. Perry was up to in this house that was the same as, yet different from, all the other seaside houses.

Organizing from Left to Right

What do you do when you walk into a room or a place where you have never been before? You might look at every object and in every corner, turning your head from left to right. As a writer, you can do the same for your readers. When you take them into a new place, you can help them see a place by writing details using left-to-right organization.

After a visit to the Laura Ingalls Wilder Museum in Mansfield, Missouri, a student made these notes about the kitchen Laura Ingalls Wilder had designed.

Left:
big white sink
slanted countertops

→

Middle:
cupboards—white with
silver hinges
whole wall

→

Right:
big windows
sunlight

Take a Look

Here is the description of the kitchen designed by Laura Ingalls Wilder. Notice how the organization of the description follows the writer's notes.

To the left, a big white sink was attached to the wall. On both sides of the sink were countertops to hold dishes and other things. The countertops were slanted toward the sink. This was so the dishwasher could put wet dishes there and have the extra water flow back into the sink. On the next wall were cupboards. They were side-by-side and from ceiling to floor. They were painted bright white and had neat little silver hinges and door handles. We could only imagine what was inside all those cupboard doors. Two very big windows were in the wall to the right. The sun streamed in so that the whole kitchen was bright and warm, even though it was a chilly October day.

A Road Map for Readers

How will your readers know what method of organization you use in your descriptive writing? You will use signal words to guide readers through your description. Often, signal words are prepositions or prepositional phrases. They can be adjectives or adverbs as well.

Look back at the description of the seaside house on page 166. The writer uses a number of signal words to let readers know where things are—from top to bottom.

> *at the top*   *below*   *second-floor*

Now look at the description of Laura Ingalls Wilder's kitchen on page 167. The signal words are different because the writer chose a different method of organization—left to right.

> *to the left*   *on the next wall*   *to the right*

Try It!

Look around the room where you are. Describe what you see, turning your head slowly from left to right. Use signal words as you describe what you see.

Reading Your Writing

Writing a description helps the reader "see" people, places, and things in both fiction and nonfiction works. There are several different ways to organize the details in a description. Choose one that works best for the thing you want to describe. Use signal words to guide the reader's journey through your writing.

Tips for Writing a Descriptive Paragraph

Prewriting Make a Plan

▶ Look at your journal and other pieces of writing you have done. Decide on a description you can add to one of them.
▶ Use a graphic organizer to gather details about how your subject looks, sounds, smells, tastes, and feels.
▶ Decide whether to use top-to-bottom, left-to-right, or some other type of organization for your description.

Drafting Get Your Thoughts on Paper

▶ Write your description.
▶ Follow your graphic organizer and stick to the type of organization you chose.
▶ Use signal words so readers can follow your description.

Revising Be Sure It Makes Sense

▶ **Ideas** Do I include enough sensory details?
▶ Will my description interest my readers?
▶ **Organization** Do I follow a logical pattern? Do I use signal words to let my readers know how the details are organized?
▶ **Voice** Does what I see show in my writing?
▶ **Word Choice** Have I chosen words that show exactly what my subject looks, sounds, smells, tastes, and feels like?

Editing/Proofreading Look Closely at the Details

▶ **Conventions** Begin each sentence with a capital letter and end each one with an appropriate end mark. Double-check for misspelled words, missing words, and incorrect punctuation.

Publishing Get Your Description Ready to Share

▶ **Presentation** Write or type a final copy of your description.

Observation Report

In an observation report, you record information that you observe using some or all of your senses. There are many reasons for writing an observation report. Here are some examples.

▶ A concerned parent observes traffic at a busy school intersection, then writes to local officials about the smell, the noise, the speed, and the number of cars that pass through there.

▶ A homeowner uses a lawn product which causes his grass to die. He writes what has happened to his grass based on what he has seen. He writes a letter to the manufacturer and includes his observation.

▶ A scientist in a lab sprays plants with different chemicals to see how they react. She writes an observation report to sum up her results.

Using Your Senses

Usually we think observing means "seeing." Observing something means more than seeing. When we observe something we use all of our senses. For example, the parent who wrote about the traffic near his children's school included smell as part of his observation. He mentioned that the exhaust fumes from the cars were so strong that some people choked on them. That proves that observation is more than just seeing.

Try It!

Use your senses to observe an everyday scene, such as eating in the lunch room. What do you observe?

A Science Observation Report

Probably the most common type of observation report is written about science experiments. You might have to write a report or observations of a process for a science project you do at school. It is a good way to summarize your project. It also helps your teacher know what you did, how you did it, and what you learned.

Scientists take careful notes on what they observe. From these notes, they write their observation reports. Here are one student scientist's notes on a fruit fly observation.

Day	Number of Flies and Larvae	Observations	Questions, Comments, or Conclusions
1	7 Flies 0 Larvae	Flies sit or crawl on apple slice (with skin); some are flying around in jar.	Some flies are larger than others.
7	7 Flies 0 Larvae	Little marks or dimples appear on the skin of the apple.	The flies made the marks on the apple.
20	7 Flies 8-10 Larvae	Larvae are crawling on paper; one crawls out of the apple slice; flies continue as before.	Did the flies lay eggs in the fruit?
30	3 Flies 12 Larvae	More larvae appear; some flies have died.	Why did some of the flies die?

Brianna Camron
Gr. 4, Mr. Tiberi

Fruit Fly Observation Report

Procedure: On Day 1, I captured seven fruit flies in a jar, using an apple slice with the skin attached as bait. I put a small piece of construction paper under the apple slice, on the bottom in the jar. Then I plugged the opening of the jar with a loose wad of cotton.

Observations: The apple slice was always the main area of activity. The adult flies sat or crawled on the apple slice in the jar. There were two different sizes of flies. The smaller ones have a dark tip at the end of their bodies.

On Day 7, I saw tiny marks on the skin of the apple. The marks looked like dimples. I figured the flies must have made these marks.

On Day 20, I saw eight to ten tiny grayish-white worms. They were fruit fly larvae that must have just hatched. When I first looked, they were crawling on the paper. When I looked later, I saw one crawling out of the apple.

By Day 30, four flies had died, and there were twelve larvae crawling on the paper.

Conclusions: While the flies were crawling on the fruit, some of them laid eggs inside. The larvae hatched from the eggs inside the apple slice and crawled out onto the construction paper.

Reading Your Writing

Check your word choices when you revise your observation report. Circle all the words that paint a visual picture for your readers. Make sure you use words that really show readers what you observed.

Tips for Writing an Observation Report

Prewriting   Make a Plan

▶ Try to use as many of your senses as possible as you observe.
▶ Take careful notes as you observe.
▶ Record your notes in a chart or table so they are in order.

Drafting   Get Your Thoughts on Paper

▶ Write your observation, following your notes.
▶ If you remember other details, add them to your report.

Revising   Be Sure It Makes Sense

▶ **Ideas** Have I recorded *all* of my observations?
▶ Have I told readers just what I observed in a way they can follow?
▶ **Organization** Do I follow my notes and keep details in order?
▶ **Word Choice** Do I use adjectives, adverbs, nouns, and verbs that accurately describe what I observed?
▶ **Sentence Fluency** Have I used some short and some long sentences in my observation?

Editing/Proofreading   Look Closely at the Details

▶ **Conventions** Check all sentences for beginning capitalization and closing end marks.
▶ Include a heading or title at the top of your report.
▶ Make sure you clearly labeled sections titled "Procedure," "Observations," and "Conclusions."

Publishing   Get Your Observation Report Ready to Share

▶ **Presentation** Write or type a neat, error-free copy.
▶ Display your observation report with your science project so that others can see the results as well.

Forms of Writing

Persuasive Writing

Persuasive writing encourages readers to think or feel a certain way. It can also motivate readers to take action. Sometimes persuasive writing can do both of these things at the same time. To do this, you, the writer, must get and keep the attention of your readers. The following lessons will show you how.

Persuasive Writing

In persuasive writing, a writer tries to make readers think, feel, or act a certain way. Unlike in other types of writing, persuasive writers may make their opinions known. For example, a person might write about the need for a traffic light at a certain corner. The writer's opinion is clear in this example. He or she wants someone to change the situation.

You probably read persuasive writing every day. It is on bus stop benches and billboards. It's in magazines and even on T-shirts. Advertisers use persuasive writing to make you think you *need* their products or services. The newspaper also contains persuasive writing. Letters to the editor are sometimes called "opinion pieces." In those letters, writers state their opinions about various issues.

How Does Persuasion Work?

Is it enough for a persuasive writer to state his or her opinion? Will that make readers agree with the writer? Probably not. Persuasive writers use certain techniques.

Support Opinions with Facts

One technique is to support opinions with facts and reasons. Here's an example.

> The intersection of Monty Road and 4th Street needs a traffic light. The traffic at the intersection has increased by 20 percent in the last two years. In the past six months, 14 accidents have occurred, involving 31 vehicles.

In the first sentence of this example the writer states his opinion. The next two sentences are facts the writer uses to support his opinion.

Appeal to Emotions

Sometimes persuasive writers appeal to the emotions of their readers. By getting emotions involved, the writer hopes to get people to take action, lend a hand, or change their minds about something. Here's the traffic light argument with an emotional appeal.

> The corner of Monty Road and 4th Street needs a traffic light. My neighbors are afraid to cross the street at that corner because the traffic goes by so quickly. They walk four extra blocks to get to the bank or the post office.

In this paragraph, the writer states his opinion in the first sentence. In the following sentences the writer wants readers to be concerned about people crossing the street.

Building a Persuasive Argument

Like other forms of writing, persuasive writing has an introduction, a body, and a conclusion. Grab your readers' interest—or emotions—in the introduction. Also, state your opinion clearly. In the body, state your facts and reasons, or make your emotional appeals. You may choose to state your strongest reason first, or you may choose to build up to your strongest point and use it last. In the conclusion, state your opinion again and tell your readers what you want them to think, feel, or do.

Purpose and Audience

Whenever you write, you should know why you are writing and for whom. When you write to persuade, your purpose for writing should be clear and specific. Ask yourself what you want others to think, feel, or do. Second, know who your audience is. To get others to think or act a certain way, you should have some idea what your audience needs or wants.

Advertisements

An advertisement uses words and pictures to communicate a specific message to an audience. Advertisements can be found in many places, such as magazines, newspapers, and on billboards. Even a sign for a garage sale is an advertisement. People who create advertisements have one purpose in mind: to make people buy their products or services. But how do the advertisements make us buy?

Advertisements are a type of persuasive writing. Persuasive writers try to get their audience to think, feel, or act in a certain way. In the case of advertising, the purpose of the persuasive writing is to get people to buy things.

The Message of Advertisements

Advertisements communicate messages to audiences in a number of different ways. Some use the "feel-good" approach. They connect good feelings, such as happiness, excitement, and hopefulness, with a product, whether it's a television, a car, or a frozen dinner. According to an ad like this, if a person buys the product, he or she will experience these good feelings.

Another type of message in an advertisement expresses people's need to fit in. This kind of message is called the bandwagon appeal. These ads suggest that if we don't have this product, we will be left out or rejected by other people.

Other advertisements try to make consumers feel smart, successful, or special. These ads use snob appeal to make consumers want their products and services. This type of advertisement usually uses celebrities. Seeing a celebrity using a product is supposed to make people think that they, too, will be "successful" if they use the product or service.

Advertisements and Audiences

Children and Parents

The makers of a breakfast cereal know that they must communicate their message to two different audiences in an advertisement. For the children who will eat the cereal, they make the cereal look fun and tasty. For the grown-ups who will actually buy the cereal, the company takes the feel-good approach. Parents are supposed to feel good that their children are starting the day with a big bowl of nutritious cereal.

Teenagers

Advertisements that have teenagers as their audience often use bandwagon appeal. Makers of skin-care products, clothing, musical recordings, and other products teenagers buy and use know about a teenager's need to fit in. They make it look as if kids who buy their products are part of the accepted "crowd."

An Older Audience

People like your grandparents have different needs than you do. They want to feel as if all their years of hard work have paid off. They want to be respected. They feel that they deserve some comforts in life. Some ads use people who are the same age to make the audience feel that they will receive the same sort of respect and treatment that the celebrity does. These ads also suggest that older people deserve to enjoy life.

Try It!

Make up a new food product, such as a hot cereal or a spaghetti sauce. Create three different advertisements for the same product using a different audience for each.

Reading Your Writing

Remember that an advertisement communicates a message to a specific audience. In order to grab your audience's attention, your writing should be clear and to-the-point. The words and pictures in the advertisement should be balanced and visually appealing to your audience.

Tips for Writing a Print Advertisement

Prewriting — Make a Plan

▶ Decide on your product and your audience.
▶ Focus your ideas. Your advertisement must send a clear message to your audience.
▶ Jot down some notes about how words and pictures work together to communicate your message.

Drafting — Get Your Thoughts on Paper

▶ Write the words for your advertisement. Keep your audience and purpose in mind.
▶ Draw or find pictures for your advertisement.
▶ Arrange the words and pictures different ways to see which works best.

Revising — Be Sure It Makes Sense

▶ **Ideas** Is the message of your advertisement clear to your audience?
▶ **Organization** Do the words and pictures go together?
▶ **Word Choice** Do you use words that will convince your audience to buy or use a product or service?
▶ **Sentence Fluency** Do you use short sentences to grab your reader's attention?

Editing/Proofreading — Look Closely at the Details

▶ **Conventions** Punctuate all sentences with an end mark.
▶ Capitalize the first letter of each important word in the headline of your ad.

Publishing — Get Your Advertisement Ready to Share

▶ **Presentation** Create a neat, error-free copy. If it is available, use computer software.
▶ Show your ad to your audience. Get their reactions.

Letter to the Editor

Have you ever read an article in a magazine or newspaper that made you upset, feel inspired, or feel terrific? If so, perhaps you should write a letter to the editor.

Many people write letters to the editor to express themselves. They may write to respond to a letter to the editor written by someone else, to an article, or simply to state their opinion.

Not all letters to the editor get published, but many do. The letters are usually published in a special section in a newspaper or magazine. Even though a letter to the editor is addressed to the editor of a newspaper or magazine, the real audience is the publication's readers.

Business as Usual

The format of a letter to the editor is just like any other business letter. The letter has a heading that includes the sender's name and address. The date is written under the heading. The inside address follows. Next comes the salutation, which ends with a colon, not a comma. The text in the body should be brief and to the point. Finally, the closing and the signature are added at the end of the letter.

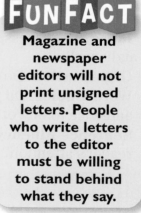

FUN FACT

Magazine and newspaper editors will not print unsigned letters. People who write letters to the editor must be willing to stand behind what they say.

Persuasive Tools

The basic reason for writing a letter to the editor is to express an opinion. However, in expressing an opinion, the writer may also want to persuade others to think, feel, or do as he or she does about the issue.

Using Facts and Reasons to Persuade

In the following letter to the editor, a reader responds to an article printed in a newspaper. She states her opinion right away. Then she uses facts to support her opinion. Notice that the writer gives her name and where she works. The writer wants people to know who she is and that she stands by her opinion.

Take a Look

Dear Editor:

Les Tarentini's article titled "Kids and Pets" in the Wednesday, November 8, Family section carried an important message about the benefits of family pets. The article did not, however, mention the importance of planning for a pet and making a good, sound decision. Too many parents do not think carefully about their decisions to buy a pet, especially during the winter holidays. During the holidays, puppy and kitten sales increase by 40 percent at local pet stores.

At the River Valley Humane Society, two of the busiest months are January and February. Dozens of "holiday puppies" are brought in. Their owners say they didn't think the puppy would be so active, or their children weren't ready yet, and so on. Think of the children's disappointment. All the disappointment and trouble could have been avoided if these parents had not made a hasty decision to buy a pet as a gift for a child.

Sincerely,

Marge Beckman

Marge Beckman, Director
River Valley Humane Society

Using Examples to Persuade

In the next letter, the writer uses examples to support his opinion. In his response to a previous letter to the editor, he disagrees with the writer's opinion.

Dear Editor:

   I do not agree with Lou Marshall's opinion (printed here on 5/26/07) that all teenagers show too little respect for the world around them. Some teenagers do behave differently—for example, eighth-grader Mary Wells recently organized a 3K run for students and teachers. All the money raised for the race went to the local chapter of the American Heart Association. And two brothers, Matt and Cal Apponte, recycle aluminum cans. With their earnings, they buy coats and donate them to the homeless shelter.

   It's true that people should earn respect. But if teenagers are shown a little respect up front, there's no telling what we might do.

Sincerely,

Mark Vadillo

Mark Vadillo, Ninth Grader
Teller Junior High

Persuading by Offering a Solution

   In this letter, the writer disagrees with something that's happening in her community. She offers her own solution to the problem.

Dear Editor:

   The City Council recently announced its plan to hire a consultant to study the needs of our city. The cost for this consultant, whose office is in New York City, is estimated to be $15,000. Surely there are better ways to spend that money. It seems to me that the citizens of this city know more about it than any consultant could ever learn. Why not ask the citizens to offer their ideas about what the city needs? We would save money, and maybe we could use it to <u>do</u> something about those needs.

Thank you,

Amber Miller

Tips for Writing a Letter to the Editor

Prewriting   Make a Plan

▶ What is your purpose? State your opinion clearly.
▶ Who will read your letter? Make sure you know your audience.
▶ Write down the facts or examples that support your opinion. Organize them from least to most important.
▶ Check the publication to see where and to whom to address the letter.

Drafting   Get Your Thoughts on Paper

▶ Write your letter, using your facts or examples in the order of importance.
▶ Include all parts of the letter—the heading, the salutation, the body, the closing, and your name.

Revising   Be Sure It Makes Sense

▶ **Ideas** Is your opinion clear and supported by facts or examples? Did you refer to the article or letter to which you are responding?
▶ **Organization** Have you stated your facts or examples in a logical order?
▶ **Word Choice** Are the words you use precise enough to convince readers that your opinion is one they should hold?
▶ **Sentence Fluency** Do you use different lengths and styles of sentences for variety and for emphasis?

Editing/Proofreading   Look Closely at the Details

▶ **Conventions** Make sure that parts of your letter to the editor are correctly formatted. Check that any proper names begin with a capital letter.

Publishing   Get Your Letter to the Editor
                 Ready to Share

▶ **Presentation** Neatly write or type your letter.

Persuasive Report

In a **persuasive report,** a writer expresses an opinion. He or she must back that opinion up with facts and reasons. Like other persuasive writing, the purpose of a persuasive report is to make readers think, feel, or act in a certain way. Supporting an opinion with facts and reasons is important to successfully persuade readers.

When Should I Use a Persuasive Report?

People in your school and community use persuasive reports to get things done. Your parents may use them at work, too. Here are some examples.

▶ An employee writes to her supervisor to explain why she thinks a new company rule is unfair.

▶ A senior citizen writes to the city transportation director to state his disagreement about changes made in bus routes.

▶ A concerned student sends an article to a local newspaper about the importance of cutting the amount of fuel used by automobiles.

Introduction, Body, and Conclusion

This structure probably sounds familiar. Many kinds of writing need an introduction to grab readers' attention and let them know what's coming. In the body, the writer lays out the facts and reasons that support his or her opinion. The conclusion restates the writer's opinion and makes it clear to readers just what the writer expects them to think, feel, or do.

Planning to Persuade

The easy part of a persuasive report is your opinion. You know what that is, of course. The next part is backing up your opinion with facts and reasons that will have an effect on your audience. It's important to identify your audience before you write. Remember, you must choose just the right things to say to your audience, or your attempts to persuade them will be unsuccessful.

Depending on your topic, you may have to do some research to find facts that support your opinion. Kyle used the Internet to find information he needed on fuel consumption. Here's the web he used to organize his supporting facts.

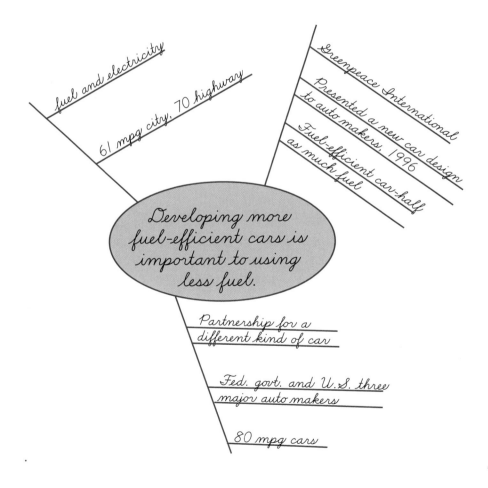

Kyle Schultz

The Answer Is Less, Not More

The world's 500 million cars will increase to 2.3 billion by the year 2030. Will there be room for them all on our roads and highways? Will we still be able to breathe? The more fuel we burn in our cars, the more harm we do to ourselves, our pocketbooks, and our air. How do we take care of ourselves and our Earth? The answer is "Use less fuel." But how do we do that and still get around? We can create cars that burn less fuel.

Greenpeace International, an environmental group, presented a new car engine design to automobile makers back in 1996. Greenpeace engineers changed the engine of a popular European car. They made a car that used half as much fuel as the most fuel-efficient model then available. Greenpeace's purpose was not to sell its own car but to prove that an inexpensive fuel-efficient car can be made.

While Greenpeace was working on its car, another group began working in the United States. The federal government and America's three major automobile makers created a program called Partnership for a New Generation of Vehicles (PNGV). The project is supposed to figure out how to build a car that gets 80 miles per gallon. Unfortunately, the project has not met many of its goals. It doesn't look as if they're going to make it.

When gas prices increased during the summer of 2000, people started looking for smaller cars that burned less fuel. One new vehicle got a lot of attention. It runs on both fuel and electricity. It averages 61 miles per gallon in the city, and 70 on the highway. That's about two times better than other cars of the same size.

Greenpeace's automobile and others prove that it can be done. Now it's up to us to tell the big auto manufacturers that we'll only buy a car that burns less fuel. Big companies should share the responsibility of taking care of the environment. People should step forward and remind them of what they must do.

Kyle's Report

Kyle ended up with a five-paragraph report. Notice that the three paragraphs in the body of his report match the information in the three "arms" of his web.

Kyle felt that his strongest point was the existence of a fuel-efficient car that is actually on the market. As it turned out, his points were also in time order. That adds to the logic and order of his report.

Beginnings and Endings

Kyle used a fact in his first sentence to catch his readers' attention. Other ways to draw readers in are to use a quotation, to address the reader directly, to ask a question, or to make a humorous statement.

The end of a persuasive report should *never* leave readers thinking, "What does this person want?" Instead, the writer must make his or her opinion clear to readers. In Kyle's report, he wants his readers to let automobile manufacturers know that they are also responsible for producing cars that do less harm to the environment.

Try It!

Think of an issue about which you have a strong opinion. Come up with three facts you could use to support your opinion.

Reading Your Writing

When writing a persuasive report, remember to include facts and reasons to support your opinion. Just presenting your opinion alone will not be enough to persuade readers to think about an issue differently.

Tips for Writing a Persuasive Report

Prewriting Make a Plan

▶ State your opinion in a sentence. Use this sentence to help you stay on topic.
▶ Determine who your audience is.
▶ Use a web to organize the reasons and facts that support your opinion.

Drafting Get Your Thoughts on Paper

▶ Write your report, following your web.
▶ Make sure your introduction grabs your readers' attention and your conclusion restates your position.

Revising Be Sure It Makes Sense

▶ **Ideas** Do your facts and reasons support your opinion?
▶ **Organization** Do you include a good introduction and an effective ending?
▶ **Voice** Do you sound confident and informed about your topic?
▶ **Word Choice** Do you use language appropriate for your audience?
▶ **Sentence Fluency** Do you connect the facts and reasons in your argument using transition words in sentences?

Editing/Proofreading Look Closely at the Details

▶ **Conventions** Proofread your report for spelling mistakes and missing words.
▶ Begin each sentence with a capital letter and end each one with an appropriate end mark.

Publishing Get Your Persuasive Report Ready to Share

▶ **Presentation** Write or type a neat copy of your report.
▶ Share your report with the audience for which it was written.

Forms of Writing

Poetry

Poetry is very different from other forms of writing. For one thing, it looks different. Think of some poems you have read. They look very different from stories or articles. The capitalization and punctuation are different. The familiar patterns of sentences and paragraphs are not present in poetry.

There is something else about poetry. It can describe things in a way that you may never have thought about before. Poetry often contains thoughts and feelings of the writer. It also contains images, or word pictures, that can make a deep impression on readers. The following lessons will give you a chance to explore some different kinds of poetry.

Rhyming Poetry

When a writer combines the sounds *and* the meanings of words to create ideas and feelings, the result is a **poem.** Poems express all kinds of feelings and create all kinds of pictures. As a reader, a poem may make you feel happy, sad, or anything in between.

Some poets use a capital letter to start each line of poetry. It does not matter whether the line is a complete sentence or not. Other poets use the regular rule for capitalization in sentences. They capitalize the first word of each complete sentence in their poetry. The most important thing is to choose one system and stick to it throughout the piece of writing.

How Poets Do It

Poems can be short or long. For all kinds of poems, poets choose their words very carefully. In addition to *choosing* words carefully, they *arrange* words in special ways.

Rhythm

Poets put their words together in a way that makes rhythm. **Rhythm** is a pattern of accented and unaccented syllables. Notice how the rhythm in this short poem sounds like soldiers marching.

> Soldiers marching to and fro,
> Marching past my window.
> Lined up straight and lined up tall,
> I will conquer one and all.

Here's a poem that has a much gentler rhythm to match its message about an autumn day. Can you hear the leaf falling?

> I heard it behind me, but no one was there.
> I heard it again, but the sidewalk was bare.
> And then, in an instant, and to my surprise,
> A leaf floated down, right in front of my eyes.

Rhyme

Many poems contain **rhyming words.** Usually the rhymes fall at the ends of lines.

> I have seen a little kitten
> who looked as woolly as a mitten.

When rhyming words fall within a line of poetry, the rhyme is called **internal rhyme.** Here is an example.

> Mary, Mary, quite contrary
> How does your garden grow?

The name *Mary* rhymes with *contrary.* Here's another example.

> If you please, is the moon made of cheese?
> Maybe so. I don't know.

In this example, there are internal rhymes in both lines. The word *please* rhymes with *cheese*, and *so* rhymes with *know.*

Stanzas

A **stanza** is a set of lines of poetry that are grouped together. Stanzas may contain two lines, three, four, or many more than that. A two-line stanza is called a **couplet.** Couplets in rhymed poetry always contain end rhyme. The kitten rhyme, above, is a couplet. Here's another poem made up of couplets.

> Would you rather eat a bug?
> Or would you rather eat a slug?
>
> Michael ate an ant.
> Lucy said she can't.
>
> I'd rather eat a bug
> Than a slimy old slug.
>
> Mom says it's lunch time.
> Maybe I'll wait 'til next time.

A three-line stanza is a **triplet.** All three lines in a triplet rhyme.

> The waters blew a salty breeze
> And rose about our knobby knees,
> Then ran away, like a bashful tease.
>
> We ranged across the sparkling sand,
> With ocean lapping all the land,
> A sunny, funny, happy band.

A four-line stanza is called a **quatrain.** There are no set rules for rhyming patterns in quatrains, but two patterns are the most common. In some quatrains, only lines two and four rhyme, as in these first two stanzas from "Lemonade Stand," by Myra Cohn Livingston.

> Every summer
> under the shade
> we fix up a stand
> to sell lemonade.
>
> A stack of cups,
> a pitcher of ice,
> a shirtboard sign
> to tell the price.

In other quatrains, lines one and three rhyme, and lines two and four rhyme.

> See how the 'scrapers stand so proud,
> All lined up in a row.
> Perhaps they'll even touch a cloud,
> If one should come so low.

Tips for Writing Rhyming Poetry

Prewriting　　**Make a Plan**

▶ Look through a journal or other writing notebooks for ideas.
▶ Think about who will read your poem. What kind of poem would they enjoy?
▶ Freewrite for several minutes to get ideas for poems.

Drafting　　**Get Your Thoughts on Paper**

▶ Write your poem.
▶ Rhyme line endings as you go, but if you get stuck on one spot, skip it and go on. What happens in line five may inspire you for line four.
▶ Say your lines out loud. Hearing the words may help you find rhymes. It also helps you hear the rhythm of the lines.

Revising　　**Be Sure It Makes Sense**

▶ **Ideas** Have you captured the feelings or ideas that you wanted to convey?
▶ **Organization** Does the rhythm match the tone and message of your poem?
▶ **Word Choice** Have you thought about *every* word to make sure it's just right?

Editing/Proofreading　　**Look Closely at the Details**

▶ **Conventions** Have you chosen a method of capitalization and followed it consistently?
▶ Have you spelled all words correctly?

Publishing　　**Get Your Rhyming Poetry Ready to Share**

▶ **Presentation** Write or type a final, neat copy of your poem. Center your poem on the page.
▶ Organize a poetry reading with your classmates. Take turns reading your poetry aloud to an audience.

Nonrhyming Poetry

Nonrhyming poetry has no "rules" at all about rhyme. Here are some examples of nonrhyming poetry.

Cinquain

A cinquain is a five-line poem that follows a pattern. Here's the "recipe" for a cinquain.

Line 1   1 word that names the subject
Line 2   2 words that describe the subject
Line 3   3 action words about the subject
Line 4   2–4 words that express a feeling or describe the subject (usually 6–8 syllables)
Line 5   1 word that sums up the subject

> Butterfly
> Bright, silent
> Fluttering, flitting, resting
> Difficult to capture
> Marvelous

Diamante

A diamante has a set, seven-line pattern that results in a diamond shape.

Line 1   1 word—a noun   **Line 2**   2 words—adjectives
Line 3   3 words—participles   **Line 4**   4 words—nouns
Line 5   3 words—participles   **Line 6**   2 words—adjectives
                    Line 7   2 words—nouns

> Race
> short, fast
> stretching, panting, sweating
> runners, lanes, elbows, legs
> running, fearing, straining
> hot, painful
> exhaustion, victory

Free Verse

Free verse poetry has neither rhyme nor rhythm pattern. It simply expresses a poet's thoughts or feelings with carefully chosen words.

> Otters—this way
> Black eyes, gleaming coat
> Dive
> Spin
> Dive

Tips for Writing Nonrhyming Poetry

Prewriting   Make a Plan

▶ Freewrite for several minutes to get ideas for poems.
▶ Use a web to collect all of your thoughts or feelings on a topic.

Drafting   Get Your Thoughts on Paper

▶ Write your poem.
▶ Focus on creating an image or feeling with each line.
▶ Read your lines out loud as you work. Hearing the words may help you create more vivid pictures.

Revising   Be Sure It Makes Sense

▶ **Ideas** Does your writing match your topic? Do you provide original ideas? Do you create clear pictures for your readers?
▶ **Voice** Have you expressed your feelings or ideas to your audience?

Editing/Proofreading   Look Closely at the Details

▶ Did you choose a method of capitalization and follow it throughout the poem?

Publishing   Get Your Free Verse Ready to Share

▶ **Presentation** Write or type a final, neat copy of your poem.
▶ Read your poem aloud to classmates.

Pattern Poetry

Can you recite "Twinkle, Twinkle, Little Star"? You have probably known it for years, and its pattern and rhythm are very familiar to you. Sometimes it's fun to create a poem by changing one with which you're already familiar. Use the same patterns of rhyme and rhythm, but switch topics or certain key words to create something new.

Take a Look

Here's a familiar rhyme. Below it is a new version. Notice how the rhymes and rhythms are the same. What details are different in the new version?

Little Jack Horner sat in a corner,
Eating his Christmas pie.
He put in his thumb
And pulled out a plum,
And said, "What a good boy am I."

FUN FACT

One of the earliest collections of children's rhymes in English was printed in 1781.

Little Jim Warner sat in a corner,
Playing a video game.
He played it so much,
His thumbs lost their touch,
And he even forgot his own name.

Try It!

Try your own poem that matches the rhythm of "Little Jack Horner." Notice that lines two and five rhyme, and lines three and four rhyme.

Here's another rhyme. Notice that the first and third lines contain internal rhyme. Also, the second and fourth lines have end rhyme. Following the original version is a new version.

Take a Look

Little Miss Muffet sat on a tuffet
Eating her curds and whey.
Along came a spider and sat down beside her
And frightened Miss Muffet away.

Old Nelly Blair sat on a chair
Tending her nails and hair.
Along came her grandson, who hadn't his socks on,
And begged Nelly Blair for a pair.

Finally, here's a rhyme that follows the rhythm and rhyme pattern of "Twinkle, Twinkle, Little Star."

Scurry, scurry, little mouse,
Wandering all about the house.
Sniffing here and sniffing there,
Finding small crumbs everywhere.
Scurry, scurry, little mouse,
Wandering all about the house.

Reading Your Writing

Read or sing your new poems aloud so you can hear their rhyme and rhythm. Your ear will tell you if you've matched the original version or not.

Forms of Writing

Timed Writing

Sometimes you will be asked to write an explanation about something you have learned about, a story about something that has happened to you, or a summary of a story you have read in a set time period. You will learn how to write about each of these possibilities and learn how to use the time you are given wisely.

Expository

There will be situations in the future where you will be asked to write a paper in a certain amount of time. This might be a special writing assignment during class or the writing portion of a standardized test. Learning how to write well "under pressure" will prepare you in many ways to be a better writer overall.

The following five-step strategy will help you calm down, gather your thoughts, focus on the assignment, complete it on time, and end up with an adequate piece of writing:

Timed Writing Strategy

1. Circle the directions for writing the paper.
2. Underline each reminder.
3. Take a few minutes to make notes about your topic.
4. Write your paper.
5. Check: Did I complete each reminder?

Take a Look

Remember that **expository writing** explains how to do something or presents information about something. Some examples of expository writing are news stories, research reports, summaries, essays, and book reviews.

The following is an expository writing prompt for a timed test:

If you could visit any two places in the world, what would they be, and why? Write a composition about why those two places excite you and what you would do while you were there. You will have 30 minutes to complete your composition.

Reminders:

▶ Write about the two places you would like to visit.
▶ Explain why those places excite you and what you would do there.
▶ Make sure each sentence you write helps the reader understand your composition.
▶ Make sure your ideas are clear and easy to follow.
▶ Write your ideas in detail and use descriptive language.
▶ Use correct spelling, capitalization, punctuation, grammar, and sentences so the reader understands what you are saying.

As Mina got ready to take this timed test, she took a deep breath, pencil in hand, and read the directions and reminders. She thought of the two places she would like to go and began to take some brief notes.

—Italy—Dad was born there
—Africa—I want to go on a safari
—Italy—eat tortellini like Grandma's
—eat real Italian ice
—learn to paint
—Africa—safari to see animals in the wild
—take new expensive camera

Then she was ready to write:

If I could visit any two places in the world, I would go to Italy and Africa. Italy is such a beautiful old country, and Africa is so wild and rugged. My dad was born in Italy, and I have some family members there. I would love to learn more about my Italian heritage. I don't know anyone in Africa, but I have always wanted to go on a safari. I would love to see animals in their wild habitat.

When I got to Italy, I would try a new kind of pasta every day. I would start with tortellini like my Grandma used to make me. I would have real Italian ice after every meal. I would learn how to paint beautiful pictures. I would go to the beach with my easel and paint pictures of the ocean for hours.

In Africa, I would find the best guide and go on a safari every day. I would take photos of the wildlife with my professional camera. I wouldn't be scared to get really close to the animals and take pictures of them in their natural habitat. Hopefully, someday I will really be able to visit these two amazing places.

Narrative

Another type of timed writing you will be asked to do is a **narrative,** a form of writing that tells a story or gives an account of an event. The five-step strategy you learned for timed expository writing will still apply. Let's review it.

Timed Writing Strategy
1. Circle the directions.
2. Underline the reminders.
3. Take notes for a few minutes.
4. Write your paper.
5. Check off completed reminders.

Just like expository writing, narratives can take many forms—a biography, a realistic story, historical fiction, a folktale, fable, play, or personal narrative. The following is a narrative writing prompt for a timed-test:

> *Life is full of new challenges. Write a composition about something you did/tried for the first time. What were you thinking? How did you feel? Describe your experience and the thoughts and emotions surrounding it. You will have 30 minutes to complete your composition.*

Reminders:

▶ Write about an experience you had for the first time.
▶ Describe your thoughts and emotions during your experience.
▶ Make sure each sentence you write helps the reader understand your composition.
▶ Make sure your ideas are clear and easy to follow.
▶ Write your ideas in detail and use descriptive language.
▶ Use correct spelling, capitalization, punctuation, grammar, and sentences so the reader understands what you are saying.

Linen was prepared for this timed test. She read through the directions carefully. She brainstormed for a couple minutes and decided to write about her first time on an airplane. She began to quickly take notes.

—nervous when they searched my bag
—couldn't believe how big plane was
—take-off was scary, then exciting
—my ears popped
—loved it

Linen was ready to start writing.

The first time I rode on an airplane, I was so nervous I was sweating in the middle of winter. I was so thankful my aunt was with me, although I didn't talk to her the entire time we were in the airport. I was too tense. She understood, smiled and squeezed my hand.

When it was finally time to board, I thought I might pass out. The airport security asked to search my bag, and I thought I was in trouble! Whew! I was safe. As I walked the long boarding tunnel, I tried to imagine what the inside of the plane would look like. I couldn't believe how big it was inside!

Before I knew it, it was time to take off! I started shaking so badly I could hardly fasten my seat belt. I was sitting by the window, but I was afraid to look. As the plane accelerated, my heart beat faster and faster. The plane finally lifted off the ground. Believe it or not, I thought the steep climb to our desired altitude was thrilling. My ears popped, but I just kept chewing the gum my Aunt Kik gave me.

I enjoyed every minute of our flight and even got to peek in on the pilot. By the time we landed, I felt like a pro at flying. I can't wait to fly again!

Summarizing

As you know, a **summary** is the main idea and main points of a piece of writing. You can summarize anything just by putting the main ideas in your own words.

When you are asked to write a summary as part of a timed-writing assignment, your strategy will be different from an expository or narrative timed writing. A piece of writing will already be selected for you. Your job will be to summarize it in your own words.

Here are some things to remember when writing a timed summary:

1. Read the material once to get the general idea.
2. Find the topic sentences and other main points.
3. Circle or mark main points and important words.
4. Jot notes in the margins if you would like.
5. Begin your summary with the main idea.
6. Add main points. Use your own words.
7. If any time remains, look over the original text and your summary to see if you are missing anything important.

Here is an article given during a timed writing assignment:

One Author's Journey

If you've read any of the *Howie Grotto* series, did you know that Kell Kramer is not the author's real name? His real name is Archibald Kellen Theodore Badswinski. As Archibald dreamed of someday becoming a published author, he knew he would need a shorter name. Since his friends and family called him "Kell," and Kramer was the name of his favorite childhood dog, Kell Kramer was the obvious choice.

Kell began writing poems at the age of four. As he got older and became proficient at reading and writing, Kell wrote longer poems. Then he started writing stories in a journal. If Kell wasn't writing, he was reading anything he could get his hands on—cereal boxes, newspapers, even department store ads.

Kell's teachers, recognizing his talents, gave him special writing assignments to further develop his skills. Upon graduation, he received several writing scholarships and attended college virtually for free. He majored in writing and graduated early.

So, understandably Kell was shocked when his first book manuscript was rejected by eight different publishers. He was crushed. Writing was his life. He had always been told he was so gifted at it. Why did no one want to publish his book?

He decided he would quit writing. One of his friends convinced him otherwise. "Kell," he said. "You're an amazing writer. You've just written the wrong book. You're using all these big words and sounding so intelligent. But the average reader can't understand your writing. Why don't you write something for normal people? Something funny, lighthearted, and interesting? How about a series of books about an odd writer-guy that no one understands?"

Kell quickly penned "*Howie Grotto*," a humorous novel for young adults about an aspiring young writer. The publishers loved it. Six books later, Kell Kramer is a star.

Kell Kramer is the pen name for the famous author of the Howie Grotto books. He began writing poems at an early age, and from then on, he read and wrote nonstop. He dreamed of someday becoming an author. He did well in school, received college scholarships and graduated early. After receiving eight rejections from publishers, he thought about giving up his dream. A friend persuaded him to write a book the average reader could relate to. Howie Grotto was the first step toward Kramer's successful career.

Writing Strategies

Like anything else that's worth doing, writing requires some skill and a lot of practice. The lessons in this unit will help you learn some of the skills that make good writing better. Just like athletes or musicians, writers learn the skills they need to improve, and then they practice, practice, practice. Look for new ways to improve your writing as you read these lessons.

Writing Strategies

Ideas

Writing starts with an idea. Coming up with ideas can be fun and very creative. When you begin thinking of ideas for your writing, there are many factors to be considered. Some of these are your audience, your characters and the general mood of your writing.

You will learn how to include all of these details in your writing.

Evaluating Writing Growth

Even though everyone is a writer, no two writers are alike. Each writer has his or her own unique skills, interests, and techniques. Because everyone is different, you shouldn't compare yourself to other writers.

All writers should have one thing in common though. They should make it their goal to constantly improve their writing. Each time you write, you improve your old skills and learn new skills. You expand your knowledge and establish your own personal writing style.

Evaluating your own growth as a writer will help you continue to grow. A journal is a helpful tool. You can record your thoughts about your writing as well as new things you have learned. As you look back at entries over the weeks and months, you will be amazed at how far you have come in your writing journey!

You might journal about:

- ▶ new words you have learned that enhance your writing
- ▶ techniques you have learned to vary your sentences
- ▶ how you are beginning to incorporate humor into your writing
- ▶ telling a story in a more interesting way
- ▶ learning to plan well before you begin writing

January 5, 2007

I just finished writing a personal narrative about helping my grandpa on the farm. I read it to my class, and I could tell they were all really interested. When I first started writing stories about myself, I think they were kind of boring. They sounded more like a textbook. I'm learning to make personal stories sound more informal—like I'm having a conversation with my readers.

I also added some sentences that made them want to know what would happen next. Like, "I definitely wasn't ready for what was waiting for me in the barn." And, "Do you know what a cow does when she's scared?"

I'm trying to work on adding good sensory details, too. Instead of saying, "the black and white cow," I wrote, "the white cow looked like she'd been spattered with black paintballs."

Generating Additional Ideas

Good writers are always looking for ways to improve their writing. Sometimes deleting unnecessary information can make your story better. In other cases, adding new information is the key. Additional details can make your story more lively and interesting.

Here are some tips to help get your creative juices flowing:

▶ Brainstorm! Grab a piece of paper, and for three to five minutes write whatever comes to mind on any topic.

▶ Draw a picture to illustrate the story you're telling. What do you see in your picture that you might have left out of your story?

▶ Make a list of all the descriptive adjectives you used in your story. What sensory words could you add to make your descriptions really pop?

▶ Create a graphic organizer such as a story map or main-idea web. Sometimes seeing your ideas in a visual manner will help generate other related ideas.

Take a Look

Ideas

Ideas are the foundation of your writing. Ideas are the main points and the supporting details that make your topic clear to a reader. Good writing has ideas that

▶ are clearly stated.

▶ are interesting or important to a reader.

▶ tell the reader something he or she might not know.

▶ include main points with supporting details or examples.

Read the two paragraphs below. Both are about a trip to the beach. Compare the ideas in these paragraphs. Which paragraph is full of details and creates a vivid picture?

A. It's fun to go to the beach. I went last summer with my family. We drove there in a van. I have one brother named Hank. He's six now.

B. It's fun to go to the beach. I like looking for things in the sand. Last summer as I walked along the beach, I spotted something pink in the sand. I walked closer and poked it with my toe. It was a seashell. I dug up the shell and ran to show it to my family.

Getting and Narrowing Ideas

Once you've figured out your task, audience, and purpose, you have to figure out exactly what you will say. Brainstorming ideas and writing them down helps you see the many ways you can cover your topic. Even if some of your ideas seem useless, write them down.

Here are David's ideas.

bald eagle

- they are not on the Endangered Species list anymore

- there used to be lots of eagles

- eagles are awesome birds

Here are Nazanin's ideas.

panthers (Florida)

- they are big and wild cats

- they live in the woods

- people take their land and build houses

David and Nazanin looked at their lists. They both realized that they did not know much about eagles and panthers. They needed to get the facts on eagles and panthers. Then they could begin to narrow their ideas. David and Nazanin took a trip to the library together. The librarian helped them find books on eagles and panthers. After they collected their information, they were able to think about how they could narrow their ideas.

David's new list looked like this.

Nazanin's new list looked like this.

Eagles

- Eagles were taken off the Endangered Species List in 1999.

- DDT was a pesticide used in the 1950s. It nearly wiped out the eagles.

- Eagles eat fish mostly.

- Scientists helped the eagle population to grow again.

Florida Panthers

- Panthers are big and wild cats, but they are a lot like regular house cats.

- Panthers have a hard time finding places to live.

- Panthers don't live in trees. They climb trees to get away from dogs chasing them.

Try It!

Think about and list as many ideas as you can for one of these writing tasks. Which ideas from your list would you choose for a topic?

▶ A persuasive essay on why we must protect the environment
▶ A funny story about the weather

Locating Information

There is more to research than finding an encyclopedia article on your topic. Encyclopedias include helpful summaries, but good researchers use more than one source when investigating a subject. As a researcher, you must decide which resources will be most helpful for your particular investigation.

Examples of Information Sources:
- encyclopedias
- atlas
- books
- magazines
- interviews
- documentaries
- newspapers
- Internet
- films
- journals

Why is it so critical to use multiple sources? There are several good reasons. Perhaps the most important is your need to cross-check information. Cross-checking simply means making sure that information is correct. You can't always believe everything you read, but if more than one source gives the same information, it is most likely true. Also, different sources provide different types of data, giving you a broader view of your topic.

Interviews

Interviewing a witness to a crime or a prize-winning scientist will give the interviewer insight into the story or topic of interest. Conducting an interview will show emotions and a personal side to the story, which wouldn't be learned from reading a book or a magazine article.

Observations

Researchers must be careful to state only the facts in their reports. But news reporters will also include observations, which will be based on what he or she knows, hears and sees, but are not necessarily facts.

Character Sketch Revising

No one wants to read a story with a boring main character. You probably enjoy reading about characters that seem to jump off the page, characters you can picture vividly in your mind as soon as you read the author's description. But how do you make a character come alive on paper?

It is all in the details—sensory words that show not only what your character looks like but give insight into his or her personality as well. Read the following description of an elderly woman named Myrtle. Notice the sensory details in the paragraph.

Spunky little white-haired Myrtle was the most popular resident in the neighborhood. Everyone adored her—adults, kids, even dogs. Just under five feet tall, she had tight curly hair, glasses, a dimple on each cheek, and a smile as big as a crocodile's. She ambled along with a slight limp, stopping every few yards to catch her breath and chat with her neighbors. As she talked, her large brown eyes danced like jitterbugs. She would speak with her hands, waving them wildly in circles or wide, sweeping motions. Her tiny frame would tremble with excitement whenever she shared a story. Her neighbors affectionately called her Mile-a-Minute Myrtle.

Try It!

What is your impression of Myrtle based on the description you just read? Which sensory details gave you clues about her physical appearance and personality?

Adding Details

They say that a picture is worth a thousand words, but a good writer can fashion a picture in readers' minds using far less words than that. The best way to create vivid and visual stories, plays, and character sketches is to add lots of sensory detail. When you use descriptive adjectives, adverbs, nouns, and verbs, your readers will be able to see, hear, smell, taste, and feel things as though they had actually been plopped down into the story itself. A good writer will capture readers' attention, drawing them in from the first word and not letting them go until the last.

When adding sensory detail to a character sketch,
▶ *a hat* can become a *flimsy straw hat that looked like it had been through a war*
▶ *a frown* can become *a fierce scowl so deep that the turned-down corners of his mouth nearly touched his pointy chin*
▶ *a skinny* man can become *a six-foot-tall toothpick with clothes on*

Using Figurative Language

Figurative language is language that goes beyond the literal, dictionary meaning of the words. Some examples of figurative language are called figures of speech. Writers use figures of speech to help create pictures in their readers' minds.

In this lesson, you will learn about four figures of speech: simile, metaphor, personification, and exaggeration. You might already be using some of these techniques in your writing. If not, now is the time to start!

Simile

A **simile** compares two things that are not alike by using the words *like* or *as*. Of course, not every sentence that uses *like* or *as* is a simile.

Take a Look

Here's an example. Look for the *like* or *as* and decide what two things are being compared.

> The rainbow spread across the sky like a colored snake.

What is being compared? If you said a rainbow and a snake, you were right.

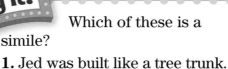

Which of these is a simile?

1. Jed was built like a tree trunk.
2. He was strong and tall.

Metaphor

A metaphor compares two things that are not alike, without using *like* or *as*.

Take a Look

Here are some examples.

> The lake was a mirror.
>
> The cloud was a cream puff in the blue sky.
>
> The rainbow was a colored snake spread across the sky.

Below are more examples of metaphor.

▶ From *The Bridge Dancers* by Carol Saller:

> <u>Our bridge is just a shaky old skeleton</u>, a tangle of ropes and boards that ripples and swings in the breeze.

▶ From *Medicine Walk* by Ardath Mayhar:

> A boy lost in the desert says, "<u>I was one huge ache. A dry ache</u>."

Try It!

Which of these is a metaphor?

1. Love is a powerful emotion.
2. When you're sick, love is medicine.

Personification

Did you ever write about something as if it were alive—when it wasn't? For example, did you ever make a doll or a car talk in a story? You were using **personification.** Personification is a figure of speech in which an object is given human qualities by the writer.

▶ "I looked at the narrow winding road that climbed across the mountains." (Roads can't really climb, but people can.)

▶ The tree stood tall and proud. (Trees can't be proud, but people can.)

Try It!

Which of these sentences uses personification?

1. Germs are sneaky.
2. Germs are dangerous.

Exaggeration

Exaggeration is a writer's way of stretching the truth to add humor or interest to a statement of fact. Like other kinds of figurative language, it is not meant to be taken literally.

Take a Look

Statements of Fact

This bag is packed too full.

My soup is very salty.

He yelled loudly.

The man answered in a voice that frightened his listeners.

Exaggerated Statements

This bag is packed so full that there isn't room for a toothpick.

My soup has more salt than the Pacific Ocean.

He yelled so loudly that they heard him in the next state.

The man answered in a voice that chilled the blood of his listeners.

Exaggeration is often used to add humor. In "The Case of the Gasping Garbage" by Michele Torrey, Gabby calls Drake and tells him: "There's a huge giant bloodsucking monster in my garbage can and it's growing bigger and bigger every second and I'm alone in the house and it's going to gobble me up and I don't want to be someone's dinner!" This would never happen, but when real events are exaggerated, they can be funny.

Try It!

Which of these is an example of exaggeration?
1. She was so angry that her face turned red.
2. She was so angry that steam came out of her ears.

Similes, metaphors, personification, and exaggeration can help create clear pictures in your readers' minds. Just make sure that your figures of speech are based on your readers' experiences. If they have never seen a farm plow, for example, using one to exaggerate the strength of the wind will only confuse them. Figures of speech are meant to clarify your message, not disguise it.

Reading Your Writing

Figures of speech can give a special voice to your writing. They can make it a reflection of your thinking and your personality. You can use them in poems, short stories, and articles. Just choose your figures carefully to match your audience.

FUN FACT

The word *simile* is based on the same Latin word as *similar*. A simile tells how two unlike things are similar.

Using the Sound of Language

As you read poetry and some stories aloud, you might notice that some of it sounds almost like music. That happens because the writers carefully chose words with certain sounds in them.

In this lesson, you will learn more about the sounds of words. You will learn about alliteration, assonance, repetition of words and phrases, onomatopoeia, end and internal rhyme, and rhythm. You might decide to use some of these techniques when you write poetry. Some of them, such as onomatopoeia, also work well in other kinds of writing, especially stories.

Alliteration

Alliteration means repeating the consonant sounds at the beginning of words. The repeating sound can be in two or three words or more depending on the effect the writer is trying to get.

Take a Look

The sentences below all have examples of alliteration.

> **P**eter **P**iper **p**icked a **p**eck of **p**ickled **p**eppers.
> She had a **b**ig, **b**right, **b**eautiful smile on her face.
> The **s**mall **s**nake **s**lithered on the ground.
> The story took place in the **d**eep, **d**ark woods.

Try It!

Find the repeating consonant sounds in these sentences.

The sheep was white and wooly.

There were rows and rows of birds resting on the telephone wires.

Assonance

Assonance is similar to alliteration. However, it uses vowel sounds, not consonant sounds. **Assonance** means to repeat vowel sounds in words.

Take a Look

The sentences below all have examples of assonance.

> The **team** was **lean** and **mean.**
> Here's my **advice:** don't think once, think **twice.**
> Nothing is so fine as a **day** in **May.**
> I couldn't **believe** how **relieved** I was.
> The wind outside my window **moaned** and **groaned.**

Try It!

Which of the words in the sentence show assonance?
I know you're feeling low.

Repetition of Words and Phrases

Writers also make their writing sound musical by repeating whole words and phrases.

> I have a place where I go
> When I need peace and quiet.
> I have a place where I go
> To think, and be me.
> I have a place where I go
> To count all my blessings.
> And when I come back,
> I'm right back on track
> And as fine as a person can be.

Onomatopoeia

Say these words aloud: *squeak, hiss, clang, thump.* They are examples of **onomatopoeia,** the use of words that imitate a sound. You can use these "sound words" to add drama and liveliness to your writing. Maybe you already do!

Take a Look

Onomatopoeia can be used in poems and other kinds of writing. Here are some examples.

> The noise of trash cans being emptied wakes him: clankity, clunkity, bang.

Try It!

What do each of the words make you think of?

swish   swoop   boom

End Rhyme

Not all poems rhyme. In many poems, however, the last words in certain lines rhyme. This is called **end rhyme.**

In some poems, the first and second lines rhyme, and the third and fourth lines rhyme. The stanza from *The Microscope* by Maxine Kumin is an example.

> Anton Leeuwenhoek was <u>Dutch</u>.
> He sold pincushions, cloth, and <u>such</u>.
> The waiting townsfolk fumed and <u>fussed</u>
> As Anton's dry goods gathered <u>dust</u>.

In some poems, only the last words in the second and fourth line rhyme. Can you find the rhyming words in this part of the poem *Lemonade Stand* by Myra Cohn Livingston?

> Every summer
> under the shade
> we fix up a stand
> to sell lemonade.

Internal Rhyme

Some poems have **internal rhyme.** This means that words in the middle of some lines rhyme. Here is an example from *The Acrobats*, a poem by Dorothy Aldis.

> Ladies spangled like the sun
> Turn just <u>so</u>, and then let <u>go</u>—

Rhythm

Poems often have rhythm, or meter. The words in many poems are arranged in a rhythmic pattern of accented and unaccented syllables. For example, try reading aloud this part of *The Germ* by Ogden Nash. Say the underlined parts with a little more force.

> A <u>migh</u>ty <u>crea</u>ture <u>is</u> the <u>germ</u>,
> Though <u>small</u>er <u>than</u> the <u>pach</u>yderm.
> His <u>cus</u>tomary <u>dwell</u>ing <u>place</u>
> Is <u>deep</u> with<u>in</u> the <u>hu</u>man <u>race</u>.

As you emphasized certain words and parts of words, you were following the pattern that the poet created by his choice of words for this poem.

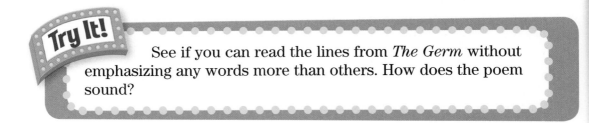

Try It!   See if you can read the lines from *The Germ* without emphasizing any words more than others. How does the poem sound?

Reading Your Writing

You can use alliteration, assonance, onomatopoeia, rhyme, and rhythm to add music to your poems and other writing. Make your writing please your readers' ears as well as their brains.

Making the Context Real

Context is the specific time, place, and circumstances that surround a particular event you are writing about. When you set out to write historical fiction, your story and characters are made up, but the setting of your story (time, place, and circumstances) is real. It plays a major role in how your characters act and how your story goes.

As a writer of historical fiction, you must make the context seem real to your readers. You want them to believe that your story really could have happened. Your plot must match the actual historical setting. Details you include about history must be accurate. You will need to do careful research about real people and events you choose to include in your fictional story.

Errors to Avoid:
▶ Do not mention anything (inventions, buildings, cities) that would not have existed when your story takes place. (*Example: Your character riding aboard the Mayflower in the 1600s should not drive a car later in your story.*) Details must stay true to your setting.
▶ Do not alter or distort actual historical events. (*Example: Do not write about Abraham Lincoln surviving the assassination attempt at Ford's Theatre when he did not.*)
▶ Your characters should not know about future events. (*Example: A slave girl in 1861 should not know that the slaves will soon be freed.*)
▶ Your characters' dialogue should be true to who they are and when/where they lived. (*Example: A 20-year-old southern belle in the 1800s would not use slang terms like a 10-year-old girl in 2007.*)

Conveying a General Mood

When you read a story out loud, it is easy to create a certain mood. If you want your listeners to think the story is sad, you can put on a dejected frown and pretend to sniff back tears while you read. If your story is supposed to be exciting, you can read loudly and dramatically, pausing every once in a while to add suspense.

When your audience is reading your story for themselves, however, conveying a particular mood is more difficult. You cannot rely on your own voice inflection and facial expressions. You must make sure that your words themselves communicate sadness, happiness, excitement, or whatever other mood you choose.

Take a Look

Read the following excerpt from Katarina's story:

Greta stomped up the stairs as loudly as she could, marched into her bedroom, and slammed the door. She threw herself on her bed, and the tears began to flow. Just thinking about her horrid little brother made her want to punch something.

It never failed. Jimmy would pester and annoy her until she couldn't take it any longer. Then, she'd let her irritation get the better of her and hit him or give him a shove. And sure enough, he'd go crying to Mom, and Greta would be busted yet again. Jimmy never got in trouble!

"Why do I let him do this to me?" she muttered under her breath. "Ugh! He knows exactly how to push my buttons, and I fall for it every time!"

Try It!

What mood is Katarina trying to convey in her story? Which words or phrases does she use to create this particular mood?

Taking Notes

Below is one of Sarah's note cards. Notice the heading she has written on the card. The headings will help her organize her notes later.

Description
P. falcon-fastest bird in the world
Peregrine Falcons, p. 2.

◀ Heading
◀ Fact
◀ Title and
  Page Number
  of Book

On the Internet, Sarah skims the lists of Web sites offered by the search engines. She clicks on the most promising sites and skims them. She looks for sites set up by colleges, government agencies, or other knowledgeable groups. Sarah skips sites set up by elementary classes and bird clubs. Sarah knows that no one checks the information in these sites to make sure it is correct. She prints a copy of the sites she wants to use so she can go back to them later, if necessary. Sarah makes note cards for the facts she finds. On each note card, she writes the title of the source where she got the information.

Taking Notes

Taking notes usually involves three steps: skimming, reading carefully, and paraphrasing.

First, Sarah uses her school library's card catalog to find the newest books about peregrine falcons and endangered species. Next, she checks the table of contents in the front of each book for chapters about peregrine falcons. Then, she checks the index in the back of the book to see if they are listed there.

When she finds information about the falcons, she **skims** it. That is, she reads the headings and the first sentence of several paragraphs on the page. When she locates information she might use in her report, Sarah **reads carefully.** She writes each fact on a separate note card. Most of the time, she **paraphrases** what she reads. That is, she summarizes the information in her own words. She often writes just a few words and uses abbreviations.

Sometimes Sarah finds a fact written in an interesting way. Then she writes down the exact words and puts quotation marks around them. On all of her note cards, she includes the title of the book and the page number.

Understanding the Main Idea and Details

Each paragraph you write should contain a **main idea** and details. The main idea is usually stated in your topic sentence—the very first sentence in your paragraph. The main idea is the most important sentence in a paragraph, because it informs your readers what the rest of the paragraph will be about. **Details** are pieces of information that further explain the main idea. When you include a main idea and details in each paragraph, your readers can follow your story more easily.

Take a Look

Emperor penguins have several different ways of getting from place to place. When they are on the land, they waddle, or wobble back and forth on their short legs. They can also slide across the ice on their bellies, using their feet and wings to propel themselves forward. Penguins can slide faster than they walk. When they are in the water, they are even faster. They swim quickly and dive deeply in search of food or just for fun.

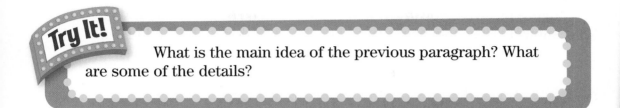

Try It!

What is the main idea of the previous paragraph? What are some of the details?

For each paragraph you write, ask yourself the following questions: Is my main idea clearly stated in my first sentence? Does each of the other sentences provide details that further explain my main idea? If a sentence does not support your main idea, it should not be included in your paragraph.

Graphic Organizers

Graphic organizers are helpful planning tools. They can help you figure out what you know and what you need to know about your subject. They also help you arrange information in a useful order.

There are many different kinds of graphic organizers. Some graphic organizers work better than others for certain written products. A time line is great if you are writing a biography. However, it wouldn't be very helpful for a description of a place. On the following pages are some examples of graphic organizers that writers use for different purposes.

Main-Idea Web

A main-idea web is useful for sorting your ideas into categories. Here's how one writer planned a report about humpback whales.

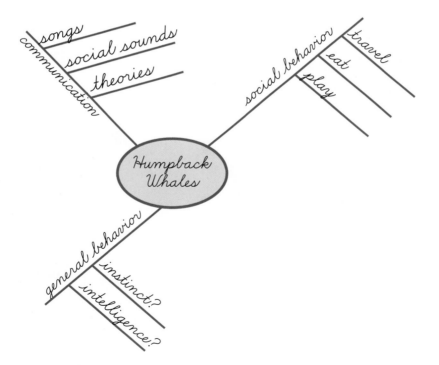

Cause-and-Effect Map

Cause-and-effect relationships are important in many different subjects. Science reports and papers about historical events might focus on cause-and-effect relationships. Here is part of the map one student created to help him write a report about the story "Magnetism" by Rebecca Hunter.

Cause

Effect

Magnets have north and south poles.

→

North poles attract south poles and repel other north poles.

If you stroke a nail with a magnet ...

→

The nails becomes magnetic.

Venn Diagram

For comparing two items, a Venn diagram is the best tool. It shows how two things are alike and how they are different. This Venn diagram helped a student writer discover that two species of owl have less in common than he had thought.

Northern Owl   Great Horned Owl

Different   **Alike**   **Different**

14-21 in. long   young fly at   18-25 in. long
                      8-10 weeks
heart-shaped face   distinct ear tufts
                      eat rodents and
nests in attics, old other small   nests in abandoned
buildings, coves   mammals   bird nests

lays 5-11 eggs   lays 2-3 eggs

Expository Structure

If you are writing to give information, it is helpful to organize your ideas into main topics and subtopics. Doing this during the prewriting phase will make both researching and writing much easier.

The following chart shows one way to plan and organize the main topic and subtopics for a piece of expository writing. This sort of organizer also helps you discover whether you need to do more research.

Topic: New Allosaur Fossil		
Subtopic: Archaeological find	Subtopic: Allosaurs	Subtopic: Importance of find
1. northern Wyoming 2. many paleontologists working together 3. must preserve site before winter	1. meat-eaters 2. ferocious predators 3. lived 136-190 million years ago	1. oldest complete skeleton found in U.S. 2. skeleton seems to be a "teenager"

Story Map

A story map is useful for planning the plot, or events, of a story. As you write, you may make changes to your story map. You might find that an idea doesn't work, or you might come up with new ideas. A story map gives you a place to start. Where you end up might be a surprise.

Title: Pirate Day

Characters: Haley and Jed, sister and brother, ages 10 and 12; various pirates

Setting: (1) rainy day in Monterey, California; (2) 18th-century pirate ship

Plot
Beginning: Haley and Jed are bored and unhappy on a rainy day. They fall asleep while reading a book about pirates.
Middle:
1. Haley and Jed "wake up" on a deserted pirate ship anchored off an island.
2. Children explore ship.
3. They hide when sailors return from island.
4. Haley and Jed must use all of their cleverness to keep from being discovered.

End: Children escape in a small rowboat. They "wake up" to discover that they shared the same adventure in their dreams.

Time Line

A time line helps you see in what order events occurred. It may also reveal relationships between events or help you draw conclusions about why certain things happened. Time lines are especially useful if you are writing about historical events or people.

Here's one format for a time line. Josie is writing a report about her great-great-grandfather who was a doctor. She recorded some of the major events in his life.

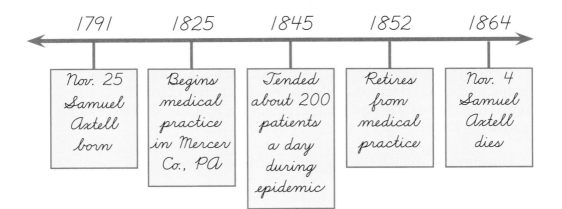

Try It!

What kind of graphic organizer would you use to plan a report about the similarities and differences between airplanes and helicopters?

Reading Your Writing

Graphic organizers are useful tools that help writers collect their thoughts and information. Different organizers are used for different kinds of writing. Organizing your ideas before you begin writing will help you create stronger stories and reports.

Using a Problem/Solution Organizer

A problem/solution organizer is a great way to visually demonstrate the scientific process. As you conduct a scientific experiment, you will encounter a series of questions or problems. Each of these will have an answer or a solution. A problem/solution organizer shows all of the steps of an experiment in order.

Miguel wanted to know if the *color* of gelatin affected people's perception of its *taste*. Miguel made three flavors of gelatin—lemon, peach, and grape. He took half of each flavor and added red food coloring. He spooned a small portion of each kind (lemon, peach, grape, red-colored lemon, red-colored peach, red-colored grape) onto three plates. He had his friends try each of the six kinds and guess the flavor.

Question 1—Which flavors will my friends guess?

Answer 1—Amy guessed lemon, peach, grape, strawberry, cherry, strawberry.
Lanere guessed lemon, peach, grape, cherry, raspberry, grape.
Benton guessed lemon, peach, grape, lemon, peach, strawberry.

Question 2—Would they guess differently if their eyes were closed while tasting the gelatin?

Answer 2—All three friends guessed the gelatin flavors correctly when their eyes were closed.

Question 3—What did my results show?

Answer 3—My results showed me that color affects people's perception of flavor.

Using a Semantic Web

A well-written report is comprised of a primary focus and many details that branch off from that main idea. A semantic web is a great way to visually organize your ideas, starting with your main point and expanding your ideas from there. Picture your main idea as a tree trunk with your supporting details as branches. You can even have smaller limbs (secondary details) branching off your supporting details.

There is plenty of sunlight.

Power plants wouldn't need much maintenance.

There are many advantages to using solar power instead of electricity.

While being used, solar power produces no pollution.

Sunlight is free.

Revising for Importance

Good writing does not happen by accident. You should always write with a purpose in mind. Before you begin any assignment, decide what that purpose will be. Ask yourself—"Why am I writing this? What do I hope to accomplish through this piece? What is the most important thing I want to express?"

Try to write your purpose in a single statement. For example:
- ▶ I want my story to express my emotions when my grandpa got sick.
- ▶ I want to persuade people that recycling paper is an important thing to do.
- ▶ I want to explain how tadpoles turn into frogs.
- ▶ I want to explain the role Abraham Lincoln's childhood played in his later presidency.

As you revise your writing, reflect on the importance of the information you have included. If it does not meet your purpose, it does not belong in your writing. You will also want to determine *how* important each piece of information is. Generally, the most important item should be shared first and the least important last.

Try It!

Think of a report or story you are working on currently. Write the purpose of your story or report in a single sentence.

Revising Using a Checklist

Revision can be an overwhelming task if you do not have a plan. You might start by looking for spelling errors and then notice that quite a few of your sentences begin with the exact same words. You start to fix that when you realize that one of your descriptions is lacking good sensory details. You get sidetracked again and again, not getting anything accomplished. It is enough to make you want to give up!

A checklist is a handy tool for revising your writing in a systematic way. You can use a checklist to help you look for one problem or pitfall at a time. Answer the questions on the checklist, making revisions to your story based on your answers. As you correct your paper and are able to answer "yes" to a question, check it off the list.

Sample Checklist for a News Story:
▶ Did you tell who, what, when, where, and why?
▶ Is the lead to your news story interesting?
▶ Did you organize the background information in a logical way?
▶ Have you ended with a sentence that summarizes your story?
▶ Have you used specific, interesting words instead of general ones?
▶ Did you delete unnecessary words?
▶ Did you use active voice in your sentences?
▶ Will the subject of your news story interest your audience?

Try It!

To use a Checklist, you must:

1. Reread your draft of your news story.
2. Read the first question on the checklist.
3. Go through your draft, revising it so that you can answer "yes" to the question.
4. Repeat 1–3 for each question on the checklist.
5. You are done!

Writing Beginnings and Endings

Did you ever read the beginning of a story or article and then decide not to read the rest of it? Think about your reasons. Was the beginning boring or confusing? Did you think the rest would be, too?

Did you ever come to the end of a story or article and turn the page? Were you looking for another paragraph or two to tie up loose ends?

If you learn to write strong beginnings and endings, your readers will not have these problems. Your beginnings will get their attention and make them want to read more. Your endings will summarize what happened or give your readers something to think about. They will know they have reached the end.

Effective Beginnings

Here are some ways to get your readers interested, along with an example of each one.

▶ Tell about a problem.

> I used to like to make wishes. I don't anymore. You see, sometimes getting what you wish for isn't always so great. I know. The day I wished I had a million dollars was the beginning of the worst week of my life.

▶ Describe something in an unusual or exciting way.

> Piercing shrieks destroyed the peace of the night. The screams and howls of the hyenas terrified the jungle campers.

▶ Invite the reader to imagine something.

> Imagine yourself as a beginning debater. Across the stage from you is the best debater in the school. She looks calm and relaxed. You feel the sweat running down your neck. When you try to wipe it away, you notice your hands are trembling.

▶ For a story, begin with dialogue.

> "Well, you're certainly in a fine mood," Mom said as I danced into the kitchen. "What's going on?"
> "Oh, nothing much," I giggled, but I couldn't hold back the laughter. "All right, I'll tell you if you promise not to tell another living soul."

▶ For an article, tell an interesting or surprising fact.

> There were once billions of beautiful passenger pigeons in the United States and Canada. There were so many pigeons that when they flew, they darkened the skies, completely shutting out the sunlight. Today, not a single passenger pigeon lives.

▶ Ask a question. For an example, read the first two paragraphs of this lesson!

▶ Tell something that happened to you or someone else. For example, if you were going to write about the school's volleyball program, you might begin by describing a game you played in or watched.

If your writing doesn't begin in an interesting way, no one will read it long enough to find out that it gets more interesting later on. Begin in a way that makes readers curious. Make them want to read more.

Effective Endings

Good writers make sure their endings are effective, too. An effective ending might summarize what you have explained or give readers something to think about.

Take a Look

In an article or report, the ending often summarizes the main points. Ending with a meaningful quotation is also a good idea.

Here is the ending from *Food from the 'Hood A Garden of Hope* by Marlene Tang Brill. It's an article about a group of high school students who created a vegetable garden that became a successful business.

> New students apply to *Food from the 'Hood* each year. About 40 percent work other jobs in addition to going to school but find time to garden. After more than five years, the business is here to stay. A small group of inner-city teenagers have proven that anyone can achieve success if they try.
>
> "What comes from that garden is hope," said Carlos. "From anything—even the riots—amazing things can grow."

Here is another example of a ending that summarizes. It is from a report about how the game of basketball has changed in the last one hundred years.

> To sum up, I found out that the game of basketball has changed in many ways. The baskets, the ball, the court, the shots, and especially the rules have all changed since the game was invented one hundred years ago.

Endings That Encourage Reflection

In both articles and stories, you can encourage readers to think or reflect on what they've read. You can help them gain some insights about their own lives from others' experiences.

Take a Look

▶ This ending is from *Toto*, a book by Marietta D. Moskin about a baby elephant who was rescued from a lion.

> It was good to be back home, Toto thought contentedly. Let the moon and the sun and the birds travel beyond the hills if they wished. His place was here.

▶ This ending is from *Mae Jemison, Space Scientist*, a biography by Gail Sakurai about the first female African American astronaut.

> Besides her work with The Jemison Group, Mae spends much of her time traveling around the country, giving speeches and encouraging young people to follow their dreams. Mae Jemison believes in the motto "don't be limited by others' limited imaginations."

As you think about the ending of your story or article, ask yourself these questions.

▶ Should I just summarize what happened?
▶ Is there something here that readers should think about?

Not all articles and stories lend themselves to reflection. Still, don't overlook this opportunity when it fits your writing.

Reading Your Writing

Readers judge writing by the way it begins—and ends. If you begin in an interesting way and end in a thoughtful way, your readers will be eager for more!

Story Structure

Where do you start when you begin a story? Do you start with a problem and then think of characters to solve it? Do you start with interesting characters and then think of a problem they might face? The answer is you can start wherever you please. However, you need to be familiar with all the parts of a story.

Plot

A **plot** is a series of events that present a problem and attempt to solve it. At the end of most plots, the problem is solved. A good plot has a clear beginning, middle, and end. Toward the end is the climax, the most exciting part of the story. During the climax, the characters struggle hardest to solve the problem.

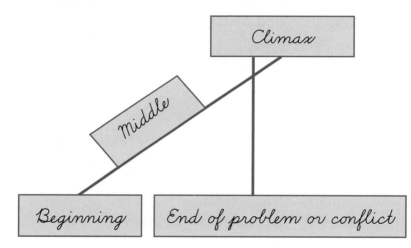

The **beginning** of a plot introduces the problem. At the beginning of the plot of Cinderella, for example, she is being treated badly by her family. During the **middle** of the plot, her problems grow worse. She wants to go to the ball, but she can't. Then her fairy godmother gives her a dress and coach.

However, Cinderella has not solved her problems. Like other main characters, Cinderella struggles through a series of conflicts. Her family keeps getting in her way. Then she gets to the ball, but when the clock strikes midnight, she must run away.

At the **climax** of the story, her family doesn't want Cinderella to try on the glass slipper. Will the prince leave without finding her? Then the prince manages to slip the shoe on her foot. In the **end** of this story, Cinderella forgives her selfish family and they all live happily ever after. All her problems are solved.

When you create your plot, think of an interesting but difficult problem for your characters to solve. Make people want to keep reading to find out what happens next.

Characters

You can create characters by showing how they act, think, feel, and speak. You can also show how others react to them. For example, Antonio Hernández Madrigal creates the character Erandi in "Erandi's Braids." He never **tells** us that Erandi loves and cares about others. Instead, he **shows** us in these ways:

By how Erandi acts: Erandi helps Mamá prepare the dough for the tortillas and separate the small fish from the large fish.

By what Erandi thinks: Erandi hopes to get a new dress for her birthday, but she thinks about Mamá using the money for a new net that they desperately need.

By what Erandi says: After the barber tells Mamá that her hair is not long enough, Erandi says she will sell her braids because her hair is long enough.

By how Erandi feels: Erandi hands turned cold and her eyes filled with tears when the barber cut her braids. After the sacrifice she makes, she knows her braids will grow back as long and pretty as before.

By how other characters react to her: Mamá is proud of Erandi. She now has enough money to buy a net and a doll for Erandi.

When you create characters, think of how they would act, speak, think, and feel. Consider how others would act towards them. Then your characters will seem like real people.

Point of View

Point of view refers to the way the author tells a story. The story is told by a character in the story or by a narrator who is not in the story.

First-Person Point of View

A story that is told by a character can be told from a first-person point of view. For example, in "A Covered Wagon Girl: The Diary of Sallie Hester, 1849–1850," the character Sallie tells the story. The first-person pronouns *I, me, my, we,* and *our* in the story help show Sallie as the person telling the story. We see only what Sallie sees and learn only what that character thinks and feels. We can guess what the other characters think and feel, but we don't know for sure.

Third-Person Point of View

Mrs. Frisby and the Crow by Robert C. O'Brien gives details about the thoughts and feelings of the characters in the story, especially Mrs. Frisby. However, it is told by a narrator who is not in the story. The narrator uses third-person pronouns, such as *he, she, they, him,* and *them,* to refer to Mrs. Frisby and the other characters. Still, the story is from Mrs. Frisby's point of view, so the narrator tells us only what she is thinking and feeling.

In some third-person stories, the narrator tells us the thoughts and feelings of several characters. We learn what each character thinks and feels.

Before you write a story, decide who will tell it. Choose whether to tell it in first person or third person. There are many ways to write a good story!

Setting

Setting includes both the place and the time when a story happens. In some stories, the location of the events is very important. For example, location is very important in "Island of the Blue Dolphins." Will Karana leave the island and find her people? In other stories, such as *Mrs. Frisby and the Crow,* the setting is not so important. A mouse and a crow might meet each other in many places.

Some stories depend totally on their settings. For example, suppose a story takes place during an historical event such as the Revolutionary War. It could not take place during other times, not even during other wars.

Try It!

Think of some stories you have read that could not be told in a different time or place. Tell a classmate the ones you've chosen.

Reading Your Writing

You cannot write a good story without paying careful attention to the plot, characters, point of view, and setting. Make all of these things work together to create a story that will interest your readers.

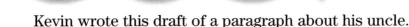

Combining Ideas

Kevin wrote this draft of a paragraph about his uncle.

> I have an uncle. His name is Jack. He is in the Army. He is in Germany. He will be home next week. Our family is coming to our house. Everyone wants to see him.

Is Kevin's paragraph well written? Not really. First, his sentences are all too short. They also don't have enough details to be interesting. Three of them begin with *He*. That's boring!

The sentences in Kevin's paragraph need to be combined so they are different lengths. He also needs to expand them with interesting details. This lesson will help Kevin and you learn ways to combine and expand your sentences.

Combining Sentences

Let's review the types of sentences.

▶ A **simple sentence** has a subject and a verb and expresses a complete thought. All the sentences in Kevin's paragraph are simple sentences.

▶ A **compound sentence** combines two or more simple sentences. Let's do that to the first two sentences in Kevin's paragraph: *I have an uncle, and his name is Jack.*

▶ A **complex sentence** combines a simple sentence and a dependent clause. Let's try it with two more of Kevin's short sentences: *Although Jack is in Germany, he is coming home next week. Our family is coming to our house because everyone wants to see him.*

By combining six sentences into three, we have improved Kevin's paragraph. We might leave one short sentence: *He is in the Army.* Then Kevin's sentences will be different lengths.

More Ways to Combine Sentences

We are just getting started on ways to combine sentences. We can also rearrange words and ideas. For example, here are other ways to combine Kevin's sentences:

> **Draft:** I have an uncle. His name is Jack. He is in the Army. He is in Germany.
> **Revision:** My uncle Jack is in the Army in Germany.
>
> **Draft:** Our family is coming to our house. Everyone wants to see him.
> **Revision:** Our family is coming to our house because everyone wants to see him.

Take a Look

Here is our revised paragraph so far. Combining sentences has made it more interesting. Notice the different sentence lengths. None of the sentences start with the same words now, so that is no longer a problem.

My uncle Jack is in the Army in Germany. He will be home next week. Our family is coming to our house because everyone wants to see him.

Expanding Your Writing

Now it's time to add some interesting details to Kevin's paragraph. We could write additional sentences. We could also add adjectives, adverbs, prepositional phrases, and clauses to the original sentences.

Try It!

What questions might readers have about Kevin's uncle? What kinds of details could he add to his paragraph?

Here is how Kevin expanded his ideas. The <u>added parts are underlined</u>. Kevin has made sure that his sentences are not all the same length. Notice how the new information makes Kevin's paragraph not only more interesting but also clearer. We have a much better understanding of why Kevin is excited.

> My uncle Jack, <u>who is 28 years old</u>, is in the Army in Frankfurt, Germany. He has been in Germany for nearly a year. He and his wife <u>Sharleen</u> will be home early next week. Our whole family is coming to our house to have a big dinner to welcome Jack and Sharleen home.

Matching Parts of Sentences

Amber needs some help too. She is writing to the editor of her local newspaper. She wants everyone to help fix up a school playground in her neighborhood. In this paragraph from her draft, she is describing the problems on the playground.

> The swings are broken. The seesaw has a big crack in it. The slide has rusted. The grass is very high. It is very full of weeds. There are very muddy puddles under every swing.

Amber knows she has too many short sentences. She combines her first three sentences into a compound sentence.

The swings are broken, the seesaw has a big crack in it, and the slide has rusted.

As Amber reads her new sentence aloud, it doesn't sound right. The words don't flow smoothly. Mr. Williams, her teacher, helps her figure out why.

He explains that the three parts of her new sentence do not match. Mr. Williams writes examples on the board to show how words or phrases in the same sentence should match. For example, they should all be verbs or all be adjectives.

1. The house was huge, dark, and scared them.
   Better: The house was <u>huge</u>, <u>dark</u>, and <u>scary</u>. (Now the words in a series are all adjectives.)
2. In the bag were some leaves, a twig, and a cocoon was in there, too.
   Better: In the bag were some <u>leaves</u>, a <u>twig</u>, and a <u>cocoon</u>. (Now the words in the series are all nouns.)
3. Either to stay or going was okay with her.
   Better: Either <u>staying</u> or <u>going</u> was okay with her. (When you use *either/or* or *neither/nor*, the words that follow these conjunctions should match each other.)

Amber knows that her new sentence is a compound sentence made of three short simple sentences. She revises it so the ending words in each simple sentence are the same part of speech. Now she likes the way it sounds when she reads it aloud.

The swings are <u>broken</u>, the seesaw is <u>cracked</u>, and the slide is <u>rusted</u>.

Try It!

Which version of this sentence has matching parts?
1. The playground is dangerous and a risk for children.
2. The playground is dangerous and risky for children.

Using Synonyms

Now Amber notices her word choices. In her last three sentences, she used *very* three times. She knows her readers will get tired of reading this word over and over. As she revises, she combines two of the sentences.

Amber's draft:

> The grass is very high. It is very full of weeds. There are very muddy puddles under every swing.

Her revision

> The grass is high and full of weeds. There are muddy puddles under every swing.

Beginning Sentences in Different Ways

Luis wrote this paragraph about video games.

> Video games are fun. I get really excited. They keep my attention for hours. Some of them are violent. They show shooting and violence. They don't have to do that to be fun.

Luis knows he has too many short sentences. He also notices that most of his sentences begin with *they*. Look at Luis' first revision on the next page. Can you find the words he added to begin his sentences in different ways? Can you see where he combined some short sentences?

First revision:

> To me, video games are fun and exciting. When I have time, I like to play them for hours. Unfortunately, some of them are violent. They show shooting and violence, but they don't have to do that to be fun.

Now Luis checks his word choices. He realizes he has used two similar words: *violent* and *violence*. He has also used *fun* twice. Here is his revision.

Final revision:

> To me, video games are fun and exciting. When I have time, I like to play them for hours. Unfortunately, some of them are violent. Some videos show shooting and explosions, but they don't have to do that to keep my attention.

In his last sentence, Luis used *Some videos* instead of repeating *They*. He replaced *violence* with *explosions* to be more specific. He also replaced *be fun* with *keep my attention*.

By combining sentences, beginning sentences in different ways, matching sentence parts, and choosing his words carefully, he has added interest and clarity.

Reading Your Writing

Try to avoid writing short, choppy sentences that all start the same way. When you're finished with your first draft, improve those sentences!

Adding Dialogue

Dialogue is the written conversation between characters in a story. Most stories get better when dialogue is added.

▶ **Dialogue helps show what characters are like.**

In *The Bridge Dancers* by Carol Saller, Callie shows her excitement about being away from her mother's watchful eye.

"Burst into jubilant song!" she cries. "The everlasting chains are loosed and we are free!"

(A less dramatic character might have said, "Mom's gone.")

▶ **Dialogue makes stories seem more real.**

In *Louis Braille: The Boy Who Invented Books for the Blind* by Margaret Davidson, Louis' friends are concerned about him.

"You never sleep!

"Half the time you forget to eat!"

"And for what?" a third boy snapped. "A wild goose chase! That's what!"

▶ **Dialogue keeps readers interested.**

In *Eddie, Incorporated* by Phyllis Reynolds Naylor, Eddie has found a dog carrying around one of the advertisements for his new business. The dog belongs to the paper boy.

"Hey, where'd he get this?" Eddie called after the boy.

The paper boy shrugged. "I don't know. It was blowing around on the street back there."

(Readers will wonder what happened to the rest of Eddie's advertisements.)

▶ **Dialogue moves the story along.**

In *Charlotte's Web* by E. B. White, Wilbur the pig escapes from his pen. Mrs. Zuckerman, the farmer's wife, calls for help.

"Ho-mer!" She cried. "Pig's out! Lurvy! Pig's out! He's down there under that apple tree."

"Now, the trouble starts," thought Wilbur. "Now I'll catch it."

Writing Dialogue

After you write dialogue for a story, read it aloud. Ask yourself if it sounds like a real person talking. If not, say out loud what you want your character to say. Experiment until you find words that sound like real talking.

As you write, put the exact words each person says inside quotation marks. Each time a new person starts talking, start a new paragraph. You don't have to tell who is talking every time. However, do it often enough so that the reader doesn't lose track of the speaker. For example, read this conversation.

"Hurry up," called Carlos. "We'll be late for school."

"I can't find my math book," said Hank.

"Did you look in your locker?"

"Twice!"

Who said "Twice!"? Are you sure? Not identifying the speaker too many times in a row can confuse readers.

Be careful not to use quotation marks with indirect quotations. Notice the difference:

Direct quotation: Kendra said, "The bus is coming."

Indirect quotation: Kendra said that the bus is coming.

FUN FACT

Dialogue is from a Greek word that means "to converse."

Try It!

Listen to people talk and write down what they say. Does this dialogue look different from what you expected? In what ways?

Reading Your Writing

Writing realistic dialogue takes some practice, but it's worth it. Good dialogue will make your stories more interesting and believable.

Using Elements of Persuasion

The purpose of persuasive writing is to influence your readers to think or act in a certain way. There are two techniques you could use. One is to support your request or opinion with reasons and facts. The second way is to appeal to your readers' interests or feelings.

How do you decide which approach to use? You must consider both your purpose and your audience. Can you back up your request or opinion with reasons and facts? If not, you can appeal to your readers' interests and feelings. Let's say you have facts you can use, along with an appeal to feelings. Then decide whether your audience is more likely to be persuaded by facts or by feelings.

After you decide on your approach, organize your points. One good way to do this is by asking and answering a question. A second technique is to present your points in order of importance, ending with the most important one. This lesson will show you how to use both persuasive approaches and ways to organize your points.

Persuading with Facts and Reasons

In this approach, you present facts and reasons that prove that your opinion is true or your request makes sense. Chan and Maya both want to persuade other students at their school. Chan's goal is to convince them to bring in cans of food for the food drive. Maya wants to persuade them to apply to be afternoon crossing guards. They both decide to use facts and reasons to support their requests.

Try It!
Read Chan's paragraph. What facts did he use? Remember that a fact is a statement that can be proved.

Try It!
Read Maya's paragraph. What facts did she include? Do you agree that she placed her most important reason last?

Here is Chan's paragraph. He organized it by asking and answering a question. Notice how he repeats his request at the end of the paragraph.

> Why should you bring in cans of food for people you don't know? The food will go to the Mid-State Food Bank. This bank provides food for more than 350 families every month. The food is given only in emergency situations. Each family can receive 10 cans of food a month. That means the bank needs at least 3,500 cans of food every month. Won't you help these hungry families get through their emergencies?

Here is Maya's paragraph. She also used facts and reasons, but she put her reasons in order from least to most important.

> Please fill in an application to be an afternoon crossing guard. As a guard, you will leave school a few minutes early and go to your corner. You will tell students when to cross and tell cars when to wait for them. Only 12 crossing guards are selected every year. They are very important because they keep students safe. Complete your application right away.

Persuading with Interests and Feelings

Knowing your audience is always important for writers. However, when you try to convince people by appealing to their interests and feelings, you must really study them. You must figure out what they care about and what they want.

Some people may be convinced to do something if it will solve a problem for them. For example, television commercials often present a problem. Then they show how a certain product will solve that problem. Some people can be persuaded if they think that others, especially people they admire, are doing the same thing. The people they admire might be movie stars or sports heroes.

At the same time, people may act in a certain way if they think this action will make others admire them. Writers of television commercials know that viewers want to look better, have more friends, be more successful, and so on. The commercials promise or hint that these things will happen if viewers just buy a certain product.

As an experiment, Chan and Maya decide to rewrite their persuasive paragraphs. This time, they try to appeal to their readers' interests and feelings. See which approach you think works better in each case.

Take a Look

On the next page is Chan's second version. This time, he wrote it to appeal to readers' interests and feelings. He is using the question–and–answer approach again. Notice how he presents a problem and then tells readers how to solve that problem.

Do you feel selfish or guilty when you think about the hungry people in our community? You know that you have all the food you need at home. Well, you don't have to feel selfish or guilty. You can help! Just bring in cans of food for our food drive. Every can our school gives to the food bank will show how much we care about others. Bring in your first can tomorrow!

Try It! Which of Chan's paragraphs do you think is more convincing? Why?

Now here is Maya's second version. Like Chan, she wants to appeal to readers' interests and feelings. What interests and feelings does she select? Does she still present her reasons from least to most important?

Here is your opportunity to be selected as one of the 12 afternoon crossing guards. Becoming a guard is an honor. You get to leave school early. No one crosses the street at your corner until you say so. You get to tell cars when to stop and go. Most importantly, you might save someone's life! Don't miss this chance! Complete your application right away.

Try It! Which of Maya's paragraphs do you think is more persuasive? Tell a classmate. What would you change about her second paragraph, if anything?

Writing Strategies

Organization

Words, sentences, and paragraphs are the building blocks of writing. In this section, you will find out how sentences and paragraphs are constructed. You will also learn how to combine short, choppy sentences into one flowing sentence. You can use what you learn in these lessons in many different kinds of writing.

Using Transition Words and Phrases

Details, details! Does it really matter how you organize them in your writing? Yes, it does! If you don't get organized, you can't expect readers to try to figure out what you meant to say. This lesson explains three ways to organize your ideas: by chronological order, by spatial order, and by order of impression.

Time and Order

Use chronological order when you want to tell when or in what order events happen. You'll need two kinds of signal words.

Time transition words and phrases tell when things happen.

this morning	at noon	tomorrow
last Monday	after lunch	in two days

Order transition words tell in what order things take place.

first	next	finally	then
meanwhile	before	later	after

Try It!

The paragraph below is from *Breaking into Print* by Stephen Krensky. Transition words show when each event happened. Can you find them?

In almost no time at all, printing grew beyond the reach of one man or firm. New printers were setting up shop as fast as they could learn the craft. A generation earlier, printers had produced a single book in a few months. Now they were printing thousands of books a year.

Using Time and Order in Your Writing

You can use chronological order when you write to **inform.** For example, in an essay about what you did last summer, you could describe the months in order: June, July, and August.

When you write to **explain** how to do something, you definitely will use order words. You need to make it clear what to do first, what to do next, and so on.

Try It!

These instructions explain how to organize notes for a research report. They are in the wrong order. What is the correct order?

_____ Divide each main topic into subtopics.

_____ Separate your note cards into piles by their main topics.

_____ Take notes on note cards.

You might also use chronological order when you write to **entertain.** Most stories, for example, are best told in this way. Paula Paul uses transition words to show the order of the events in this part of *You Can Hear a Magpie Smile.*

At first, she couldn't see too clearly, so she leaned closer to the door. Just as she did, the door opened from the inside, and Lupe tumbled forward, sprawling on the floor and looking at a pair of sandals.

Spatial Order

Not everything can be organized by time and order, of course. When you are describing how something looks, you might use **spatial order,** or order by location. There are many ways to do this. You might go from top to bottom or right side to left side. You might tell how something looks on the outside and then how it looks on the inside.

Here are some signal words for spatial order.

through	between	beside	right, left	above
into	next to	across	overhead	under

Using Spatial Order in Your Writing

You could use spatial order when you write to **inform.** For example, in science class you might want to describe the climate in the United States. You could start in the northern states and move south, in a top-to-bottom organization.

Take a Look

In her diary, Anne Frank used spatial order to describe her family's hiding place. Can you find the transition words?

There is a steep staircase immediately opposite the entrance. On the left a tiny passage brings you into a room which was to become the Frank family's bed-sitting-room, next door a smaller room, study and bedroom for the two young ladies of the family. On the right a little room without windows containing the washbasin and a small W.C. compartment, with another door leading to Margot's and my room.

As you **explain** how to do something, spatial order can help you tell where to put things. Here is how Steve used spatial order to explain how to address an envelope.

Write your address in the upper left corner. Put a stamp in the upper right corner. Then write the person's name and address in the middle of the envelope. Put it a little to the right of the center.

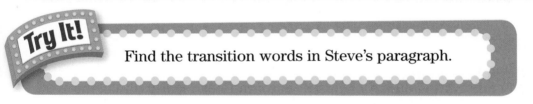

Try It!

Find the transition words in Steve's paragraph.

You could also use spatial order when you write to **entertain.** For example, you might want to describe something in a story. You could use spatial order and transition words to do it.

Take a Look

In this story, Jennifer's grandfather took her to a fancy restaurant for her birthday. Below, the writer describes the menu from the top to the bottom.

At the top of the menu were the appetizers. Grandpa wanted Jennifer to order stuffed mushrooms, but she wasn't that hungry. In the middle part of the menu were the dinners. On the right were all kinds of chicken dishes. On the left were beef dishes. Which one did she want? Then she spotted the desserts across the bottom of the menu. Where was the birthday cake?

Order of Impression

When you describe something, you might want to start with the most important part of it—what you noticed first. Let's say you are describing a special neighbor. You might start with her smile. Perhaps you are writing about an exciting basketball game. In this case, you might start with the loud cheering.

Here are some transition words you might use for order of impression. The ones in the first row below can help you point out what was most important to you. The words in the second row tell readers that more information follows.

most	best	first	important
also	in addition	too	as well as

Using Order of Impression in Your Writing

When you describe something, order of impression is often a good choice. In *The Early Houses*, Barbara Beck clearly thinks the fireplace was the most important part of the Pilgrims' homes. She describes it first and in the most detail.

Each house had a large fireplace, in front of which everyone gathered for warmth, food, and light. Cranes were used to hold large brass and iron cooking pots and kettles over the wood fire. A huge table, a stool or two, some plain wooden chairs, a chest, and beds took up most of the space in the tiny house. At bedtime, the children went up the ladder to the sleeping loft.

FUN FACT

The word *spatial* is based on a Latin word meaning "space." When you use spatial order, you tell how something is arranged in space.

Let's say you want to describe the main living area of your home by order of impression. Where would you start? What is the most important thing in that room, in your opinion?

Order of impression also works well when you are writing to **entertain.** Robert O'Brien used order of impression when he described a cat named Dragon in "Mrs. Frisby and the Crow." Most people might begin describing a cat by telling its color. O'Brien wanted his readers to know just how scary Dragon was.

He was enormous, with a huge, broad head and a large mouth full of curving fangs, needle sharp. He had seven claws on each foot and a thick, furry tail, which lashed angrily from side to side. In color he was orange and white, with glaring yellow eyes; and when he leaped to kill, he gave a high, strangled scream that froze his victims where they stood.

Other Ways to Get Organized

You might have noticed that none of these three ways to organize was used for persuasive writing. If you are trying to convince someone to do something, you must organize your ideas in a different way. First, you choose the reasons you think are most likely to persuade your reader. Then you put them in order of importance—important to your reader, that is. You will end with your most persuasive reason.

Reading Your Writing

Being able to organize your ideas is a valuable skill, one you will use your entire lifetime. The three types of organization in this lesson will help you share what you're thinking. Learn them and use them. You and your readers will be glad you did!

Does your writing need some glue? Transition words, or signal words, are the "glue" that can help your ideas fit together. They can make your sentences read more smoothly. These words can show how your ideas are organized.

What are some specific ways they can help? Transition words can be used to show location. For example, they can tell how characters in a story move from one place to another. They can also show time so readers know when something happened.

Transition words also tell order so readers understand what came first and what came next. In addition, these words can be used to compare and contrast things or ideas. They help you tell how things are the same and how they're different.

Showing Location

Transition words that tell location help readers picture what is happening. Several transition words for location are listed in the previous lesson under spatial order. More are listed below.

among	around	behind	below	over
beneath	down	near	outside	against

In this part of *One TV Blasting and a Pig Outdoors* by Deborah Abbott and Henry Kiser, the transition words for location are underlined. Imagine how confusing these sentences would be without these transition words.

Halfway to school, my best friend, Adam, yells from behind me, "Wait up, Conan! I can't walk that fast this early."

In school, the clanging of lockers echoes through the halls. I skip into my classroom just as the bell rings.

Showing Time

When you're reading, does it matter if you can't tell when something happened? Of course it does! That's why you need to use transition words for time in your own writing. Some of these words were listed in the previous lesson under Time and Order. More time transition words are listed below.

after	during	until	today	soon
later	then	when	as soon as	yesterday

Take a Look

Pearl Buck used time transition words throughout *The Big Wave* to show when events took place. Here is part of what she wrote.

> <u>One evening</u>, Kino climbed the hill behind the farm and looked toward the volcano. The heavy cloud of smoke had <u>long ago</u> gone away, and the sky was <u>always</u> clear <u>now</u>. He felt happier to know that the volcano was <u>no longer</u> angry, and he went down <u>again</u> to the house.

A boy named William revised his writing by adding time transition words. He thinks the transition words make his sentences more interesting and informative.

William's draft:

I was chosen for the baseball team! I can't wait for our first practice.

His revision:

An hour ago, I was chosen for the baseball team! I can't wait for our first practice Saturday morning.

Showing Order

Transition words that show order tell what happened first, second, next, and last. They are especially helpful when you are explaining how to do something. Several order transition words were listed in the previous lesson. Some transition words, such as *before, during, after,* and *finally,* can tell time or order.

Take a Look

Here is part of some instructions that Charlotte wrote about how to give a dog a bath. Notice how much clearer they became after she added order transition words.

Charlotte's draft:

Get out your dog's shampoo, a lot of old towels, a tub, and a plastic pitcher. Put about 6 inches of water in the bath. Put your dog into the tub and get him wet. Squeeze some shampoo onto his back. Rub it in and spread it around. Be careful not to get it in his eyes.

Her revision:

First, get out your dog's shampoo, a lot of old towels, and a plastic pitcher. Second, put about 6 inches of water in the tub. Next, put your dog into the tub and get him wet. Then, squeeze some shampoo onto his back. Rub it in and spread it around. Meanwhile, be careful not to get it in his eyes.

Signal Words

Using Transition Words to Compare

When you are giving readers new information, it often helps to compare the new information to something familiar. For example, if you're writing about a lynx, you might tell how it is like a house cat. Transition words can help you do this, including the words *like, in the same way,* and *also.* Here are some examples.

▶ The *Mayflower,* like all ships of that time, was built to carry cargo, not passengers.

▶ The space shuttle *Endeavour* perched on the launch pad like a great white bird waiting to take flight.

Using Transition Words to Contrast

You can also use transition words to show how two things contrast, or are different. These transition words and phrases will help you show contrast.

but	however	on the other hand	although
yet	otherwise	nevertheless	

FUN FACT

Transition means "a change." These words tell readers that a change is coming.

In the examples below, notice how the second clause contrasts with the first one.

▶ The morning was sunny, <u>but</u> the afternoon was rainy.

▶ I liked both books, <u>although</u> the mystery was more exciting.

Reading Your Writing

Transition words smooth the way for your reader. They tell where, when, and in what order. They help you to compare and contrast.

Try It!

Find two transition words that show comparing or contrasting in one of your books.

Using an Outline to Organize Information

Hopefully by now, you realize how important organization is to the writing process. Taking time to organize your thoughts and notes before you begin writing will save you much time in the long run.

An outline is one of the most helpful organization tools. It helps you sort through your notes and focus on the main ideas you want to address. An outline also helps you decide where each tidbit of information fits most logically into your writing.

An outline does not have be detailed or complicated. It is simply a rough sketch of what your story or report will look like. Think of yourself as an artist, drawing a quick sketch of your subject in pencil. Later, you will fill in the details, add color, and paint your masterpiece.

Here is Felipe's partially-completed outline for his persuasive report about expanding the art program at his school:

Hawthorne Elementary should expand its art program.

I. Current art program

A. Students are not given enough time each week for art.
1. 45 minutes a week is not even enough time to complete one project.
2. Students have 225 min. of science and 100 min. of recess per week.

B. Students are not engaged in enough varieties of art.
1. There is more to art than cutting, drawing and painting.
2. Artistic students want to sculpt and build and take photos and design web sites.

II. What we need

A. Three days of art each week (45 minutes each day).
1. Each week can be devoted to one form of art
2. Mondays=painting, Wednesdays=sculpting, Fridays=photography, etc.

B. More art supplies available to students
1. Clay, building materials, cameras, computers, etc.
2. More field trips devoted to art.

III. How to make it happen.

A. Subtopic
1.
2.

B. Subtopic
1.
2.

Creating a Summary

Create a Summary from a Single Sources

If a friend casually asks you about the movie you saw last night, you would probably give a *summary*, not a detailed description of every scene in the movie. A summary is short and to the point. The main idea is the focus, not the details.

When you take good notes from a source and organize those notes well, writing a summary is easy. Look at Caroline's notes about lianas (a kind of rainforest plant) and the brief summary she wrote from her notes.

Lianas

What They Look Like
— liana means woody vine
— resemble ropes in size, shape, color
— grow to size of your arm

How Where They Grow
— start growing on the ground
— do not have strong roots
— wind themselves around trees
— trying to get to light at top of rainforest

Why They are Useful
— form bridges across canopy top of rainforest
— animals use them to climb from tree to tree
— one species of liana is called "monkey ladder"

Take a Look

Lianas are a type of plant found only in rainforests. They are woody vines that look like ropes and can grow to be the size of your arm. They start growing on the ground, but their roots aren't strong. They wind themselves around trees, trying to reach the sunlight at the top of the canopy. Then they form bridges from tree to tree and animals use them as tightropes. Smaller animals, like monkeys, often use lianas to help them escape from predators.

Create a Summary from Multiple Sources

You will recall that a summary is a short, basic paragraph stating only the most important ideas on your topic. Look carefully at your notes, pull out the main things you want to focus on, and gather them together in a concise and logical paragraph.

When you write a summary comparing and contrasting two different things, there are a couple ways to organize it. Maggie is writing a summary about squirrels and chipmunks. She has already taken notes on both animals. She could briefly discuss each heading in her notes, or she could give facts about squirrels and then tell how chipmunks are similar to and different from them.

Read Maggie's summary about squirrels and chipmunks. Which method of organization did she use?

Take a Look

Squirrels and chipmunks are closely-related rodents, but they each have many unique characteristics. Squirrels are bigger than chipmunks and have big, bushy tails. Squirrels live in trees and bury food for the winter underground. Chipmunks are actually a type of squirrel, too. They are small animals with stripes down their backs. Like squirrels, they store food for the winter, but they gather it in their chubby cheeks and build large burrows for storage. Unlike squirrels, chipmunks live on the ground.

Try It!

Notice that Maggie used the words *too*, *like*, *but*, and *unlike* to show comparison and contrast. Can you think of any other words?

Organizing Multiple Paragraphs

Organizing a Multi-Paragraph Composition

When you write a piece that has several paragraphs, you must decide on the best way to organize them. When writing a biography or recounting a historical event, you should organize your ideas in chronological (time) order. When explaining how to do something, you can use sequential order (first step to last). When describing a space or object, you can use spatial order (top to bottom or left to right). You can also use order of importance to organize your ideas (most important first).

When you write a book review, you will most likely use time order. In other words, you will follow the same order the author used in the book. Then your reader will be able to better understand the events as you describe them.

The first step of writing a multi-paragraph composition is to draw up some pre-writing plans. You might choose to make an outline, create a graphic organizer, or just jot notes and ideas down on paper. When your prewriting stage is complete, you are ready to draft your book review.

Sample Book Review Structure:

Introduction—introduce the book, briefly share why you liked/disliked it

Supporting Paragraph 1—begin describing the book's plot (add personal opinions)

Supporting Paragraph 2—continue describing the book's plot (add personal opinions)

Supporting Paragraph 3—finish up describing the book's plot (add personal opinions)

Conclusion—wrap up your personal thoughts and opinions

Remember—a book review is not just a summary of the book; you are giving your own opinion of the book as well. It is best to support your opinions with details from the book. You can draw on your personal knowledge and experience as well.

Use your own judgment when deciding when and where to add your opinions within the book summary. There are no set rules for this. No two book reviews will be the same. Your goal is to find a balance between sharing what the book is about and expressing your thoughts and opinions about it.

Forms of Writing

Vocabulary

The words and phrases you choose to include in your writing will make a huge impact on the overall outcome of your ideas. Making your writing understandable to your friends can be quite easy. But using those same phrases might make it impossible for your grandparents to understand what you are talking about. You will learn how to write so both groups can understand your thoughts.

Formality of Language

A college professor speaks *formally* when teaching a class. However, he probably speaks quite *informally* when talking to his two-year-old daughter at home. The formality of our language depends on the setting, who we are talking to, and what we are talking about. If you are invited to meet the president, you will probably speak more formally to him than you speak to Billy out on the school playground.

This same concept will show up in your writing assignments. Some of your writings will be more formal (more precise, organized, textbook-sounding) than others. A biography or explanation of a scientific process will sound more technical while a friendly e-mail will be more informal (casual and conversational in tone).

Read these two excerpts written by Madison. The first is the introductory paragraph to her report on John Adams and the second is part of a personal e-mail she wrote to a friend. Notice the formality of her language in each one.

It wasn't easy playing second fiddle to George Washington. John Adams was the second President of the United States, yet the average person knows very little about him. He was our nation's Vice President for two terms under President Washington. Known for his great intellect, he found the role of Vice President to be quite boring. Since then, that office has changed. In 1797, Adams became President for four years.

I just can't believe I got the part! Can you? I mean, we've both always wanted to play Annie someday, and now I get to! I wish you still lived here, so we could do it together. Except then you might have beat me out for the part! Do you think you could talk your mom into letting you come to opening night? I know it's a five-hour trip, but Mom said you could spend the night at our house. Please, please, please say you can come!

Try It!

Which of these writing assignments will require formal language and which will be more relaxed or informal?

▶ a report on magnetism

▶ a personal story

▶ a tall tale

▶ a biography on Thomas Edison

▶ a newspaper article

Revising with Precise Word Choice

Finding the precise word for your story is a good feeling. A *tasty* pie becomes *mouth-watering*. A *thirsty* boy becomes *parched*.

A thesaurus is an invaluable tool for finding the right word to make your story come to life. Maybe a character in your story runs through a forest. Will you have him just *run*, or will he *race* through the forest? *Hurry, speed, hasten,* or sprint through the forest? Maybe he will *dart* through the forest or *scamper* or *dash*.

Read the following paragraph from Tyler's personal narrative. Think about his word choice as you read.

> Grampy and I took our first fall walk through his woods. We watched the colored leaves fall to the ground. Suddenly, a strong wind blew all around us, and more leaves fell. I walked slowly down the path. The trees formed an arch over my head. It was a red, orange, and yellow arch. I picked up a leaf and looked at it. It had so many details. I could see all the small lines and types of orange. I love fall.

Try It!

Choose five words from Tyler's paragraph, and think of more precise words to replace them.

This is Tyler's paragraph after he revised it using precise word choice.

> Grampy and I took our first autumn walk through his woods. We gazed in amazement as the brilliant leaves fluttered to the ground. Suddenly, a blustery wind blew all around us, and more leaves cascaded to the ground. I ambled leisurely down the leaf-strewn path. The trees formed a warm-colored canopy over my head. I picked up a leaf and peered closely at it. It had so many fine details. I could see all the tiny lines and various shades of orange. I love autumn.

Revising to Eliminate Irrelevant Information

Have you ever heard of the term "fluff?" As it relates to writing, "fluff" is another word for unnecessary information that is not relevant to the topic. Fluff is unimportant, nonessential; it does not matter. You are a great writer with a lot of important things to say. Why would you waste space on fluff?

Fluff gets in your readers' way and makes it difficult for them to focus on what is really important. Read one of the paragraphs from Dayne's rough draft titled, "How to Make Grandma Helen's Healthy Granola." What information in his paragraph could be considered irrelevant?

The first thing you'll want to do is preheat your oven to 250 degrees. Get out a large bowl. It should be pretty big so it can hold everything. Maybe not the biggest bowl you have, but close. In the bowl, you'll put in two cups of rolled oats, one cup of slivered almonds, three-fourths cup of whole wheat flour, and one-half cup of natural bran. Next stir in one-half cup of maple syrup, one-half teaspoon of cinnamon, and one-fourth teaspoon of salt. Mix all that together really well and pour onto a sheet pan. Cook for one hour. You'll probably want to stir the mixture every 15 minutes. Remove the pan from the oven and put the granola into a large bowl. Enjoy your healthy granola!

This is Dayne's revised paragraph.

Preheat the oven to 250 degrees. In a large bowl, combine all the ingredients listed on the recipe, making sure to stir the mixture well. Pour the mixture onto a sheet pan. Bake for one hour, stirring every fifteen minutes. Remove the pan from the oven and transfer the granola to a large bowl. Enjoy your healthy granola!

Writing Strategies

Voice

When writing a journal entry, you write as you would speak to your friends. But do you write the same way when writing a newspaper story or informative report? No. You use different slang terms and vocabulary words when you are writing depending on your audience.

You use your writing voice to communicate your ideas, thoughts and feelings. Learning how to draw in your audience is one of the most valuable writing tools.

There are times when you write just for yourself, perhaps in a journal. However, most of the time, you write to communicate with other people.

You might want to share a new idea, a good story you've thought of, or something exciting that happened to you. You might be answering a question from your science textbook. You might be writing a thank-you note to someone.

No matter what you write, keep two things in mind: your purpose, or reason, for writing and your audience, or readers. Don't begin writing until you know your purpose and have identified your reader or readers. Good writers never forget about their purpose and their audience. That's what makes them good!

Writing with a Purpose

Here are the main purposes for writing:
▶ to inform (pass on new information)
▶ to explain (tell how to do something)
▶ to entertain (tell a story, a poem, or a play)
▶ to persuade (influence readers to do something or think in a certain way)

Now, how do you decide the purpose of a piece of writing? Begin by identifying your goal. What do you want your readers to do? Do you want them to learn something? Then you're writing to inform. Do you want to show them how to do something? Then you're writing to explain.

As they read, do you hope they will laugh, cry, or be on the edge of their seats? You're writing to entertain. Do you want to influence them to do something? Your purpose is to persuade.

Try It!

What is the purpose of each topic below—to inform, explain, entertain, or persuade?

1. the history of recycling
2. why people should recycle
3. how to prepare materials for recycling
4. what happened the first time your family began to recycle

Sometimes you can have two purposes for your writing. For example, you could write a story about fourth grade to entertain your readers. At the same time, you might use the story to persuade your readers to treat each other with more respect.

Writing for an Audience

Have you ever picked up a book and immediately known that it was too easy—or too difficult—for you to read? Think about how you could tell. Was it the length of the book? Was it the number of words on each page? Was it the kind of words that were used? Maybe it was the number of pictures.

Somehow, you knew that you were not the intended audience for that book. The writer had a different audience in mind.

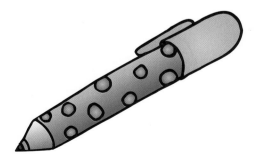

Analyzing Your Audience

When you write, you must have a clear audience in mind, too. Otherwise, you might use words that are too simple or too difficult. You might include information that your readers already know. On the other hand, you might leave out important information that your readers need to know.

If you haven't thought about your audience, your writing might be too formal or too relaxed. You wouldn't write to your best friend in the same way that you would to a person you don't know.

These questions will help you analyze your audience.

▶ Who is likely to read this piece of writing?

▶ What does this reader already know about the topic?

▶ What would the reader probably like to learn about it?

▶ What does the reader need to know about it?

▶ What words will this reader understand? Which ones should I not use? Which ones should I define if I decide to use them?

▶ Let's say you're writing to explain how to do something. Has this reader ever done anything like this before? If so, what?

▶ Let's say you're writing to persuade. What opinions does this reader probably have about this topic?

FUN FACT

Audience is based on a Latin word that means "to hear." However, an audience includes people who read, watch, or listen.

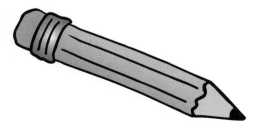

Each example below shares the same information with two different audiences. Notice how the word choice in the message to the cousin shows the writer's excitement. The message to the teacher uses more formal words and more details.

Here's a sample for a seven-year-old cousin.

> Yesterday, we got a new puppy! He is black and white. He loves to lick my face!

Here's the same information for a teacher.

> We have a new pet in our family. He's a two-month-old cocker spaniel. He is black and white and very friendly.

Here are two more examples of writing for different audiences. Notice how the review for the friend draws on the experiences shared by the reader and the writer. A book review for the school's Web site.

> *The Bridge Dancers* by Carol Saller tells how a girl named Maisie finds out how much courage she has.

Here's a review of the same book for a friend.

> You really ought to read *The Bridge Dancers*. The main character reminds me of my neighbor Brenda. Do you remember how afraid she is of crossing bridges?

Reading Your Writing

To accomplish your goal in writing, start with a clear purpose. To meet your readers' needs, identify your audience. These two steps will start you on your way to a really good piece of writing.

Convincing Opening Paragraphs

The first paragraph of a story, report, letter, or any other kind of writing should be **cogent.** In other words, it should get right to the point and make your reader want to read more. There is no better way to start off your writing than by clearly telling your readers exactly what the point of your story will be. Your first paragraph should convince them that the rest of your piece is well worth reading.

Read the following two introductory paragraphs Joe wrote for his composition on former U.S. Presidents. Which one do you think he should use for his paper?

Convincing Opening Paragraphs

Millard Fillmore was President of the United States from 1850 to 1853. He was the 13th President. Franklin Pierce was President right after Fillmore. There were other Presidents named Chester Arthur and Grover Cleveland. We mostly know about famous Presidents like George Washington and Abraham Lincoln. We also know about recent Presidents like George W. Bush and Bill Clinton. We don't know very much about people like John Tyler and Martin Van Buren.

OR

Have you ever heard of Millard Fillmore? If you answered no, that's not surprising. As a matter of fact, he was the 13th President of the United States. Imagine being the President. You're famous all over the country. Everyone knows your name. You're the most important person in America. Now fast forward a couple hundred years. Most kids today have never even heard of you. Martin Van Buren? Who's he? Benjamin Harrison? Chester Arthur? I think it's time we got to know some of our lesser- known Presidents, don't you? Come join me while I introduce you to a few of them.

Paragraph two definitely packs more punch, doesn't it? Not only is the reader's interest piqued, but Joe clearly states what lies in store for the rest of his report.

Facts and Examples

Presenting Facts and Examples Objectively

Can you describe a food you dislike to your readers without letting them know you do not like it? This is what we call being **objective**. When you write objectively, you present only the facts. You do not allow your personal feelings, opinions, interpretations, or biases affect what you're writing. When you present facts objectively, readers cannot tell how you personally feel about the topic.

The opposite of *objective* is *subjective*. Subjective writing is writing that emphasizes the writer's own mood, attitude, and opinions on the topic. Friendly letters, personal narratives, persuasive paragraphs, book reviews, and even poems and songs can be subjective.

Other forms of writing should present facts and examples objectively. Here are some examples:

▶ research report
▶ biography
▶ news story
▶ scientific process
▶ summary

Read Mark's news story he wrote for the school newspaper. The story is about the high school boys' soccer team, and Mark's older brother, James, is one of the star players. Mark does not share his personal feelings, though, about how much he loves watching his brother's team play. He presents only the facts and states examples as objectively as possible.

"This is our year," said Coach Hal Sutton when asked about his 11-0 Northland Yellow Jackets soccer team. "We've come close to winning the state championship in the past, but this is definitely it."

Northland has always been strong athletically. Their sports programs have done quite well against other schools in their league. In the 30-year history of the school, they have won 15 state championships—in basketball, wrestling, volleyball, and cross country. They have not yet been the best soccer team in the state.

The Yellow Jackets have one regular season game left before they head to the play-offs. "As long as we stay healthy," forward James Link said, "we're confident we can go all the way." James is the team's leading scorer with 18 goals on the season.

The team admitted that winning a championship will not be easy. They will meet some other undefeated teams along the way.

One of those teams is the Great Forest Blackhawks. "Northland is good," admitted Jon Drake, the Blackhawks' leading scorer, "but we'll beat 'em."

The Yellow Jackets have a grueling four weeks ahead of them. Only time will tell if they make it to the championship game and bring home the trophy.

Using Visualization to Highlight a Memorable Moment

If a word is **concrete,** it is something you can actually touch or see—trees, people, buildings, toys, food. Concrete sensory details are descriptive words used to make those objects come to life in your writing. Adding this kind of detail to your writing helps readers engage their five senses and hop right into your story.

You might know you need more sensory detail in your story, but you cannot figure out the right words to use. So, what do you do? One idea is to **visualize** what your character or setting looks like. After you have formed a mental image or picture in your mind, it might be helpful to actually draw it on paper. Then you can look at your drawing and write about what you see in front of you.

If drawing is not your strong suit, you can use visualization in a different way. Look for photographs in magazines or on the Internet that match the things you are trying to describe. Then look at those photos while you write concrete sensory details to describe them.

Again, a thesaurus is a great place to find descriptive words.

Examples:
▶ a book = the tattered pages of the worn, dark-brown leather volume
▶ a window = the old, cracked window streaked with dirty fingerprints
▶ a rug = the deep goldenrod yarn braided with dark shades of red and green
▶ a girl = her coal-black ringlets of hair bounced up and down every time she moved

Try It!

Use visualization to add concrete sensory detail to the following nouns:

▶ a tree   ▶ a horse   ▶ a cabin   ▶ a boy

Many people today are publishing *memoirs*—an account of their personal experiences and things they have observed while going through life. The experiences most people have are far from extraordinary, but you can make them meaningful to readers by writing about them in an interesting way.

A memorable moment in your life is one that helped you learn something about yourself or about the world. Not all of life's moments are good topics for personal narratives. Some might be *too* personal—like an experience your family wouldn't want you to share. Some just aren't interesting enough—like "How I Brush My Teeth" or "My New Sweatshirt." You will have to decide whether or not a topic is appropriate.

Here are some ideas:
▶ *My grand slam that won the game*
▶ *My trip to England to visit my grandparents*
▶ *The pig I named Wilbur*

After much thought, Julio decided to write about helping his grandpa take care of a newborn calf. He tried to make his introductory paragraph as interesting as possible.

I know a baby who weighed over 40 pounds when he was born. You think that's amazing? Well, there's more. He was no more than two hours old when he stood up and began to walk! Sure, he was a little shaky at first, but soon he was walking like a pro. I know this is true, because I was there in the barn when he was born. My Grandpa even let me name him. I called the little black-and-white calf Jack.

Try It!

What techniques did Julio use to create immediate interest at the beginning of his story? Was he successful?

Choosing a Topic

Choosing a writing topic can be difficult. Some writers cannot think of a single thing to write about. Others have many ideas swirling around in their brains and cannot narrow them down to just one.

Your teacher might give you a fairly specific writing assignment, like "write a report on a sea creature of your choice" or "write a report on one of America's former Presidents." Then your task will be a bit easier since your topic choices have been limited. Other times, you might be given no direction at all other than "write a historical fiction story" or "write a personal narrative."

Whichever the case, you will need two things, a plan for generating topic ideas and a method for choosing just one.

Paulo's teacher has asked the class to write a report on a sea creature. Paulo first decides to make a list of sea creatures he might like to research. He brainstorms 15 different sea creatures. Then he narrows his list down to four ideas.

- ▶ bottlenose dolphins
- ▶ orcas
- ▶ lionfish
- ▶ starfish

He chooses dolphins because he thinks they are fascinating to watch. Now that he has chosen an animal, it is time to narrow his topic. He decides to go to the library and browse through a book on dolphins for some topic ideas.

Here is his list:

- ▶ why dolphins in the wild do acrobatic tricks
- ▶ how dolphins use echolocation to communicate
- ▶ how dolphins are used in the military
- ▶ the social life of dolphins in pods
- ▶ how dolphins are trained

Paulo makes his final decision and chooses "how dolphins use echolocation to communicate." Now, he is ready to begin researching and then writing!

Choose a General Topic
and Narrow It Down

Sarah is writing an informative report for science class. She has chosen *endangered animals* as her general topic. To narrow down this topic, she uses a word web. She has added the names of four endangered animals to her web.

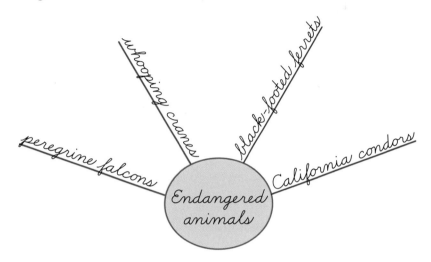

Sarah has heard about breeding rare animals in zoos and laboratories. However, she doesn't know much about it. She looks up "breeding and zoos" in an online encyclopedia. An article on this topic explains that scientists have helped breed the four kinds of animals she included in her word web.

Form a Question about the Topic

Sarah knows that writing an informative report means answering a question. She avoids questions that can be answered *yes* or *no*. Better research questions begin with *why, how,* or *what.*

Sarah wants to know how the falcons were saved, so she chooses that as her research question. She thinks that the falcons were bred in zoos and then released into the wild. Now she will find out if she is correct.

Writing Strategies

Sentence Fluency

The beginning of your sentence can either make people really interested in your writing, or make them stop reading. You don't want people to stop reading! Learning new and exciting ways of creating sentences can generate a real interest in your writing. Get creative!

Varying How Sentences Begin

Have you ever read a piece of writing where all the sentences began in the exact same way? How did you feel when you were done reading it? Bored? Disinterested? Relieved?

One of the easiest ways to make your story dull is to over-use the word "I" as a sentence-starter like this:

I looked at the clock. I saw that it was 10:15. I was almost late for my dog's first haircut. I had promised Mom I wouldn't be late. I began to panic. I ran downstairs. I grabbed my dog's leash. I put it on her and we ran to the dog groomer's. I got there just in time.

Read the revision to the paragraph above and notice how much better it sounds.

I looked at the clock and saw that it was 10:15. "Oh, no! I thought. "I'm going to be late for Jalopy's first haircut!" Mom had made me promise to be there on time. Running down the stairs, I grabbed Jalopy's leash. I put it on her and we ran to the dog groomer's. Out of breath, I flung open the door and dragged Jalopy inside. Glancing up at the clock on the wall, I noticed I had one whole minute to spare. "Why did I bother rushing?" I asked myself with a smile.

Adding Variety to Your Sentences

One way to improve your writing is to use a variety of sentences. To add variety, you can
▶ begin some sentences with adverbs
▶ end or begin some sentences with prepositional phrases
▶ write some simple sentences
▶ write some compound sentences
▶ write some complex sentences

Adding Variety with Adverbs

Adverbs describe verbs, adjectives, and other adverbs. Beginning sentences with adverbs lets your readers know right away how or where something is or when something happens. For example, look at the differences between the following sentences.

> *Joe walked home.*
>
> *Slowly, Joe walked home.*

The first sentence does not tell anything about how Joe walked. However, the second sentence lets the reader know right away that Joe walked slowly. If a detail like this helps make your ideas clearer, you should include and begin some of your sentences with adverbs. You can read more about adverbs on page 355.

Varying Types of Sentences

Adding Variety with Prepositional Phrases

A **prepositional phrase** is a group of words that begins with a preposition and ends with a noun or pronoun. Beginning or ending some sentences with prepositional phrases gives your writing variety and lets your readers know where, when, and how long something is or happens. Here are some examples.

> *We ate sandwiches.*
> *After the concert, we ate sandwiches.*

Compare the two sentences in the box above. The first sentence does not give as much information as the second one. The second sentence tells exactly when *we ate sandwiches*. Sometimes giving your readers information right away is important. Often the added details make your writing more colorful and keep your readers from becoming bored. You can read more about how to use prepositional phrases in sentences on page 361.

Rosa has already made some changes in the paragraph below. She

looked up the spelling of several words. She thought of a missing word. However, all her sentences begin very much the same. They all start with *ferrets* or with the pronoun *they*, which takes the place of *ferrets*. Here is how Rosa changed the beginnings of some of her sentences. She decided to begin some sentences using adverbs and prepositional phrases for variety.

Ferrets do not make good pets. Unfortunately, ferrets can be very destructive. They chew up houseplants. Ferrets tear open garbage bags. Under furniture and on floors, they leave a trail of trash. Ferrets spread the mess all over everything.

Adding Variety with Simple, Compound and Complex Sentences

Have you ever read something that has too many short, choppy sentences? You can easily correct this problem in your writing by combining some short sentences. Don't combine all your sentences, though. Interesting writing includes a variety of sentence lengths.

Most short sentences are simple sentences. Many beginning writers create only simple sentences. To create medium and long sentences, you can combine short sentences to make compound and complex sentences. Two simple sentences joined together with a comma and a conjunction (*and, or, but*) form a compound sentence. A simple sentence and a clause joined together make a complex sentence. You can read more about how to form compound and complex sentences on pages 366 and 367.

Rosa decided to change some of her sentences in the last paragraph of her draft. Here's Rosa's paragraph before the changes.

> Ferrets are not good pets. They are too expensive. They cause too much trouble. They might be cute. Cuteness isn't everything. Dogs and cats are better. Don't you agree?

Rosa combined and added words and a comma to two sentences to make a complex sentence. Here's the new sentence.

> Since they are destructive and too expensive, they are too much trouble to keep.

Rosa combined two other sentences in her paragraph to create a compound sentence. Here's the new sentence.

> They might be cute, but cuteness isn't everything.

By using adverbs and prepositional phrases in sentences and writing different types of sentences, you can create variety. Variety in your writing will help keep your audience interested.

Writing Strategies

Conventions

Having a spelling error or completely leaving out a word can really change the meaning of a sentence or paragraph. To keep this from happening in your writing, proofreading is the answer. Proofreading is made easier with symbols and shortcuts. Learn these and you are on your way to mistake free writing.

Proofreading

Proofread Using Symbols

As you know, one of the most important steps in the writing process is proofreading (editing) your rough draft. When you wrote the draft, your biggest concern was getting your thoughts and ideas down on paper. You were not worried about getting everything perfect. Now, it is time to go back and check your draft for errors in spelling, punctuation, and grammar.

Do you recall the chart of **proofreading symbols** on page 36? Remember that these symbols are like editing shortcuts. Without them, your rough draft could get so cluttered with scribbled notes and arrows that you might find it difficult to even understand what you wrote. The symbols are simple and easy to learn and make the editing process move quickly and smoothly.

Since Danny has memorized the proofreading symbols, he was able to quickly and easily make the following corrections to his friend Jillian's story:

My grandpa had to move from his home into an assisted living center last year. At first I was so upset about it. I just cried and cried. I loved Grandpa's house. I have so many wonderful memories there—wading by the creek, playing croquet in the yard, picking rasberries in the woods. What would happen to Grandpa's house? More important, by what would happen to Grandpa?

¶ My Grandpa had always been so strong and helthy. Then he fell and broke his hip. He wasn't able to take care of himself while he recovered. He tried to make me feel better. He said, "Jillian, you can still come visit me. We'll still have fun together. It will be just like old times." But I knew it wouldn't.

A year has gone by now, and I was right. It's not like old times. But I've been suprised to find that grandpa and I are still having a wonderful time together. No, it's not the same as it used to be, but we're making new memories together. We play chess and dominoes. We take walks around thecare center and visit with the other residents. I bring photo albums and home videos, and we pop popcorn and reminisce about old times. It's really special. I love making new memories with my Grandpa.

Writing Strategies

Presentation

Everyone knows the more interesting a book cover looks, the more likely you are to read that book. Same goes for your writing. The more creative you are about the way in which you present your ideas, the more people will want to read your thoughts and concepts. Using technology to enhance the presentation your writing will make your writing a hit!

Referencing a Source

Any time you present an informational report, you must provide a bibliography of your sources. Referencing your sources takes a little time, but it is an essential part of the research process.

Why is it so important to reference each source you use when writing a research paper? There are actually several reasons.

1. To give credit to those people who provided you with information and ideas.

2. To prove that you actually got that information from other sources and did not make it up.

3. So that you will remember where to find this information if you should need to continue your research.

4. So that your teacher can check to make sure your words in your report have been paraphrased, not plagiarized (copied word for word without quoting).

5. So that others who read your report can find additional information on your topic if they are interested.

Try It!

Can you think of any other reasons why referencing sources is important? What could happen if you do not cite each source?

Take a Look

Each type of source has its own unique referencing format. You must follow the format precisely so that your readers will understand how to find your source if needed. Here are some examples of the most common types of sources:

Making a Bibliography

At the end of her report, Sarah lists her sources in a **bibliography.** As Sarah gathered information, she made a separate bibliography card for each source. Then she put the cards in alphabetical order. To create a bibliography for her report, she simply wrote or typed the information from the cards.

Here is the information from one of Sarah's bibliography cards. Can you find the title, the author, the publisher, and the date of publication?

> *Pendleton, June. Peregrine Falcons: Saved by the Law. Nature Publications, 2000.*

Other Kinds of Entries

The example above shows what to record in your bibliography for a book. You may also need to record information from other sources. Some of them are shown below. Pay attention to order of the information and the punctuation.

Magazines:
Westin, Adrienne. "How Smart Are Elephants Really?" *Zoopers for Kids* September 2005: 30–38.

Encyclopedias:
Black, Margaret. "Elephants." *Animal Encyclopedia*. 2004: 115–116.

Web Sites:
Newman, Aline Alexander. "Cool Things About Elephants." National Geographic Kids. June 2006. http://www.nationalgeographic.com/ngkids/0606/

CD-ROM Sources:
Van Buren, Blake. Life Encyclopedia. 2006. Keyword: Elephant.

Using Multi-Media Sources to Publish a Paper

What if you had been a fourth-grader 20 or 30 years ago? What kind of technology do you think would have been available to you? You might not realize just how much technology has progressed in the last few decades. When your parents were your age, computers were new on the scene and not very common in schools. When your grandparents were in school, they probably didn't even know what computers were. What kind of technology do you use on a daily basis?

The term media generally refers to methods used to communicate information, such as sound, video, and written words. Multi-media sources refer to combinations of several media, such as a computer program that combines sound, video, text and graphics.

In the past, when students gave reports in school, they read the report orally and perhaps drew a picture to illustrate their topic. Today, multimedia sources like the Internet, interactive DVDs, and laptops can enhance your reports and presentations in creative ways.

Here are some examples of using multi-media sources:

▶ Internet: insert images, charts, graphs into your paper
▶ video: use to present ideas and highlight key points
▶ laptop computer: show a slideshow presentation
▶ digital camera: create a computer slide show of photos
▶ CD-ROMs: demonstrate an interactive activity on your topic

Try It!

What kind of multi-media sources do you think will be available to students 20 years from now?

Using Multi-Media Sources to Illustrate a Paper

Most people are visual learners. They acquire information better and retain it longer if they can *see* what they are learning, rather than just *hear* it. When presenting a research report, you can help your classmates understand it better if you include images, photographs, or illustrations in your paper and show them to the class at appropriate times during your report.

The Internet makes it easier than ever to find images to illustrate your report. You can check out websites and copy images from those sites directly into your paper.

Jaden did a research report on the life of painter Vincent van Gogh. He checked a search engine on the Internet for images of van Gogh's most famous paintings. Then he copied 10 of his favorites into documents in a word processing program. He enlarged each image to nearly cover an $8\frac{1}{2} \times 11$ piece of paper. Then he printed out a copy of each on a color printer and bound them in a spiral binder.

Jaden also made a slideshow presentation of each painting. He showed the paintings using a computer while he read his report. Then he passed around the binder for students to take a closer look. He had the class vote on their favorite painting. When he handed the paper in to his teacher, he placed it inside the binder as well.

Depending on what computer programs are accessible to you, you can illustrate your papers in many different ways.

Vocabulary

If you made a list of every word you know and use, that would be your vocabulary. As a writer, you need to keep adding to that list, no matter how long it is. The more words you know, the better chance you have of communicating exactly what you want to say to your readers.

Compound Words

A **compound word** is made by joining two short words. If you know the meanings of the two shorter words, you can sometimes figure out the meaning of the compound word. For example, a *haystack* is a stack of hay. A *scarecrow* scares crows.

Kinds of Compound Words

Closed compound words are written as one word.

cornfield	ballplayer	raindrop	springtime

Hyphenated compound words include a hyphen.

thirty-three	take-out	good-bye	one-half

Open compound words are written as two words.

car pool	milk shake	gift wrap

Knowing When to Use Each Kind

How can you tell whether a compound word is closed, hyphenated, or open? There are no clear rules. You must look up the word in a dictionary. For example, *bookmark* is a closed compound, while *book club* is an open compound.

It gets trickier! The same compound word might be written differently when it is used as a different part of speech. For example, *clean up* is an open compound when it's a verb: *I will clean up my room.* It's a compound when it's a noun: *When does the park cleanup begin?*

Writing Connection

Compound words help you make your writing exact. It's clearer and easier to write "I met my mother at the airport," instead of "I met my mother at the place where planes take off and land."

Antonyms

An **antonym** is a word that means the opposite of another word. *Happy* and *sad* are antonyms because they have opposite meanings. *Smooth* and *bumpy* are antonyms too. You can use antonyms to show how things or ideas are different.

Take a Look

Jolene wrote these paragraphs to contrast two zoos. The antonyms she used are underlined. Can you match the underlined words that have opposite meanings? Notice how they help explain the differences between the two zoos.

> The zoo in our city is <u>small</u>, but the one in Columbus is <u>huge</u>. Our zoo has only a <u>few</u> of each kind of animal. The Columbus Zoo has <u>many</u> of each kind of animal.
>
> The animals in our zoo are shut up in cages. Those in the Columbus Zoo are free to roam in open spaces that are fenced in. I thought that the animals in the Columbus Zoo seemed <u>relaxed</u> and <u>content</u>. Those in our zoo often look <u>nervous</u> and <u>unhappy</u>.

Try It!

What is an antonym for the word *laugh?*

Writing Connection

Using antonyms in your writing helps you explain how things are different from each other.

FunFact

Ant- and *anti-* both mean "opposite." *Antonyms* have opposite meanings. *Antifreeze* means "to prevent from freezing."

Synonyms

A **synonym** is a word that means the same or nearly the same as another word. For example, *damage* and *harm* are synonyms. These two words have almost the same meaning.

As you write, you must choose the word that is exactly right for your sentence. For example, you might use *damage* to write about pollution damaging the environment. You might use *harm* to write about pollution harming a person's health.

Being Specific

Jose has found three words that are synonyms: *center*, *core*, and *middle*. Here is his sentence: *The _____ of Earth is very hot.* All three of these words might fit here. Jose knows that the best choice is *core*, the name for the center or middle of Earth. He chooses *core*.

Take a Look

Lily wrote a paragraph about the season that she likes best. As she read over her paragraph, Lily realized that she used the word *like* too many times. Here's how she revised her paragraph.

> Spring is the season I like best. During the spring, the plants
> start to grow again. I also ~~like~~ springtime because of its storms.
>   ^ am fond of
> I ~~like~~ the lightning and thunder that often fill the sky during the
>   enjoy
> spring.

Writing Connection

Synonyms make your writing better in two important ways. First, they help you express your meaning exactly. Second, they make your writing more interesting because you don't use the same words over and over.

Analogies

An **analogy** shows how words are related to each other. An analogy has two pairs of words. The two words in each pair are related to each other in the same way. For example, both pairs of words might be synonyms, or both pairs of words might be antonyms.

Take a Look

Here are examples of two kinds of analogies.

Synonyms:

Stop is to *end* as *fix* is to *repair*. (*Stop* means the same as *end*, and *fix* means the same as *repair*.)

Big is to *huge* as *glad* is to *happy*.

Start is to *begin* as *have* is to *own*.

Antonyms:

Dark is to *light* as *bitter* is to *sweet*. (*Dark* is the opposite of *light*, and *bitter* is the opposite of *sweet*.)

Arrive is to *leave* as *fix* is to *break*.

East is to *west* as *friend* is to *enemy*.

Try It!

Think of a word that completes this analogy.
Find is to *lose* as *open* is to _____.

Completing analogies can be fun, just like solving riddles. You might have seen analogies in puzzle books.

Writing Connection

When you create and complete analogies, you think about how words are related. Knowing how words are related to one another helps you choose the right words when you are writing.

Homophones

Homophones are two or more words that sound the same but have different spellings and different meanings. For example, the words *to*, *too*, and *two* are homophones. Since each of these words has a different meaning, you must choose the word that fits your sentence.

> I am going <u>to</u> the store. (*To* means "movement toward a place.")
>
> My brother is coming, <u>too</u>. (*Too* means "also.")
>
> We will buy <u>two</u> loaves of bread. (*Two* means "2.")

Here are other homophones that you must be careful to use correctly.

1. I need to <u>buy</u> a new pencil at the store.
   I walk right <u>by</u> the store every day after school.
2. My sock has a <u>hole</u> in the toe.
   Are you going to eat that <u>whole</u> sandwich by yourself?
3. Sue and James are bringing <u>their</u> grandmother to the talent show.
   She lives in Colorado, and she is flying back <u>there</u> soon.
   Sue and James told me <u>they're</u> going to visit her soon.
4. May I borrow <u>your</u> math book?
   <u>You're</u> in my math class, aren't you?
5. <u>It's</u> raining outside. (contraction of *It is*)
   The dog is staying dry in <u>its</u> house.
6. Let's sit <u>here</u> in the front row.
   Then we will be able to <u>hear</u> the music.
7. I'm going to <u>write</u> an article about our town's mayor.
   I must make sure that I spell her name <u>right</u>.

8. I need to <u>know</u> the capitals of all the states.
   I have <u>no</u> more time to study.

9. I <u>knew</u> you would be here!
   Is that a <u>new</u> sweatshirt you're wearing?

10. I brought a sandwich <u>for</u> you.
    I also brought <u>four</u> cookies, two for each of us.
    Before the golfer swung his club, he shouted, "<u>Fore</u>!"

11. I <u>heard</u> that the zoo has some new animals.
    It now has a <u>herd</u> of buffaloes.

12. I saw several <u>deer</u> on my walk through the woods.
    To begin my letter, I wrote "<u>Dear</u> Grandma."

13. I have <u>one</u> more page of math to finish.
    Our baseball team <u>won</u> its last game!

14. The school <u>principal</u> is your *pal*. (Both words end the same.)
    A <u>principle</u> is an important *rule*. (Both words end the same.)

15. We are leaving <u>in</u> a minute.
    We will stay at an <u>inn</u> in the countryside.

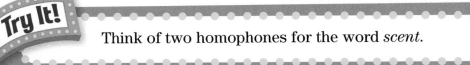

Try It!

Think of two homophones for the word *scent*.

Writing Connection
Learn the different meanings of homophones so that you write what you mean.

Homonyms

Is a *bill* a duck's beak or something you have to pay? Is a *fan* something that cools you off or someone who likes a certain musician? Some words like *bill* and *fan* are called **homonyms.** Homonyms are spelled the same and pronounced the same but have different meanings.

Here are some other words that have two meanings. You can tell which meaning a word has by reading the other words in the sentence.

1. I have a sore on my <u>gum</u>, right behind my front tooth.
   We are not allowed to chew <u>gum</u> in school.
2. Is a penguin too heavy to <u>fly</u>?
   A <u>fly</u> landed on my nose.
3. My apartment is on the second <u>story</u> of our building.
   I love to hear my grandfather tell a <u>story</u>.
4. An <u>ear</u> of corn is delicious with a little butter on it.
   I hear a buzzing sound in my right <u>ear</u>.
5. When she threw the snowball, it was time to <u>duck</u>.
   Is that a <u>duck</u> swimming in the pond?
6. My sister has a <u>date</u> with her boyfriend tonight.
   What was the <u>date</u> of Christopher Columbus's first voyage?
7. My mother works for a law <u>firm</u> downtown.
   The police officer spoke in a <u>firm</u> voice.
8. I made a sandwich with peanut butter and <u>jam</u>.
   My father got caught in a traffic <u>jam</u>.
9. The baby bird was covered with soft <u>down</u>.
   I put <u>down</u> my heavy book bag.
10. This is not the time to <u>clip</u> your toenails!
    She held her hair back with a <u>clip</u>.

FUN FACT

Homo- means "same," and *graph* means "write." Homographs are words that are *written* the *same*—but have different meanings.

Homographs

Does the word *tear* rhyme with *deer* or with *bear*? Does it mean "water that comes out of your eyes" or "a rip in your shirt"? Some words are spelled the same but pronounced differently. These words are called **homographs.** Each pronunciation has a different meaning. Here are some examples of these pairs of words.

1. I tripped and got a <u>wound</u> on my knee. (a sore area)
   Spot <u>wound</u> his leash around the tree.(wrapped around)
2. Does a pencil really have <u>lead</u> in it? (a metal)
   Would you <u>lead</u> us to the cafeteria? (guide)
3. Tie your shoelaces in a <u>bow</u>. (a knot with loops)
   The dancer will <u>bow</u> to the audience. (bend the body in greeting or respect)
4. Do you <u>live</u> on this street? (to exist)
   Is that a <u>live</u> turtle? (having life)
5. The <u>wind</u> blew down our tent. (air in motion)
   The road began to <u>wind</u> around the mountain. (turn)
6. I saw cacti and lizards in the <u>desert</u>. (a dry, sandy place)
   Don't <u>desert</u> us when we really need you! (go away)

Try It!

How can you tell whether *wind* means "air in motion" or "to turn" in this sentence?

Do you have to wind that clock?

Writing Connection

When you use homographs in your writing, you don't have to worry about mixing up their spellings. Instead, you must know their different meanings.

Learning Greek and Latin Roots

Many English words have Greek or Latin roots. When you know the meaning of these roots, you can figure out many unfamiliar English words. For example, *bio* is a Greek root that means "life." Whenever you see a word with the root *bio*, you will know that the word's meaning has something to do with life. Some words with the root *bio* include *biology* (the study of life), *biography* (a written history of a person's life), and *biotic* (relating to life).

Greek Roots

Here are three Greek roots, their meanings, and some words with each root.

geo   meaning "Earth"
geography (the study of Earth's surface)
geology (the study of Earth's rocks)
geologist (someone who studies Earth's rocks)

graph   meaning "write"
graph (information in written form)
paragraph (written sentences)
autograph (a written copy of a person's name)
biography (a written history of a person's life)

meter   meaning "measure"
kilometer (a measure of distance)
diameter (a measure of the width of a circle)
thermometer (a tool that measures temperature)

Try It!

The root *thermal* means "heat." What does *geothermal* mean?

Latin Roots

Here are four Latin roots, their meanings, and some words with each root.

aqua meaning "water"
aquarium (a tank of water)
aquatic (growing or living in the water)

aud meaning "hear"
audiotape (a tape that you listen to)
audience (people who listen)

ped meaning "foot"
pedestrian (someone who is walking)
pedal (something you push with your foot)

struct meaning "build"
construct (build)
instruct (build knowledge)

Writing Connection

Be sure to look for words with these Greek and Latin roots as you read. Knowing these roots expands your vocabulary. You will understand more words when you read and have more words to use when you write.

Prefixes

A **prefix** is one or more letters added to the beginning of a root or a base word. A prefix changes the meaning of a root or base word. Notice how these prefixes change the meaning of the base words below.

Prefix	Meaning	Examples
re-	again	redo (do again)
		rewrite (write again)
		reheat (heat again)
un-	not, opposite	unable (not able)
		untied (not tied)
		unhappy (not happy)
over-	too much	overpriced (priced too high)
		overflow (flow too much)
dis-	not, opposite	disappear (opposite of *appear*)
		disagree (not agree)
		dishonest (not honest)
mis-	wrong, not	misplace (put in the wrong place)
		misunderstand (have the wrong understanding)
		misbehave (behave wrongly)
pre-	before	preschool (before school)
		preheat (heat before)
		prepay (pay before)

Try It!

If you redo your homework, do you do too much homework, do it the wrong way, or do it again?

Here are some more prefixes and their meanings.

Prefix	Meaning	Examples
im-	not	impossible (not possible)
		impatient (not patient)
in-	not	inexpensive (not expensive)
		invisible (not visible)
non-	not	nonfiction (not fiction)
		nonsense (not making sense)
		nonviolent (not violent)
bi-	two	bicycle (a vehicle with two wheels)
		bimonthly (twice a month)
tri-	three	tricycle (a vehicle with three wheels)
		triangle (a figure with three angles and three sides)
		triplets (three children born together)

Using Prefixes

Be careful when you add prefixes to words. Certain words take certain prefixes. For example, you cannot say that someone is "dishappy." *Dis-* and *un-* both mean "not," but only *un-* is used with *happy*. On the other hand, *disappear* is correct, but *unappear* is not.

Some prefixes have several meanings. For example, another meaning of the prefixes *in-* and *im-* is "in or within."

FUN FACT

The first three digits of a phone number (not the area code) are often called the "prefix."

Try It!

What does *import* mean?

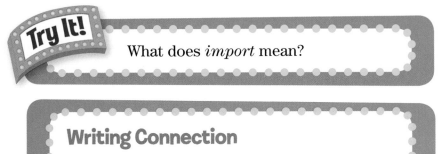

Writing Connection

Adding prefixes to words often helps you express your ideas using fewer words.

A **suffix** is one or more letters that are added to the end of a root or a base word. A suffix can change the meaning of the word or change the word into a different part of speech. For example, adding *-able* to the verb *enjoy* turns it into the adjective *enjoyable*.

When you add a suffix, you often must change the spelling of the base word. Here are three important spelling rules.

1. If a base word ends in a consonant + *y*, change the *y* to *i* before adding the suffix. Thus, *happy + -ness* becomes *happiness*.
2. If a base word has only one syllable and ends in a vowel + a consonant, double the final consonant. Thus, *sun + -y* becomes *sunny*.
3. If a base word ends with silent *e*, drop the *e* before adding a suffix that begins with a vowel. Thus, *love + -able* becomes *lovable*. However, *care + -ful* becomes *careful* because *-ful* begins with a consonant, not a vowel.

Here are some suffixes and their meanings. Notice how each suffix changes the meaning of a word.

Suffix	Meaning	Examples
-ful	full of	beautiful (full of beauty)
		fearful (full of fear)
-less	without	fearless (without fear)
		careless (without care)
-er, -or	one who	teacher (one who teaches)
		actor (one who acts)

 **Try It!**

What suffix would you use to form the word that means "without hope"? How would you spell the new word?

Notice how these suffixes change the meanings of words.

Suffix	Meaning	Examples
-*ness*	state of	kindness (state of being kind)
		darkness (state of being dark)
-*y*	being, having	rainy (having rain)
		funny (being fun)
-*ly*	like	fatherly (like a father)
		quietly (like quiet)
-*ment*	act, process	development (process of developing)
		experiment (act of experimenting)
-*able*, -*ible*	having, likely to	comfortable (having comfort)
		breakable (likely to break)

Using Suffixes

Like prefixes, suffixes must be added to words carefully. You cannot say the weather is "rainable," even though it may be raining. In the same way, someone who has friends is not "friendy." If you are unsure about the correct suffix to use with a certain word, look it up in a dictionary.

Fun Fact

Names can have suffixes too, such as -*son. Johnson* means "son of John."

Try It!

What word means "the state of being sad"?

Writing Connection

You can add many words to your vocabulary by adding suffixes to base words. Using words with suffixes can help make your writing more specific and interesting.

Using Context Clues

What do you do when you find an unfamiliar word in your reading? Do you immediately look it up in a dictionary? Do you skip over it and hope it's not important?

Instead of looking up difficult words or skipping them, you can use context clues to figure out what they mean. The context of a word can include other words in the sentence or the paragraph, plus any illustrations for that story or article. If you pay attention to clues in the sentences and pictures, you can usually figure out what a word means.

Take a Look

Chad is reading "Medicine: Past and Present," an article by André W. Carus, which includes a time line. Here is an entry from the time line that describes a discovery that was made in 1753.

> James Lind discovers that lemons and limes can cure scurvy, a vitamin C deficiency. Sailors, who frequently suffer from this disease on long ocean voyages, welcome his findings and drink lime juice.

Chad isn't sure what *scurvy* means. He reads the rest of the paragraph again and notices the words *this disease*. He realizes they refer to scurvy. Scurvy is a disease.

Then Chad wonders what *deficiency* means. He knows it has something to do with vitamin C and scurvy. Would scurvy be caused by too much vitamin C? That doesn't seem likely, so Chad decides that *deficiency* means "too little of something."

As Marlene reads *Mae Jemison, Space Scientist*, a biography by Gail Sakurai, she comes across the word *choreography*. She wonders what this word means—until she reads the rest of the sentence. The definition follows the word!

> She was also skilled at choreography, the art of creating a dance.

Philip is enjoying *Martha Helps the Rebel*, a play by Carole Charles, until he reads what Mother says to Martha.

> **Mother**: I see. Martha, ride old Jonathan as fast as you can to that soldier. Bring him back by the stream bed so no one will see him. I'll wait in the kitchen.

Philip is confused by how the word *bed* is used in the second line. Then he reads the sentence again and remembers that *bed* has two meanings: a place to sleep and the path of a stream. In this sentence, it has the second meaning.

Tips for Using Context Clues

These guidelines will help you get more from your reading.

1. If you come across a difficult word, reread the sentence and the paragraph. Look for clues to the word's meaning.
2. See if the word is defined in its own sentence or the next one. Often, the definition is set off by commas.
3. Look at the illustrations. Sometimes they help explain unfamiliar words.
4. Once you think you know the meaning of the word, reread the sentence. Substitute your meaning for the actual word. Does the sentence make sense? If so, you are probably correct.

FUN FACT

Context is from a Latin word that means "weaving together."

Try It!

Use context clues to figure out the meaning of *accelerator*.

When he pressed his foot on the accelerator, the car shot forward.

Writing Connection

You can use context clues in your own writing to help readers understand words. Always keep in mind what your readers are likely to know—and not know.

Across-the-Curriculum Words

Each subject area has its own vocabulary words. Here are some words that are used in math, science, social studies, and health.

Math Vocabulary

Bar graph: a graph that compares different amounts.

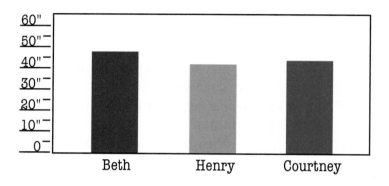

Line graph: a graph that shows changes over time.

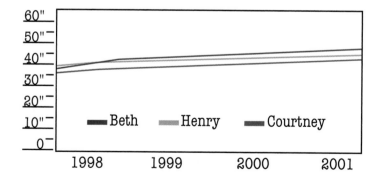

Decimal: a number less than 1. Example: 0.25 is 1/4 of 1.
Percent: part of 100. Example: 25 percent is 1/4 of 100.
Ratio: a comparison of the amount or size of two things.
Example: the ratio of 1 puppy to 3 kittens is 1:3.

Science Vocabulary

Predator: an animal that eats other animals. Example: lion.
Prey: an animal that is eaten by other animals. Example: rabbit.
Revolve: to move around another object. Example: The moon revolves around Earth.
Rotate: to spin. Example: Earth rotates on its axis.
Mass: the amount of matter in an object. Example: a brick has more mass than an empty box the same size.
Weight: a measure of the pull of gravity on an object. Example: The same object weighs more on Earth than on the moon because the pull of gravity is stronger on Earth.

Social Studies Vocabulary

FUN FACT

Vocabulary is from a Latin term that means "a list of words."

Capital: the city where a state's government is located.
Capitol: the building where a state's officials meet.
Barter: to trade one thing for something else.
Compromise: in a disagreement, each side gives up something and gets something.
Truce: a temporary halt to fighting.
Majority: more than half of the total number; most of a group.
Minority: less than half of the total number.
Urban: relating to a city.
Suburban: relating to neighborhoods or towns around a city.
Rural: relating to farming areas.
Pilgrim: a member of the first group of English people who founded a settlement at Plymouth Rock.
Pioneer: someone who is the first to explore or settle a region.

Health Vocabulary

Abdomen: the part of the body that contains the stomach, intestines, kidneys, and liver.
Diaphragm: the muscle between the chest and abdomen that helps you breathe.
Artery: a blood vessel that takes blood away from the heart.
Vein: a blood vessel that takes blood back to the heart.

Adjectives

An **adjective** is a word that describes a noun or pronoun. However, adjectives do much more than that. Adjectives can draw readers into a scene or an experience.

Many adjectives relate to the five senses: seeing, hearing, touching, tasting, and smelling. This lesson will remind you of words for each sense so you can use them in your writing.

Telling How Something Looks

To tell how an object looks, you might describe its color, size, or shape. You could use adjectives such as *bright, crooked, tiny, pale, hollow, pointed,* and *gigantic.* The adjectives used in the book *Toto* by Marietta D. Moskin help readers picture the African setting where this small elephant lived.

"On a saucer-shaped plain sheltered by the ring of blue and purple hills lived a curious little elephant. . . . With his large family, he roamed across the silvery plains of his valley, feeding on the juicy grasses and bathing in the broad green river that twisted through the land."

Telling How Something Sounds

Here are some adjectives that can help you describe how something sounds: *booming, clattering, deafening, high-pitched, harsh, hushed, hoarse, loud, purring, raspy, shrill, whispered.*

Don't the adjectives used to describe sounds make this paragraph scarier?

At first, all I heard was the pounding rain against my bedroom window. Then faint, scratching sounds seemed to come from downstairs. Were those soft footsteps in the kitchen? Then I was sure I heard a squeaking noise. Wait! The third step on the stairs always squeaked!

Telling How Something Feels

Adjectives that tell you how something feels can help readers imagine a scene in their minds. Here are some words that describe how something feels: *boiling, breezy, chilly, cuddly, dry, flaky, fuzzy, gooey, greasy, sandpapery, slippery, stinging.*

Which adjectives below describe how something feels?

> The icy air burned its way down my throat with every breath. My feet felt wooden inside my frozen boots, and my damp, rough socks were rubbing painful blisters into my heels.

Telling How Something Tastes or Smells

Our senses of taste and smell are closely related. For example, when something smells lemony, it tastes that way, too. Adjectives that describe taste, smell, or both include these and others: *fragrant, nutty, juicy, sweet, ripe, salty, smoky, rotten, sour, spicy, stale, stuffy.*

Notice how the adjectives in this paragraph describe certain smells.

> When I awoke, the medicinal smell told me where I was. The fragrance of lilacs nearby also told me that my mom was there. Then someone waved a small bottle of choking fumes near my nose, and I hurried to sit up.

Try It!

Think of three adjectives you could add to this sentence.

I took a walk along the road to the garbage dump.

Writing Connection

Adjectives can draw your readers into your stories and articles. Adjectives can help your readers see, hear, touch, smell, and taste each scene or event that you describe.

FUN FACT

Someone who is "sensible" does not have better senses than other people. A sensible person has good sense— that is, good thinking skills.

Choosing the Best Verbs

Most verbs tell about actions. The verb is often the word in the sentence that communicates the most meaning. When you write, you must decide exactly what meaning you want to communicate.

Some verbs, such as *go*, communicate a general meaning. Other verbs that mean almost the same as *go*, such as *leave*, *disappear*, and *travel*, communicate more specific meanings. When you use a specific verb, you express your thoughts clearly.

Let's say that Inez is having a conversation on the telephone. We might just write that she is talking. However, if she is telling a secret, we might write that she is whispering. If she is angry, she might be shouting. The verb we decide to use will depend on what we want to communicate.

Recognizing Specific Verbs

Below are some general verbs, followed by more specific ones. The specific verbs are not exactly synonyms, because their meanings are slightly different. The verb you choose for your writing will depend on the idea you want to express.

walk: stroll, wander, pace, shuffle, stumble, march

see: glimpse, spot, notice, view, spy

shine: sparkle, shimmer, glow, burn, blaze

take: grab, borrow, collect, gather, gain

sit: slouch, slump, perch, rest, wait

Try It!

Which verb in each sentence would you use to show anger?
1. He (glared/stared/looked) at the slip of paper.
2. Then he (put/shoved/placed) it in his pocket.

Take a Look

Here are two sentences from *The Girl Who Loved the Wind*, a folktale by Jane Yolen. Notice how the specific verbs create a clear picture of the wind's actions.

> The wind <u>danced</u> around the garden and made the flowers <u>bow</u>. He <u>caressed</u> the birds in the trees and <u>played</u> gently with the feathers on their wings.

The underlined words also help tell you that the wind was not angry or destructive. The choice of these words helps create the feeling that the wind is a positive force in the garden, not a negative one. The writer knew what she wanted to communicate and then chose specific words to do it.

Try It!

Which word expresses that the dog is very hungry?
A large dog was (eating/devouring/nibbling) its food.

Writing Connection

Specific verbs help you write exactly what you want to express. They help your readers better imagine scenes that you describe.

FUN FACT

A person who is *verbose* is not full of verbs. That person simply uses too many words to say something!

Rules for Writing: Grammar, Usage, and Mechanics

You know about rules. When you know and follow the rules of a game, you're better at the game. It's the same with writing. Knowing the rules and following them will make you a better writer.

Rules for Writing: Grammar, Usage, and Mechanics

Grammar

Grammar is about how language is organized. Parts of speech, such as nouns and verbs, are grammar. The names for different parts of a sentence, such as subject and predicate, are grammar. The names for different types of sentences, such as simple, compound, and complex, are grammar. Knowing about grammar helps you understand how to build sentences that make sense to your readers.

Nouns

Nouns are words that name everything in the world, such as persons, places, things, or ideas.

Persons:	student, Judge Taylor
Places:	room, Sacramento
Things:	traffic, *Apollo 13*
Ideas:	kindness, beauty

Kinds of Nouns

Common nouns name *any* persons, places, things, or ideas. **Proper nouns** name particular persons, places, things, or ideas. A proper noun always begins with a capital letter.

Common Nouns	Proper Nouns
mayor	Mr. Alvarez
bridge	London Bridge

Try It!

Look at the first table of nouns at the top of this page. Identify which words are common nouns and which are proper nouns.

Concrete and Abstract Nouns

Nouns can be either concrete or abstract. A **concrete noun** names something we can touch or see. An **abstract noun** names something we cannot touch or see, such as an idea or feeling.

Concrete	Abstract
tree	truth
bookmark	value
window	education

Singular and Plural Nouns

A singular noun names one person, place, thing, or idea. A plural noun names more than one person, place, thing, or idea. Here are some general guidelines for forming plural nouns.

▶ For most nouns, add -*s*.	hall—halls, patio—patios
▶ For nouns ending in *s, x, z, ch*, or *sh*, add -*es*.	cross—crosses, fox—foxes, waltz—waltzes, hunch—hunches, marsh—marshes
▶ For nouns ending in a consonant + *y* change the *y* to *i* and add -*es*.	city—cities, berry—berries, family—families
▶ For nouns ending in a consonant + *o* usually add -*es*, but sometimes add just -*s*.	tomato—tomatoes, piano—pianos
▶ For nouns ending in *f* or *fe*, change the *f* to *v* and add -*es*, or add just -*s*.	knife—knives, belief—beliefs

For many nouns, such as *mouse—mice* and *foot—feet*, there are no rules for creating their plural forms. A few nouns have the same form in the singular and plural such as *deer* and *sheep*.

Possessive Nouns

A possessive noun shows ownership of things or qualities. It tells to whom or to what another noun belongs.

Steven's sister is on the soccer team.   *Tasha's* bicycle is red.

Here are some guidelines for forming possessive nouns.

▶ To make a singular possessive noun, add an apostrophe + *s*.	Marsha's, book's, Ms. Crawford's, house's, boss's
▶ To make a plural possessive noun from a noun whose plural form ends in *s*, add only an apostrophe.	runners—runners', doctors—doctors', countries—countries'
▶ To make a plural possessive noun from a noun whose plural form does not end in *s*, add an apostrophe + *s*.	teeth's, men's, mice's

Pronouns

A **pronoun** is a word that takes the place of a noun in a sentence.

<u>Kelly</u> has a beautiful voice.   <u>She</u> has a beautiful voice.

<u>Oak and maple</u> are hardy trees.   <u>They</u> are hardy trees.

Personal Pronouns

Personal pronouns name specific persons or things. Personal pronouns can be singular or plural.

A personal pronoun can be the **subject** of a sentence.

Ian went to soccer practice.
He went to soccer practice.

A personal pronoun can be an **object** in a sentence.

Abby told her idea to Kyle.
Abby told her idea to **him.**

Some personal pronouns are possessive pronouns. A possessive personal pronoun can show possession.

Carleton's car wouldn't start.   **His** car wouldn't start.

It is important to remember to replace a singular noun with a singular pronoun, and a plural noun with a plural pronoun.

Here are all of the personal pronouns.

	Singular	**Plural**
Subject Pronouns	I, you, he, she, it	we, you, they
Object Pronouns	me, you, him, her, it	us, you, them
Possessive Pronouns	my, mine, your, yours, his, her, hers, its	our, ours, your, yours, their, theirs

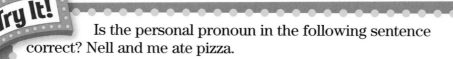

Try It!   Is the personal pronoun in the following sentence correct? Nell and me ate pizza.

Intensive and Reflexive Pronouns

Intensive and reflexive pronouns end with *-self* or *-selves*. An **intensive pronoun** draws attention to a noun or pronoun in the same sentence.

> Kay **herself** cleaned the entire room.
> We set up the tents **ourselves.**

A **reflexive pronoun** refers to the subject of a sentence and receives the action of the verb.

> Kay reminded **herself** to clean the room.
> We taught **ourselves** to set up the tents.

Note that the forms of intensive and reflexive pronouns are the same. How the words work in a sentence shows whether they are intensive or reflexive.

FUN FACT
The English word *pronoun* comes from two Latin words. The first is *pro,* meaning "for." The second is *nomen,* meaning "name." So a pronoun is a word that we use for, or in place of, a name for something.

	Singular	Plural
Reflexive and Intensive Pronouns	myself, yourself, himself, herself, itself	ourselves, yourselves, themselves

Demonstrative Pronouns

A **demonstrative pronoun** points out a particular person, place, or thing.

> **This** is a huge balloon.
> **These** are the best grapes I've ever had.

Notice that these demonstrative pronouns stand alone. *This* and *these* usually refer to people or things that are nearby. *That* and *those* usually refer to more distant people or things.

	Singular	Plural
Demonstrative Pronouns	this, that	these, those

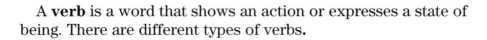

Verbs

A **verb** is a word that shows an action or expresses a state of being. There are different types of verbs.

Action Verbs

In a sentence, an **action verb** shows what the subject does. Sometimes we can see the action of the verb; sometimes we can't.

Marcy **stomped** in the puddle.   Ted **hoped** to be the winner.

As you learn about verbs, you will notice that a number of verbs do different things in sentences.

State-of-Being Verbs

State-of-being verbs are usually a form of *be (am, is, are, was, were, be, being, been).* A state-of-being verb that joins, or links, the subject of a sentence with a noun, pronoun, or adjective in the predicate is called a **linking verb.**

I **am** the hall monitor.   Marla **was** late.

There are other kinds of linking verbs. Here are common linking verbs.

Common Linking Verbs		
appear	feel	seem
be	grow	are
was	am	were
being	is	taste
been	sound	remain
smell	look	become

Some verbs can be action or state of being.

Action   Simon and Beatrice *smell* the roses.

State of Being   The roses *smell* good.

Read the following sentences. In which sentence is the word **taste** an action verb? In which sentence is it a state of being verb?

The lemons **taste** sour.   The cooks **taste** the lemons.

Helping Verbs

In many sentences, the verb is one word. In other sentences, the verb is made of two or three words. In these cases, the last word is the **main verb.** The other words are called **helping verbs.** Helping verbs help the main verb show action or state of being by telling when an action occurred or will occur.

Lou **had known** about the meeting.
Mason **will be working** after school.

Here are the most common helping verbs.

Common Helping Verbs			
am, is, are, was, were, be, being, been	can could do, does, did have, has, had	may might must	shall should will would

Helping verbs and the main verb are not always right next to each other in a sentence. Notice how some other words fall between the parts of the verb in the following sentence.

Lou **had** not **known** about the meeting.

Some helping verbs act as action verbs and main verbs in sentences. The verbs **has, have,** and **had** can be action verbs. Verbs such as **had** can be main verbs in a sentence.

Action Verb	She **has** the books.
Main Verb	Her parents had **had** enough.

FUN FACT

The English word *verb* comes from the Latin word *verbum,* which means "word."

Adjectives and Adverbs

Adjectives

An **adjective** is a word that describes, or modifies, a noun or a pronoun. An adjective usually comes before the word it modifies.

> The **loud** ring of the telephone interrupted her sleep.

Adjectives modify nouns in three different ways. Some adjectives tell *what kind*. Some tell *how much* or *how many*. Others tell *which ones*. Here are some examples.

> **What kind?**   The **fluffy** puppy ran across the floor.
> **How much or how many?**   Hugh chose **two** kittens.
> **Which ones?**   The flowers are in **this** garden.

Sometimes a linking verb lies between a noun and its modifier. A **predicate adjective** is one that modifies the subject of a sentence and is separated from it by a linking verb.

> The breeze is **chilly.**

Articles

Articles a, an, and **the** are special adjectives. They modify nouns, just like other adjectives. *The* refers to a particular person, place, or thing. It is called a **definite article.**

> Gary climbed **the** hill with ease. (**The** refers to a particular hill.)

The words *a* and *an* are indefinite articles. They refer to any one person, place, or thing. *A* is used before a noun or pronoun that begins with a consonant sound. *An* is used before a noun or pronoun that begins with a vowel sound.

> Claire pulled **a** book off the library shelf.
> (**A** refers to no particular book.)
>
> **An** egg fell from its nest. (**An** refers to no particular egg.)

Sometimes another adjective is placed between an article and the noun or pronoun the article modifies. Gary climbed the **steep** hill.

Proper Adjectives

Some adjectives, called **proper adjectives,** are formed from proper nouns. Like proper nouns, they always begin with a capital letter.

Greek islands	**Japanese** garden	**American** automobile

Adverbs

An **adverb** describes, or modifies, a verb, an adjective, or another adverb. Adverbs add more meaning to the words they modify by telling *how, when, where,* or *to what degree.*

How	Tia set the table **quickly.**
When	Tia set the table **already.**
Where	Tia moved the table **upstairs.**
To what degree	Tia cleared the table **completely.**

You will notice that many adverbs end in **-ly.** They are formed by adding that ending to adjectives. Many adverbs, though, do not follow that pattern. Here are some of the most common adverbs that do not end in **-ly.**

just	most	not	somewhat
more	never	so	very

An adverb that modifies a verb may be in one of several positions in the sentence. Here are some examples.

At the Beginning of a Sentence	**Quietly,** the mongoose *crept* across the garden.
Before a Verb	The mongoose **quietly** *crept* across the garden.
At the End of a Sentence	The mongoose *crept* across the garden **quietly.**
After a Verb	The mongoose *crept* **quietly** across the garden.

Prepositions

A preposition is a word that relates a noun or a pronoun to some other word in the sentence. Prepositions usually indicate relationships of time or place.

> We swam **until** sunset.
>
> We swam **near** the lifeguard's chair.
>
> We swam **past** her.

Here are a number of words that are often used as prepositions. Note that some prepositions have more than one word.

about	at	by	like	over	underneath
above	because of	down	near	past	until
according to	before	during	of	since	up
across	behind	for	off	through	upon
after	below	from	on	throughout	with
against	beneath	in	onto	to	within
along	beside	inside	out	toward	without
among	between	in spite of	outside	under	
around	beyond	into			

Object of the Preposition

The noun or pronoun that follows a preposition in a sentence is called the **object of the preposition.** A preposition cannot stand alone. It must have an object.

> The magician pulled the rabbit **from** the **hat.** *(Hat is the object of the preposition from.)*
>
> The rabbit made the magician disappear **into** thin **air.** *(Air is the object of the preposition into.)*

Prepositional Phrases

A **prepositional phrase** is made of a preposition, its object, and any words in between.

> Blake saw the presents hidden **in the closet.**

Conjunctions and Interjections

Conjunctions

A **conjunction** is a word that connects words or groups of words. The words *and, but,* and *or* are **coordinating conjunctions.** They connect related groups of words.

> Knights **and** squires were busy in their tents. (connects subjects)
> Some squires repaired **or** polished lances. (connects verbs)

These conjunctions can also connect independent clauses.

> One knight looked fearless, **but** he was worried.
> He had to win the contest, **or** he would lose his honor.
> No one had ever defeated him, **and** he didn't want that to change.

Subordinating conjunctions introduce subordinate or dependent clauses. A subordinate clause is a dependent clause that gives more information to another part of a sentence.

> The game is still on, **unless** you hear otherwise.

Here are some common subordinating conjunctions.

after although as	because before if	since than though	unless until when	whenever where while

Interjections

An **interjection** is a word or group of words that usually expresses strong feelings. Most interjections are followed by an exclamation point.

> **Hey!** That was *my* sandwich!

Some interjections are not as strong and are followed by a comma in a sentence.

> **Hey,** when did you get here?

Subjects and Predicates

A sentence has two parts—a subject and a predicate.

Subjects

The **subject** of a sentence names whom or what the sentence is about. The **simple subject** of a sentence is the noun or pronoun that names who or what performs the action.

> *Koko* loves picture books.
> The tabby *kitten* is Koko's choice.

Complete Subject

The **complete subject** of a sentence includes the simple subject and any words that describe it.

> *The tabby kitten* is Koko's choice.

Compound Subjects

In some sentences, two or more nouns or pronouns perform the action of the same verb. A sentence that has more than one simple subject is said to have a **compound subject.** The simple subjects may be joined by *and* or *or.*

> Did **Koko or her kitten** talk to Dr. Patterson?
>
> **Dr. Patterson and her assistant** understand Koko's sign language.

Writing Connection

We sometimes use fragments when we speak. We fill in the missing parts of our sentences by our tone of voice, facial expressions, or gestures. When we write, we cannot show our facial expressions or gestures to our readers. We can only use words on paper to express thoughts.

Predicates

The **predicate** of a sentence is the part that tells what the subject does or is. In most sentences, the predicate comes after the subject. The **simple predicate** of a sentence is the verb.

> Koko's first kitten **was** smoky gray.
> Dr. Patterson **carried** the kitten in her pocket.

Complete Predicate

The verb, plus any words that modify or complete its meaning, make up the **complete predicate.**

> Koko's first kitten **was smoky gray.**
> Dr. Patterson **carried the kitten in her pocket.**

Compound Predicates

In some sentences, the subject performs more than one action. A **compound predicate** is two or more simple predicates, or verbs, that have the same subject. The verbs may be joined by *and, or,* or *but.*

> Koko **cradled the kitten and examined its paws.**
> The kitten **loved Koko but scratched her.**

Try It!

Look at the two sentences above. Identify the simple predicates in each sentence.

Writing Connection

Knowing what complete subjects and complete predicates are will help you construct sentences and not fragments.

Direct Objects and One-Word Modifiers

Direct Objects

The noun or pronoun that *receives* the action of the verb is the **direct object.** To identify the direct object in a sentence, first find the verb. Then ask *Whom?* or *What?* Look for the answer to the question among the words after the verb. The answer is the direct object. If you can't answer the question, there is no direct object in the sentence.

> Danielle called **me** yesterday.
>
> Parents chatted in the hallways. (Parents chatted *what?/whom?* There is no answer; this sentence does not have a direct object.)

In some sentences, there is no direct object.

> Everyone laughed.

In other sentences, an object is required to give meaning to the sentence. The following sentence would not make sense without a direct object.

> Loretta dropped her **pencil.**

One-Word Modifiers

Modifiers are words that describe or add to the meaning of nouns, pronouns, and verbs. **Adjectives** modify nouns and pronouns. **Adverbs** modify verbs, adjectives, and other adverbs.

One-word modifiers are single adjectives or adverbs that make up part of the subject or predicate of a sentence.

> His **new** football felt good in Mitch's hands. (The adjective *new* modifies the noun *football.*)

> Mitch **proudly** slipped his jersey over his head. (The adverb *proudly* modifies the verb *slipped.*)

Phrases

A **phrase** is a group of words used as a single part of speech. There are several kinds of phrases.

Prepositional Phrases

A **prepositional phrase** begins with a preposition and ends with the noun or pronoun. The noun or pronoun at the end of a preposition is the **object of the preposition.** Prepositional phrases may modify nouns, pronouns, verbs, adjectives, or adverbs.

The computers **in the new lab** are fantastic.

The computers look **like expensive machines.**

The lab is popular **among teachers.**

Our lab opens early **in the afternoon.**

Appositive Phrases

An **appositive** is a noun that describes or explains another noun in a sentence. An **appositive phrase** includes the appositive and any words that modify it. An appositive phrase always occurs right next to the noun it modifies.

George Washington, **our first president,** was ambitious.

Participial Phrases

A **participle** is a verb form that acts as an adjective. A participle is formed by adding *-ed* or *-ing* to a verb. A **participial phrase** includes a participle and any modifiers or objects.

The field **covered in wildflowers** spread before us.

Overflowing with color, the field welcomed us.

Clauses

A **clause** is a group of words that contains a verb and its subject. There are two types of clauses.

Independent Clauses

An **independent clause** can stand alone as a sentence. An independent clause is sometimes called a main clause. Every sentence must have at least one independent clause.

The elephant trumpeted. (This independent clause is a simple sentence.)

The elephant trumpeted, but **the giraffe remained silent.** (These independent clauses, joined by *but*, make up a compound sentence.)

Here are two ways to join two or more independent clauses to form a sentence.

We were tired, **but** we decided to continue hiking. (with a comma and a coordinating conjunction)

We were tired; we decided to continue hiking. (with a semicolon)

When you join independent clauses with a semicolon, do not use a coordinating conjunction.

Dependent Clauses

A **dependent clause** is sometimes called a subordinate clause and must be combined with an independent clause to form a sentence. A dependent clause gives more information to the independent clause in a sentence.

Here are some sentences that have dependent clauses. Notice that when the dependent clause comes before the independent clause, the two clauses are separated by a comma.

Although we liked the movie, we preferred the book.

We will begin **whenever you arrive.**

Look at the following sentence. Would you place a comma between the dependent and independent clauses in the sentence?

I stayed indoors because of the rain.

Special words introduce dependent clauses. They are called **subordinating conjunctions.** Learning to recognize these words will help you identify dependent clauses in sentences.

Writing Connection

A subordinating conjunction introduces a clause containing a subject and a verb. Sometimes subordinating conjunctions are confused with prepositions. Remember that a preposition is followed by a noun or pronoun.

Adjective Clauses

An **adjective clause** is a dependent clause that modifies a noun or pronoun in a sentence.

Matt saw glaciers **that looked like thick flowing cream.** (The clause modifies *glaciers* and tells *what kind.*)

Matt Henson is an African American explorer **who traveled in the Arctic.** (The clause modifies *explorer* and tells *which one.*)

Adverb Clauses

An **adverb clause** is a type of dependent clause that modifies a verb, an adjective, or another adverb in a sentence.

Because of the harsh weather, Henson froze his heel. (The clause modifies the verb **froze** and tells *why.*)

Matt built a house **as soon as they arrived.** (The clause modifies the verb **built** and tells *when.*)

Writing Sentences

Variety helps make your writing more interesting to readers. One way to include variety is to use sentences of different lengths. Using a lot of short sentences makes your writing choppy and hard to read. Combine sentences or parts of sentences to add interest to your writing and make it easier to read.

Combining Sentences by Creating Compound Elements

Sometimes two sentences contain many of the same words. You can combine these sentences and leave out the repeated words. Use the conjunctions *and, but,* and *or* to make compound subjects, predicates, and objects.

> Celia drew several pictures. Peter drew several pictures.
>
> **Celia and Peter** drew several pictures. (compound subject)
>
> Peter uses markers. Peter uses colored pencils.
>
> Peter uses **markers or colored pencils.** (compound object)
>
> Tonio carves animals. Tonio sculpts people.
>
> Tonio **carves animals but sculpts people.** (compound predicate)

You can also combine adjectives and adverbs from different sentences. Use commas or conjunctions to join these sentence parts.

> Peter sketches neatly in his notebook. He sketches quickly.
>
> Peter sketches **neatly, but quickly,** in his notebook.
>
> Marta painted a rustic cabin. It is a small cabin.
>
> Marta painted a **small, rustic** cabin.

Combining Sentences with Phrases

Sometimes you can combine phrases from separate sentences to create one sentence that reads more smoothly. You might even be able to combine several sentences to avoid repeating words.

> Peter hung his pictures in the classroom. Peter hung his pictures on the wall.
>
> Peter hung his pictures **on the wall in the classroom.**
>
> The hallway was full of parents. The parents were excited. The parents were talking about their young artists' work.
>
> The hallway was full of excited parents **talking about their young artists' work.**

When you move words or phrases from one sentence to another, make sure you put them in a place that makes sense.

> The teacher asked Peter to wash his hands. He asked Peter three times.
>
> The teacher asked Peter to wash his hands three times. (This sentence does *not* contain the same message as the two original sentences.)
>
> The teacher asked Peter **three times** to wash his hands. (This sentence correctly combines the two original sentences.)

Try It!

Combine these two sentences to create one sentence that reads more smoothly.

Steven sat on a stool. Steven sat behind the easel.

Combining Simple Sentences to Create a Compound Sentence

Two simple sentences that are related can be combined to form a compound sentence. Join the sentences with the conjunction *and, but,* or *or.* A comma is needed before the conjunction in a compound sentence.

Use *and* to join two sentences that contain similar ideas.

Tia wrote the story. Peter drew the illustrations.

Tia wrote the story, **and** Peter drew the illustrations.

Use *but* to join sentences that are on the same topic but contain different ideas.

The story is sad. The pictures are beautiful.

The story is sad, **but** the pictures are beautiful.

Use *or* to join sentences that are related but show a choice between two ideas.

Are Tia and Peter finished? Are they going to add a cover?

Are Tia and Peter finished, **or** are they going to add a cover?

Try It!

Form a compound sentence with these simple sentences. Remember to choose the conjunction that best fits with the ideas in the sentences.

I enjoyed the book. I didn't like the movie.

Combining Sentences to Create a Complex Sentence

Another way to avoid repetition is to create a complex sentence from two shorter sentences. A complex sentence is made of an independent clause and one or more dependent clauses. An independent clause can stand alone as a sentence, but a dependent clause cannot. A dependent clause gives more information to an independent clause in a complex sentence. To rewrite two sentences as a complex sentence, make the idea from one of the sentences a dependent clause. A dependent clause begins with a subordinating conjunction such as *after, as if, because, before, that, though,* or *when.* Other words, such as *which* and *who,* are also used to introduce the dependent clause in a complex sentence.

> Tia submitted her story to *Stone Soup.* It is a magazine that publishes student writing.
>
> *Tia submitted her story to* Stone Soup, **which is a magazine that publishes student writing.**
>
> *Tia's cousin had a poem published. Her cousin is in fourth grade.*
> *Tia's cousin,* **who is in fourth grade,** *had a poem published.*

For some sentence combinations, the dependent clause can go at the beginning or the end of a sentence.

> Tia has high hopes. She worked so hard on her story.
> Tia has high hopes **because she worked so hard on her story.**
> **Because she worked so hard on her story,** Tia has high hopes.

Reading Your Writing

If your writing has too many short sentences and repeated words, you can improve it by combining sentences. Combine phrases, clauses, or simple sentences to create variety in your writing.

Types of Sentences

There are different types of sentences writers use to create variety in their writing.

Simple Sentences

A **simple sentence** has only one subject and one predicate.

> **Pearl S. Buck** <u>was an author.</u>

Simple sentences may have a compound subject, a compound predicate, or both.

> **Compound subject: Pearl Buck and her parents** were Americans.
>
> **Compound predicate:** Buck <u>wrote books</u> and <u>worked as a missionary.</u>
>
> **Compound subject and compound predicate: Buck and her parents** <u>lived in China</u> and <u>worked in that country.</u>

Compound Sentences

Two or more simple sentences make up a **compound sentence.** There are two ways to join simple sentences to make a compound sentence. One way is to use a comma and a coordinating conjunction. Another way to join simple sentences is by using a semicolon without a coordinating conjunction.

> Setsu was cheerful, **but** she knew Jiya was sad.
>
> Kino's father worked as usual; he told Kino to do the same.

If more than two simple sentences are joined to make a compound sentence, the first simple sentences are separated by commas. Then the final sentence is separated by a comma and joined with a conjunction.

> Father carried the boy, Mother brought a mattress, **and** Kino watched sadly.

Try It!

Which of the following sentences is a compound sentence?

Carmen and Miguel are neighbors.

Darnell cleaned his room and washed the dishes.

Complex Sentences

In a **complex sentence,** there is one independent clause and one or more dependent clauses. In some complex sentences, the independent clause is first, followed by the dependent clause. In other complex sentences, the dependent clause is at the beginning of the sentence. Separate an introductory dependent clause from the independent clause with a comma.

Independent Clause	Dependent Clause

Kino had to wait until his friend woke up.

Dependent Clause	Independent Clause

After Jiya woke up, he still was not hungry.

Writing Connection

Different types of sentences add interest. Mix simple, compound, and complex sentences when you write. Create further variety by changing the position of dependent and independent clauses in complex sentences.

Sentence Problems

Sentences and clauses that are punctuated incorrectly can confuse readers. Learning to recognize and to fix problem sentences will make your writing clearer.

Fragments

A group of words that is written and punctuated as a sentence but is missing a subject or a predicate or both is a **fragment.** Some fragments are dependent clauses. They need to be attached to an independent clause. Dependent clauses have subjects and verbs, but they do not completely express who or what did something and what happened.

> The tall weed.
> Grew out of the sidewalk.
> While we were walking.

Remember that every sentence should include information about *who* or *what* did something and *what* happened. If you cannot answer **who** or **what** did something, you need to add a subject to make a sentence. If you cannot answer **what** happened, you need to add a predicate to make a sentence.

> The tall weed **waved in the wind.** (added a predicate)
> **It** grew out of the sidewalk. (added a subject)

With dependent clauses, look for subordinating conjunctions such as **though, because,** and **while.** These words introduce a dependent clause. If you cannot find the words the clause modifies, then you will probably need to add an independent clause to make a sentence.

> **We saw it** while we were walking. (added an independent clause)

Run-on Sentences

A sentence with no punctuation or coordinating conjunctions between two or more independent clauses is a **run-on sentence.**

> I need new shoes my sister needs a new coat.

Here are three ways to fix run-on sentences.

1. Make two sentences out of one run-on sentence. Add a period at the end of the first independent clause. Then capitalize the first word of the second one.

   I need new shoes. My **sister needs a new coat.**

2. Separate the two independent clauses with a comma and a conjunction.

   I need new shoes, and **my sister needs a new coat.**

3. Separate the two independent clauses with a semicolon.

   I need new shoes; my sister needs a new coat.

Try It!

How would you fix the following run-on sentence?

Consuela drew a picture she gave it to me.

FUN FACT

Using rules for spelling and punctuation became a more common practice when William Caxton printed the first book in the English language in 1475.

Rambling Sentences

In a **rambling sentence,** a writer strings together many thoughts. Rambling sentences often have many *and*s in them.

> Last week we wrote letters and we learned how to address envelopes and then we toured the post office.

Here are two of the best ways to fix the rambling sentence above.

> Last week we wrote letters. We learned how to address envelopes. Then we toured the post office.

> Last week we wrote letters and learned how to address envelopes. Then we toured the post office.

Awkward Sentences

An **awkward sentence** is a sentence that does not sound or read well. Many awkward sentences just have too many clauses.

> Jerry thought he learned everything, but it turned out that the test was on something different from what Mr. Elder had said it would be.

To fix this sentence, break it into several shorter sentences. You can get rid of some of the words, too.

> Jerry thought he learned everything. It turned out that the test was on something different from what Mr. Elder had said.

Some have words or phrases that repeat the same thought.

> I didn't get much out of that book I was reading out of.

To fix this one, remove the words that repeat.

> I didn't get much out of that book I was reading.

Sometimes phrases do not describe the right words.

> Flapping its wings rapidly, away flew the bird.

To fix this sentence, place the noun the phrase describes immediately after the phrase.

> Flapping its wings rapidly, the bird flew away.

Sometimes words are misused.

> I called my cousin, only I got a busy signal.

Replace this misused connector with a coordinating conjunction.

> I called my cousin, **but** I got a busy signal.

Try It!

Read the following sentence aloud. Does it sound correct? If not, how would you fix it?

These are the shoes because they belong to my sister.

Kinds of Sentences

There are different kinds of sentences.

Declarative Sentences

A **declarative sentence** makes a statement. It tells something or gives information. Declarative sentences always end with a period.

Magma is the hot melted rock that blasts or pours out of a volcano.

Exclamatory Sentences

An **exclamatory sentence** expresses strong feeling or emotion. An exclamatory sentence ends with an exclamation point.

I could read about volcanoes all day!

Interrogative Sentences

An **interrogative sentence** asks a question. It always ends with a question mark.

Is the volcano, El Chichon, in Mexico still active?

Imperative Sentences

An **imperative sentence** makes a request or gives a command. Usually, imperative sentences end with a period.

Move carefully to the edge of the crater.

The subject is *you*, meaning the person or persons being spoken to. Notice that the subject is not actually stated in the sentence.

Writing Connection

Some imperative sentences can be written as exclamatory sentences. For example, *Be careful near the ledge!* takes an exclamation point because it is an imperative sentence that expresses strong feeling or emotion.

Paragraphs

A **paragraph** can be one sentence or a group of sentences that tell about one idea or topic. Many paragraphs are made of two or more sentences including a **topic sentence, supporting sentences,** and a **closing sentence.** A **topic sentence** states the paragraph's main idea. The first sentence of a paragraph is often the topic sentence. However, you may find it later in the paragraph. The other sentences provide information that supports the main idea. Some paragraphs have a closing sentence at the end that gives a summary of the paragraph and helps readers move smoothly on to the next paragraph. Here's an example of a good paragraph. Notice that the first line is indented.

Take a Look

The first line of the paragraph is indented.

The topic sentence states the main idea of the paragraph.

Supporting sentences tell more about the main idea.

The colonies were different in many ways. For example, in Massachusetts, many of the colonists came as families looking for land to settle. The Rhode Island and Pennsylvania colonies were settled by religious groups in search of freedom to worship as they pleased. The New York Colony became a very culturally and ethnically diverse colony. People from all countries began to settle there.

—from "Early America," by Trevor Matheney

FUN FACT

The original meaning of the word *paragraph* was "written by the side." Centuries ago, people used to make a mark beside the text at the spot where a new idea or topic began. They did this instead of indenting new paragraphs.

Staying on Topic

All of the sentences in a paragraph should tell about the same subject. If a writer includes information that doesn't relate to the main idea, it is confusing to the readers. The student who wrote the paragraph below realized that one of the sentences doesn't belong.

Take a Look

> The early American colonists liked art. Portraits were very popular. Wealthy families decorated their homes with large portraits of family members. Most colonial artists didn't have any formal art training. Colonists also liked to hang paintings over their fireplaces. Many of these scenes showed a favorite activity such as hunting or horseback riding. Even gravestones were decorated with carvings.

Sentences that don't stay on topic in one paragraph might fit in another paragraph. Look for ways to include interesting information instead of throwing out sentences that are out of place.

Try It!

Does the following sentence belong in the above paragraph? Why or why not?

Fireplaces were used for cooking and heat in colonial homes.

Supporting the Main Idea

Writers use different kinds of information to support their ideas. **Examples, facts,** and **evidence** can help you make your point.

Examples

In the paragraph on page 374, the writer used examples to support his main idea. To emphasize this, he even starts one sentence with the words *for example.*

Facts

Writers may also support a main idea with facts. The sample paragraph on page 375 includes facts about colonial artists. Using facts helps make your writing more believable.

Evidence

Sometimes a writer uses evidence as support for a main idea. This happens most often in persuasive writing, such as a letter to the editor. A writer may express an opinion then support that opinion with evidence as to why it is reasonable.

Try It!

What other kind of information supports the main idea of the paragraph on page 374?

Starting New Paragraphs

Paragraphs give order to what you write. Putting your ideas in separate paragraphs will help readers stay focused. When you start writing about a new idea, it's time to start a new paragraph.

Here is another part of the student's report on early American art. Notice the different ideas in the two paragraphs.

> Many painters in the English colonies were itinerant, which means they went from place to place. They painted for anyone who would hire them.
>
> Not all early artists fit this pattern, however. Charles Willson Peale had some wealthy supporters who sent him to England to study art for three years. When he returned to the colonies, he became a very popular portrait painter. John Singleton Copley was another famous colonial painter. The works of both of these artists are still known today.

In the first paragraph, the writer tells about itinerant colonial artists. In the second paragraph, she tells about artists who became famous. Because she was changing ideas, the writer began a new paragraph. The topic sentence in the second paragraph (the first sentence of the paragraph) helps connect the ideas in the two paragraphs.

Reading Your Writing

Make sure that all of the sentences in a paragraph relate to the main idea. This will help you organize your writing and help your reader follow along.

Types of Paragraphs

Writers use different kinds of paragraphs for different reasons. Choose from narrative, descriptive, expository, and persuasive paragraphs, depending on your purpose for writing.

Narrative

Narrative writing is used for telling stories. Writers should always keep in mind who their audience is. Because narrative writing is usually written to entertain, you should choose a subject that would be interesting to readers. Also use words that are probably familiar to your audience. Give context clues for terms that might be new to readers.

Look at this student's narrative paragraph. The audience is her teacher and fourth-grade classmates.

> Jeremy was dreading his trip to the doctor's office. All morning he tried to think of ways to get out of going. He couldn't say he didn't feel well—that would only be more of a reason to see the doctor. Besides, his mom was set on everyone in the family getting a flu shot. That's what Jeremy was worried about. He hated needles.

Descriptive

Descriptive writing lets readers share the writer's experiences. Many descriptions contain sensory details that appeal to some or all of the readers' five senses—sight, hearing, taste, touch, and smell.

You might include descriptive writing in a story. For example, if you were to tell what a character sees from the top of a mountain, you would use descriptive writing. You might also use descriptive writing in a science class to report what you observe during an experiment.

After a seed-growing experiment, Nick used his daily notes to write the following paragraph. He knows his audience is his teacher and, perhaps, his classmates. His purpose is to tell what happened, based on his observations. He must also tell what he learned from the experiment.

> I tried to grow a bean plant. I gave it only water and light, not soil. I put a folded paper towel and a bean seed in a clear plastic bag. I added two tablespoons of water. Then I sealed the bag and hung it in a south window. On Day 2, the seed had split open. A tiny white sprout was visible. On Day 3, the sprout was 1/8 inch tall already. Tiny, hair-like roots grew downward. On Day 5, the sprout had two small, green leaves unfolding. The whole plant was about 3/4 inch tall. The roots continued to spread, but they were still very thin. All of this tells me that a plant can at least begin to grow with only light and water.

Try It! Create a descriptive paragraph about what you are wearing.

Expository

Expository writing is used for giving information. A writer might use expository writing to inform readers, to explain something, or to explore a topic. Most newspaper and magazine articles are expository. Travel writing and biographies are also expository.

Once again, knowing your audience is important. What does the audience already know? How much do you need to tell them? What does the audience *want* to know? These are the questions to ask yourself as you plan.

Kara wrote the following paragraph explaining how to pan for gold. She explains the process in a way that makes it clear to her readers, who probably haven't panned for gold.

Kara states her main idea ▶
in the first sentence.

In the rest of ▶
the paragraph,
Kara explains
the process.

Kara uses signal words, ▶
such as *First, Then,*
continue, again, and *Finally,*
to help her readers
through the process.

Panning for gold is a slow but easy process. First, scoop some dirt and sand from the bottom of a stream into a shallow pan. Hold the pan under water and swirl it gently. The water will carry out the lighter materials, such as sand and pebbles. Then, when the pan is about half full, lift it out of the water. Tip it slightly and continue swirling until all the water is gone. Dip the pan into the water again, bring it back out, and swirl some more. Keep doing this until almost all the material is out of the pan. Finally, look for any shiny flakes or tiny nuggets that remain in the pan.

Persuasive

In persuasive writing, a writer tries to get readers to think, feel, or act a certain way. It is especially important for writers who are trying to persuade others to know their audience. This helps them choose the right "argument" to make their point.

Before writing a persuasive paragraph, ask yourself what you want to accomplish. Do you want people to act a certain way, or do you just want them to believe what you believe?

In the following paragraph, the writer states his main idea in the first sentence. In this case, the writer's main idea is an opinion. He then gives evidence that supports his main idea. In the closing sentence, he suggests how the problem could be solved.

> The author states an opinion in the first sentence. It is the paragraph's main idea.

> The first piece of evidence—kids are throwing away lots of food.

> The second piece of evidence—kids say they couldn't eat all the food.

The serving portions in our school cafeteria are too large. I stood next to the garbage cans for two lunch periods last week. On most hot lunch trays, about a quarter or a half of the food was uneaten. I asked 25 kids why they were throwing their food away. Only three kids said they didn't like the food. The other 22 said they were full or couldn't eat it all. Reducing the portions would save money for the school and would cut down on a lot of waste.

> In the closing sentence, the writer suggests a solution and gives reasons for taking this action.

Reading Your Writing

You can use different kinds of writing for different reasons—to tell a story, describe, explain, or persuade. No matter what kind of writing you do, remember to include all the parts of a paragraph.

Rules for Writing: Grammar, Usage, and Mechanics

Usage

Usage is about how we use language when we speak and write. For example, the rules of usage tell you when to use was and when to use *were*. They tell you when to use *broke* and when to use *broken*. They tell you when to use *smaller* and when to use *smallest*. Learning and using the rules of usage will make it easier for people to understand what you say and what you write.

Verb Tenses

To show when an action takes place, we use different verb forms called **tenses.**

Present Tense

In the **present tense,** the action, or condition, is happening now.

Lena **skips** down the sidewalk.
Mark **hurries** to the bus stop.

When the subject is singular, add **-s** or **-es** to the base form of a verb. When the subject is plural, do not add **-s** or **-es.**

Singular	Lena **skips.** The puppy **bites.**	Mark **hurries.** He **carries** books.	Sara **dresses.** Lou **tosses** a ball.
Plural	Lena and I **skip.** The puppies **bite.**	Mark and Lisa **hurry.** They **carry** books.	Her sisters **dress.** Dad and Lou **toss** a ball.

When the subject of a sentence is *I* or *you*, do not add **-s** or **-es** to the verb to express the present tense.

I **skip.**   I **toss** a ball.   You **hurry.**   You **carry** books.

Past Tense

A **past tense** verb tells about action that has already taken place.

Lena **skipped** down the sidewalk.
Mark **hurried** to the bus stop.

Past tense verbs use the same form for both singular and plural subjects. Form past tense verbs by adding **-ed** to the base form of the verb. In some cases, as in *skip—skipped*, double the final consonant, then add **-ed.** For verbs that end in **y,** such as *hurry,* change the **y** to **i** and add **-ed.**

laugh—laughed   toss—tossed
rattle—rattled   mop—mopped

Future Tense

The **future tense** tells about actions happening in the future. Use the helping verb *will* with the base form of a verb to express the future tense.

> Shelly **will arrive** soon.
> You **will see** her later.
> I **will think** about it.

Here are some things to remember when forming tenses for verbs.

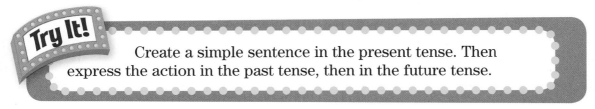

Try It!

Create a simple sentence in the present tense. Then express the action in the past tense, then in the future tense.

Action Verbs

An **action verb** tells what the subject of a sentences does. Sometimes we can see the action; sometimes we can't.

> Luke **waved** at Alex.   Luke **bought** Alex a present.

State-of-Being Verbs

State-of-being verbs tell that something exists, or they tell about the state of something. State-of-being verbs are usually a form of the verb *be*.

> Luke **was** late.   Alex **seems** sad.   Heidi **is** my pet hamster.

Helping Verbs

Helping verbs are often used to form the future tense. Helping verbs are also called **auxiliary** verbs. They help the main verb express action by telling when an action will occur.

> I **will visit** the zoo tomorrow.
> I **will think** about your answer.

Regular and Irregular Verbs

Regular Verbs

Regular verbs are verbs that take **-ed** to form the past tense.

> jump—jumped   kick—kicked   smile—smiled

For most regular verbs that end with a vowel and a consonant, double the final consonant, then add **-ed.**

> hop—hopped   trip—tripped   skim—skimmed

For regular verbs that end in **y,** change the **y** to **i** and add **-ed.**

> carry—carried   hurry—hurried   tarry—tarried

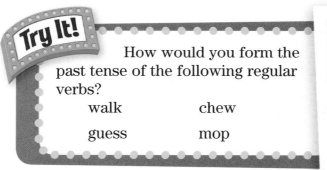

Try It!

How would you form the past tense of the following regular verbs?

walk   chew

guess   mop

Irregular Verbs

Some verbs don't follow this pattern. These verbs, called **irregular verbs,** change their form completely for the past tense. You must learn the forms of irregular verbs. See the chart on the next page for examples of common irregular verbs.

Common Irregular Verbs

Present Tense	Past Tense
am	was
are	were
come	came
catch	caught
drink	drank
eat	ate
fall	fell
fly	flew
forget	forgot
go	went
know	knew
make	made
sit	sat
sleep	slept
speak	spoke
think	thought
win	won
write	wrote

Try It!

Look at the following sentences. Which sentences are correct? Which ones are incorrect?

I slept soundly last night.

She spoke to no one.

The bus stopped at the corner.

Writing Connection

Since there are a lot of verbs that are irregular, it helps to check the dictionary to make sure the correct spelling of the past tense is used.

Subject-Verb Agreement

The verb in a sentence must agree with its subject in number. When subjects and verbs match up in this way, we say there is **subject-verb agreement.** Writers must pay attention to subject-verb agreement when they write in the present tense. In the past and future tenses, singular and plural verb forms are the same.

Singular subject and verb:	**Marian paints** well.
Plural subject and verb:	**They paint** well.

When the subject is singular, add -*s* or -*es* to the basic form of a verb. When the subject is plural, use the base form of the verb.

	Subject	Verb
Singular	Dana She Margaret	reads. marches. dances.
Plural	Children They We	read. march. dance.

Irregular verbs have plural forms that are quite different from their singular forms. Learn to recognize these forms.

	Singular	Plural
forms of *be*	am, is, was	are, were
forms of *have*	has	have
forms of *do*	does	do

The **goat is** white.	The **goats are** white.

Pronouns as Subjects

Pronouns have singular and plural forms, just like nouns do. When a pronoun is the subject of a sentence, the verb must agree in number, just as when a noun is the subject.

Singular subject pronouns: *I, you, he, she, it*
Plural subject pronouns: *we, you, they*

Pronouns *I* and *You*

The singular pronouns *I* and *you* require special treatment when it comes to subject-verb agreement. When *I* or *you* is the subject do not add *-s* or *-es* to the base form of a regular verb.

	Subject	Verb
Singular	I You He *or* She	sing. sing. sings.
Plural	We You They	sing. sing. sing.

Compound Subjects

In a sentence with a **compound subject,** two or more nouns or pronouns perform the action of the verb. A sentence with a compound subject might take a verb that agrees with a singular or a plural subject, depending on how the compound subject is formed.

When the parts of a compound subject are joined by *and,* the verb must agree with the plural subject.

> **Jan and Leah knock** at the door.
>
> My **teachers and I go** to the library.

When the parts of a compound subject are joined by *or,* the verb must agree with the *closest* noun or pronoun in the compound subject.

> The **door or the windows are** drafty. (verb agrees with *windows*)
>
> The **windows or the door is** drafty. (verb agrees with *door*)

Try It!

Check the following sentences for subject-verb agreement. Which one is correct?

Karen and Charles runs to the store.

The cat or the dogs need to go outdoors.

Pronouns and Their Antecedents

A **pronoun** takes the place of one or more nouns. The noun to which a pronoun refers is the pronoun's **antecedent.** The English word *antecedent* comes from two Latin words joined together that mean "to go before." A pronoun's antecedent is always *before* the pronoun. The antecedent can appear in the same sentence as the pronoun.

Elijah picked up the muddy **puppy** and hugged **it.**
(*Puppy* is the antecedent of the pronoun *it.*)

An antecedent may also be in a previous sentence.

Elijah saw the muddy **puppy. It** needed a bath.
(Again, *puppy* is the antecedent of the pronoun *it.*)

A pronoun may have more than one antecedent.

Jenny and **Dave** drove to St. Louis. **They** attended a concert.
(The pronoun *they* refers to both Jenny and Dave.)

Pronoun-Antecedent Agreement

If a pronoun replaces a singular noun, the pronoun must be singular. If a pronoun replaces a plural noun, the pronoun must be plural. When pronouns and their antecedents match up in this way, they agree in number. This is called **pronoun-antecedent agreement.**

The new **bridge** has just opened. **It** is the longest bridge in the state. (The singular pronoun *it* agrees with its singular antecedent, *bridge.)*

The new **stores** are open now. **They** are full of sporting goods. (The plural pronoun *they* agrees with its plural antecedent, *stores.)*

Pronouns must also agree in **gender.** A noun may refer to a male or female person or a neutral thing. Use the pronouns *he* or *him* when referring to a male person. Use *she* or *her* when referring to a female person. *It* is used to refer to a neutral thing.

> **Ben** hit the home run **he** had always dreamed of.
> **Wanda** hopes **she** is not late for practice.
> The **river** rose, but **it** did not overflow.

Pronoun-Antecedent Pitfalls

A pronoun usually follows and refers to the last noun in a sentence. Sometimes, confusing and funny things happen when pronouns and antecedents don't work together.

> Elijah saw the muddy puppy and the dirty kitten. **It** needed a bath. (What needs a bath is unclear in this sentence.)

Sometimes it's not clear which noun or nouns are the antecedents of a pronoun.

> Jenny and Dave went to visit their parents. **They** attended a concert. (Who attended a concert—Jenny and Dave, their parents, or all four of them?)

Finally, sometimes writers forget to include an antecedent at all.

> I was about to call the bus depot when **it** drove up. (The bus depot drove up?)

Try It!

Look at the following sentence. Do the pronoun and antecedent agree?

Jeremiah and Daniel said he would walk the dog.

Forms of Adjectives and Adverbs

Comparing with Adjectives

To compare two things, use the **comparative** form of an adjective. For one-syllable adjectives, add -*er*. For adjectives with more than one syllable use *more*.

> This street is **wider** than that street.
>
> Neal's project was **more difficult** than Dan's.

To compare three or more things, use the **superlative** form. Superlative forms of most one-syllable adjectives end in -*est*. Words with two or more syllables use *most* to form their superlatives.

> This street is the **widest** of all the streets in town.
>
> Neal's project was the **most difficult** of all.

Some adjectives, such as *good* and *bad*, have different comparative and superlative forms.

> good, better, best   bad, worse, worst

Comparing with Adverbs

For most short adverbs, add -*er* to compare. Use *more* with adverbs with two or more syllables.

> I jumped **higher** than you did.
>
> I visited her **more recently** than you did.

Add -*est* to most short adverbs to make the superlative form. Use *most* with adverbs of two or more syllables.

> Of the three frogs, mine jumped **highest.**
>
> She is the one I visited **most recently.**

Some adverbs, such as *well* and *badly*, have different comparative and superlative forms.

> well, better, best   badly, worse, worst

Contractions and Double Negatives

Contractions

We often shorten the negative word *not* and attach it at the end of other words. In this shortened form, called a **contraction,** *not* appears as *-n't.*

Celia was**n't** at her locker this morning.

Double Negatives

A **negative** is a word that says "no." Here are some negative words.

no no one	nobody none	not nothing	nowhere never

In English, we use only one negative word in a sentence. When two negatives occur in a sentence, the sentence is incorrect and contains a **double negative.**

Incorrect: I did **not** hear **no** phone ring.
Correct: I did **not** hear the phone ring.

Do not combine a contraction containing *not* with another negative word.

Charlie could**n't** get **nowhere** in the snow.

Correcting Double Negatives

There are two ways to correct a sentence that contains a double negative. One way is to remove the *-n't* at the end of the contraction.

Charlie could**n't** get **nowhere.**   Charlie could get **nowhere.**

Another way is to replace one negative word with its opposite, or affirmative, form.

We did**n't** do **nothing.**   We did**n't** do **anything**.

Rules for Writing: Grammar, Usage, and Mechanics

Mechanics

The rules of mechanics are very important in writing. Imagine a paragraph with no capital letters at the beginnings of sentences and no punctuation at the ends of sentences. How confusing would that be? Of course, there is a lot more to mechanics than capitalizing the first word of a sentence and using end marks. These lessons will give you what you need to know to understand and use the rules of mechanics to improve your writing.

Periods

Where to Use Periods

Use a **period** at the end of a **declarative sentence** and some **imperative sentences.**

The passengers on the *Mayflower* were below decks.
Look over there to see the picture of the *Mayflower*.

Use a period after many **abbreviations.**

mountain–mt.	inch–in.	November–Nov.	dozen–doz.

Place a period after a person's **initials.**

R. G. Vincente

Use a period in the abbreviation of a person's title.

Senator—Sen.   Mister—Mr.

If a sentence ends with an abbreviation, don't add a second period.

Please send inquiries to Sean O'Bannon, M.D.

Often abbreviations are used in street *addresses*. Place a period after each abbreviation.

street—St.	parkway—Pkwy.	road—Rd.	north—N.
217 E. Highland St.	1004 Teal Pkwy., Bldg. 4	drive—Dr.	lane—Ln.

Use a period, or a decimal point, in numbers expressed as **decimals.**

Our carnival raises 42.5 percent of our funds.

Use a decimal point to express amounts of **money.**

The cost of $3.82 for a nice lunch seems reasonable.

Where Not to Use Periods

Some abbreviations of names of agencies or organizations appear in all capital letters with *no* periods between them. These abbreviations are formed from the first, or initial, letter of each word in the name of the organization.

NASA	**N**ational **A**eronautics and **S**pace **A**dministration
FBI	**F**ederal **B**ureau of **I**nvestigation
HMO	**H**ealth **M**aintenance **O**rganization
EPA	**E**nvironmental **P**rotection **A**gency

Some of these abbreviations are pronounced as a word. These are called **acronyms.** Others are pronounced letter by letter. These are called **initialisms.**

NASA	Pronounced *na s[ə]*
EPA	Pronounced *ē pē ā*

There are some groups of abbreviations that do not require periods.

Points on a compass	
N	north
NW	northwest
Business and Commerce	
COD	cash on delivery
FOB	free on board
Units of Measurement	
kg	kilogram
m	meters

Try It!

Which of the following abbreviations take a period?

NATO   Mr   lb

When addressing envelopes to be mailed to or within the United States, use the two-letter **state abbreviations** listed below. Do not use periods with these abbreviations.

Alabama	AL	Kentucky	KY	Ohio	OH
Alaska	AK	Louisiana	LA	Oklahoma	OK
Arizona	AZ	Maine	ME	Oregon	OR
Arkansas	AR	Maryland	MD	Pennsylvania	PA
California	CA	Massachusetts	MA	Rhode Island	RI
Colorado	CO	Michigan	MI	South Carolina	SC
Connecticut	CT	Minnesota	MN	South Dakota	SD
Delaware	DE	Mississippi	MS	Tennessee	TN
District of Columbia	DC	Missouri	MO	Texas	TX
		Montana	MT	Utah	UT
Florida	FL	Nebraska	NE	Vermont	VT
Georgia	GA	Nevada	NV	Virginia	VA
Hawaii	HI	New Hampshire	NH	Washington	WA
Idaho	ID	New Jersey	NJ	West Virginia	WV
Illinois	IL	New Mexico	NM	Wisconsin	WI
Indiana	IN	New York	NY	Wyoming	WY
Iowa	IA	North Carolina	NC		
Kansas	KS	North Dakota	ND		

Try It!

Write your address for an envelope. Use only initials for your first and middle names. Then use street abbreviations. Include your city and use the abbreviations for your state.

Question Marks and Exclamation Points

Question Marks

Use a question mark at the end of an **interrogative sentence.**

Has anyone studied the Pilgrims?
Do you know anything about them?

If a question ends with an abbreviation, place the question mark after the abbreviation. If the abbreviation has a period, place the question mark after the period.

Did you mail a letter to the EPA?
Did Augustus begin his reign in 29 B.C. or 29 A.D.?

Exclamation Points

Use an exclamation point at the end of a word or sentence that expresses strong feelings, such as surprise, fear, anger, or excitement.

An exclamation point is used at the end of an **exclamatory sentence.**

Look at that ball go!
I've never seen a throw like that!

If an **imperative sentence** expresses strong feelings, use an exclamation point at the end.

Don't run that way!
Pass it! Pass it!

Use an exclamation point after an **interjection.** An interjection is a word or group of words that expresses strong feelings or emotions.

Wow! What a play!
Hey! That was a great game!

Commas

Commas are used to separate groups of numbers, words or ideas.

Numbers

Use a comma to separate groups of three digits in numbers greater than 999.

> We need $2,560,000 to build a new gymnasium.

Dates

Use commas to separate elements in a date.

> She was born on November 8, 1994.

Place a comma between the day of the week and the month.

> She started school on Wednesday, August 27, 2003.

Use a comma after the year if the date is used in the middle of a sentence.

> Harley will graduate on June 10, 2005, if he passes his final tests.

If only a month and a year appear in a sentence, no comma is needed.

> My parents met in July 1986 at a street fair.

Letters

Use a comma at the end of a greeting in a friendly letter and after the closing in all types of letters.

> Dear Cousin Kristin,   As always,

Names

Use commas to separate the names of places in a sentence or in an address.

> The town of Fish Creek, Wisconsin, is popular among tourists.
>
> Milwaukee, WI 43035

Dialogue

In dialogue, use commas to separate a speaker's words from the speaker. The comma is placed *inside* the quotation marks if the speaker is named at the end of a sentence. If the speaker is named at the beginning of a sentence, the comma is placed outside the quotation marks at the speaker tag.

"We've got to have advertising," said Eddie.

Eddie said, "We've got to have advertising."

If the speaker tag is in the middle of a sentence, place a comma inside the first set of quotation marks and at the end of speaker tag (outside the second set of quotation marks).

"What we need," she said, "is to rent a plane."

Series

Use a comma to separate three or more words in a series. Place a comma after every word in the series except the last one. Always place the final comma before the conjunction that joins the last words in the series. A series may contain single words.

Eddie, Dink, and Elizabeth were a team.

A series may also contain longer elements, such as three or more phrases or clauses. Commas are placed after each phrase or clause in the series (except the last).

Eddie walked down to the corner, looked at the ruined poster, and shrugged.

Elizabeth walked down the block, around the corner, and up the next block.

Direct Address

Use a comma to set off the name of the person or persons being spoken to.

Judy, can you help me with this?

Never fear, **Sarah,** I won't let you down.

I promise this won't happen again, **Mrs. Lewis.**

Introductory Words

When the word *yes* or *no* begins a sentence, put a comma after the word.

Yes, I am going to the game this afternoon.

No, I am staying home tonight.

Interjections

When a sentence begins with an interjection that does not express a strong feeling or emotion, place a comma after the interjection.

Well, you didn't tell me he was your cousin.

Hey, let's go kick a soccer ball around.

Introductory Phrases

Put a comma at the end of a **prepositional phrase** that begins a sentence.

In the beginning, everyone got along just fine.

At the restaurant, no one felt very hungry.

When a **participial phrase** begins a sentence, place a comma after it.

Saddened by the news, Benjamin went to his room.

Hearing the crash of thunder, he sat straight up in his bed.

Introductory Clauses

If a sentence begins with a **dependent clause,** place a comma after the clause.

> **If anyone sees my cat,** please let me know.
>
> **Because he hoped to win,** the candidate toured for three weeks straight.
>
> **Although Marlin disliked salami,** he politely ate the sandwich.

Appositives

Most appositive phrases are set off by commas. If an appositive adds information that is not important to the sentence, it should be set off by commas.

> My great-great-uncle, **Samuel McFarland,** was a friend of Colonel Sherman's. (The appositive phrase adds information to the sentence.)

If an appositive *is* important to the sentence, it should *not* be set off by commas.

> Jansen borrowed things from his friend **Mick** all the time. (This appositive phrase identifies from which friend Jansen borrows.)

Compound Sentences

In a compound sentence, place a comma before the conjunction that joins the two clauses of the sentence.

> Phil called to his mom, **but** she had already left the room.
>
> Jessica was startled by the ringing phone, **and** she trembled as she picked it up.

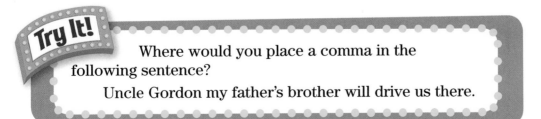

Try It!

Where would you place a comma in the following sentence?

Uncle Gordon my father's brother will drive us there.

Colons and Semicolons

Colons

Use a colon after the greeting in a business letter.

> Dear Sir or Madam:

Use a colon between the numerals that identify hours and minutes in an expression of time.

> 8:45
> If you get done before 4:30, call me.

Use a colon at the end of a complete sentence that introduces a series or a list of items.

> Our student council will focus on the following projects this year: **repair playground equipment, collect books for kids, and raise money for a mural in the cafeteria.**

Semicolons

A semicolon is used to join two clauses that have similar ideas. Use a semicolon in a compound sentence without a coordinating conjunction. Place the semicolon between two independent clauses in the sentence.

> Aaron is constantly eating; he insists he is constantly hungry.
>
> Ashley hated peas; it was their color that bothered her the most.

Try It!

Where would you place a colon or semicolon in the following words or sentences?

I am leaving today at 430.

The bus arrived at 830 it was late as usual.

Quotation Marks, Underlining, and Apostrophes

Quotation Marks

Use quotation marks to set off the exact words of a speaker. Place the end punctuation and commas inside the quotation marks.

> "Right," I answered. "Call me tonight."

> "What kind of animal is it?" Janet asked.

Place quotation marks around the titles of poems, short stories, newspaper and magazine articles, chapters in books, and songs.

> "The Grasshopper"   "The Scotty Who Knew Too Much"

Underlining

Underline if you are writing by hand, or use italics for titles of books, works of art, movies, television shows, or CDs.

> <u>Mrs. Frisby and the Rats of NIMH</u>   *Sarah, Plain and Tall.*

Apostrophes

In a **contraction,** an apostrophe takes the place of the missing letter or letters.

> we + are = we're.   he + had = he'd

To show possession, add an apostrophe + **s** to a singular noun or a plural noun that does not end in **s.**

> Mr. Assad**'s** store is closed.   The children**'s** clothes were new.

Add only an apostrophe after a plural noun that ends in **s.**

> The birds**'** calls woke me up before sunrise.

Parentheses and Hyphens

Parentheses

Use parentheses around words that add information to a sentence. If the parentheses are at the end of the sentence, the sentence's end punctuation falls outside the parentheses.

On the Arctic expedition, both men and dogs would eat pemmican (a mixture of powdered dried meat, dried berries, and fat).

If the words inside the parentheses are a complete sentence, end punctuation goes at the end of the sentence inside the parentheses.

My grandparents moved from North Carolina to New York. (Luckily, they moved before the Great Depression in the 1930s.)

Hyphens

If you have to break a word at the end of a line of writing, place a hyphen at the end of the first half of the word. Make sure that you divide the word only between syllables.

Use a hyphen in fractions that are spelled out.

The recipe calls for only **one-eighth** teaspoon of peppermint.

Hyphens are used to separate groups of numbers, such as in a telephone number.

315-555-0814

Use a hyphen in some compound nouns.

father-in-law   great-uncle   self-confidence

Try It!

Where would you place hyphens in the following sentences?

My great grandfather owns two thirds of the land in this county.

Capitalization

Sentences

Capitalize the first word in a sentence.

My hands shake a little as I set the kettle on to boil.

Proper Nouns

Use a capital letter for a proper noun, which names a particular person, place, or thing.

Rita   Atlanta   **Q**ueen **A**nne

Use a capital letter at the beginning of names of languages.

English   **H**indi   **S**panish

Capitalize the **names** of people and pets.

Megan   **M**arie   **C**omstock   **M**opsy

Capitalize family names when they are used as the person's name.

After **M**amma left, we all burst into giggles.
Whenever **G**rampa **R**ay came to visit, he cooked dinner for all of us.

Capitalize the titles that go along with people's names.

Governor Haywood

Dr. Leontis

Ms. Stevenson

Proper Adjectives

Because proper adjectives are formed from proper nouns, they must be capitalized too.

Italian	Mexican
Asian	Californian

Initials

Use capital letters for people's initials.

Pearl **S.** Buck   **R.** Collier-Morales   Reuben **L. J.** Slatkin

Acronyms

In an acronym, all letters should be capitalized.

NAFTA	AARP
EPA	NAACP

The Pronoun I

The pronoun *I* is always capitalized in a sentence.

Callie sees how **I** don't want to go.

Letters

In both friendly and business letters, capitalize the first word in the greeting of the letter. The title and name of the person being written to is also capitalized.

Dear Aunt Linda,
Dear Mr. Paxton:

In the closing of a friendly or business letter, capitalize only the first word.

Sincerely yours,
Best wishes,
Cordially,

Dialogue and Direct Quotations

Capitalize the first word of a line of dialogue or direct quotation that is a complete sentence.

"**C**ome on, Callie," I say, starting up the path.

If any words (such as speaker tags) interrupt the quotation, start the second half of the quotation with a capital letter if it follows a period and if it is a complete sentence.

"**M**ama?" I call. "**D**o you have the pansy I picked?"

If the second half of the quotation follows a comma, do not capitalize the first word after the second comma.

"**Y**es, I've got it," says Mama, "but I don't expect to need it this time."

Product Names

Use a capital letter at the beginning of names of specific products.

The **B**illy **V**eggie **B**urger at the diner is named for my uncle.

We buy **S**oftmaid tissues because we think they're softest.

Organization Names

Capitalize all important words in the names of organizations. Short words, such as *a, the, in, of,* and so on, are not capitalized unless they are the first word in the organization's name.

American **H**eart **A**ssociation

League of **W**omen **V**oters of the **U**nited **S**tates

American **F**ederation of **P**olice

United **A**uto **W**orkers

Both her parents work at **S**terling **S**oftware on Baxter Drive.

Special Events

Capitalize the names of special events.

At the 1994 **W**inter **O**lympics, Bonnie Blair won two gold medals.

Historical Periods

Capitalize the names of important historical periods.

Grandpa was born in the middle of the **G**reat **D**epression.
During the **S**tone **A**ge, humans made tools out of stone.

Months, Days, and Holidays

When you name months, days, and holidays, capitalize the first letter.

To a child, **D**ecember seemed a long, long time away.
Every **W**ednesday I floated into Miss Becky's studio for dance class.
The **L**abor **D**ay weekend was our last fling before school started.

Cities, States, and Countries

Capitalize the names of cities, states, and countries.

Did you know **L**os **A**ngeles, **C**alifornia, is the second largest city in the **U**nited **S**tates?
One city in **J**apan is nearly twice the size of **L**os **A**ngeles, however.

Geographical Areas

Capitalize the names of geographical areas.

Mt. Shasta lies in the **C**ascade **R**ange.

When you use the words *north, south, east,* and *west* as directions, they are *not* capitalized. When you use those words to refer to sections of the country, they *are* capitalized.

We turned **n**orth on Highway 5 and headed for home.
During the war, the **N**orth had an advantage over the **S**outh.

Titles

In general, capitalize the first word, the last word, and all other important words in a title. Articles, conjunctions and prepositions and other short words such as *a, and, the, it, of, for,* and *from* are not capitalized unless they are the first or last word of the title. Note that all verbs, even short ones such as *be* and *are,* are capitalized.

Capitalize the titles of written works.

Book	*The Story of Communications*
Magazine	*Kids for Saving Earth News*
Newspaper	*Milwaukee Journal*
Poem	"Surgeons Must Be Very Careful"
Important Documents	Mayflower Compact

Capitalize the titles of musical works.

Beethoven's **Piano Concerto** no. 5, or the *Emperor* **Concerto**
"**Wind Beneath My Wings**"

Capitalize the titles of works of art.

Painting: *Old Man Walking in a Rye Field,*
by Lauritz Andersen Ring
Sculpture: *Bird in Space,* by Constantin Brancusi

Capitalize the titles of visual and multimedia works, such as television programs, films, computer programs, and CD-ROMs.

Television Program	*Kratt's Creatures*
Film	*Prince of Egypt*
Computer program	*3D Home Planner*
CD-ROM	*The Way Things Work*

Writing Connection

Using capitalization correctly helps readers understand and correctly identify the proper names of people, places, and things in a piece of writing.

Glossary

A

abbreviation   the shortening of a word, such as St. for Street. Most abbreviations are followed by a period.

abstract nouns   words that name ideas, qualities, and feelings

acronym   the short form of several words, usually as in the name of an organization, such as NASA for National Aeronautics and Space Administration

adverb clause   a dependent clause that often modifies the verb in the main clause of a sentence

adverb   a word that describes a verb, adjective, or another adverb. An adverb tells how, when, where, or to what degree something happens.

alliteration   the repetition of a consonant sound at the beginning of words, such as *Jordan dreamed of a jiggling jellyfish.*

analogy   a comparison of two words based on how the two words are related.

antecedent   a word that a pronoun refers to

appositive   a noun that follows another noun to modify or rename it

appositive phrase   includes an appositive and the words that modify it

assonance   the repetition of a vowel sound in words

auxiliary verb   a helping verb that helps the main verb show action or express a state of being

B

bibliography   a list of research materials used and referred to in the preparation of an article or report

byline   the place where a reporter writes his or her name in a news story

C

caption   a sentence or phrase written under a picture or illustration that tells more about the picture or explains it

chronological order   time order, or putting events in the order in which they happened, starting with the earliest and ending with the most recent

clause   a group of words that has a subject and a verb

closed compound word   a compound word that has no space between the words, as in *popcorn*

common nouns   nouns that name any person, place, thing, or idea and start with a lower case letter

comparative form   the form of an adjective or adverb that compares two of something

complex sentence   a type of sentence that is made up of an independent clause and one or more dependent clauses

compound predicate   two or more simple predicates joined by a conjunction

compound sentence   two or more simple sentences joined by a conjunction

compound subject   two or more simple subjects joined by a conjunction

concrete nouns   words that name things you can see or touch

conjunction   a word that is used to join equal words or groups of words

context clues   words or sentences that surround an unknown word that give the reader clues about the meaning of the unknown word

conventions   the rules one follows when writing. These include spelling, grammar, punctuation, capitalization, and usage.

couplet   a type of poetry that has two lines that rhyme

D

declarative sentence   a type of sentence that makes a statement and ends with a period

definite article   the article *the* that identifies specific people, places, things, or ideas

demonstrative pronoun   points out something. *This, that, these,* and *those* are demonstrative pronouns when they take the place of a noun.

dependent clause   a group of words that contains a subject and verb but cannot stand alone as a sentence

diagram   an illustration with labels that shows how something works, or how to do something

dialogue journal   a type of journal in which two people write back and forth about a topic as if they were having a conversation

diamante   a diamond-shaped seven-line poem that has specific information in each line and an exact number of words

direct object   a noun or pronoun that receives the action of the verb

drafting   the stage, or phase, of the writing process in which a writer puts prewriting ideas on paper

E

editing/proofreading   the stage, or phase, of the writing process in which the writer checks spelling, usage, grammar, capitalization and punctuation

end rhyme   rhyming word at the end of two or more lines of poetry

expository writing   a form of writing that gives information or explains something, such as newspaper and magazine articles, textbooks, and biographies

F

fable   a tale that has a lesson or moral. Characters in a fable are often animals that talk and act like humans.

figurative language   words or groups of words that stand for more than their literal meaning, such as similes, metaphors, personification, or exaggeration

folktale   an old story that teaches a lesson about life. The characters in a folktale may be people or animals.

fragment   a group of words that is written as a sentence but is not one. It is missing a subject, a predicate, or both.

free verse   a type of poetry that doesn't follow any specific pattern of rhyme or rhythm

H

helping verb   a verb that helps the main verb express action or a state of being

homographs   words that are spelled the same but have different pronunciations

homonyms   two words that have the same spelling and same pronunciation but have different meanings

homophones   two or more words that sound the same but have different meanings and spellings

I

imperative sentence   a sentence that gives a command or makes a request and ends with a period or exclamation point

indefinite article   the articles *a* and *an* that refer to a general group of people, places, things, or ideas

independent clause   a group of words with a subject and predicate and that can stand alone as a sentence

intensive pronoun   a pronoun that ends with *-self* or *-selves* and is used to draw special attention to a noun or pronoun already mentioned

internal rhyme   words that rhyme in the middle of lines of poetry

interrogative pronoun   a pronoun that asks a question, such as *who* or *which*

interrogative sentence   a sentence that asks a question and ends with a question mark

irregular verb   a verb that does not follow the rule for adding *-ed* to form the past tense

L

lead   the first paragraph of a news story that answers the five Ws

learning log   a type of journal where you write about something you are studying

linking verb   a state-of-being verb that links the subject of the sentence with a word in the predicate

M

metaphor   a figure of speech that compares two unlike things without using the words *like* or *as*

meter   the rhythm of a poem

N

narrative writing   a form of writing that tells a story or gives an account of an event

O

object of the preposition   the noun or pronoun that ends a prepositional phrase

object pronoun   a pronoun used as a direct object or indirect object

onomatopoeia   a word that imitates or suggests the sound it describes, such as the *pitter-patter* of rain

open compound word   a compound word that has a space between the words, such as *sea horse*

P

participle   a verb form that acts as an adjective

participial phrase   includes a participle and other words that complete its meaning and always functions as an adjective

personification   a figure of speech in which an object or idea is given human qualities

persuasive report   a report that is written to change the thinking, feelings, or actions of the reader about a specific issue or to get the reader to recognize the writer's point of view

persuasive writing   a type of writing in which the writer tries to change the way readers think or feel about a topic

phrase   a group of words that does not contain subject and verb

plural   more than one

poetry   a type of writing in which the sound and meaning of words are combined to create ideas and feelings

possessive noun   a noun that shows ownership

predicate   the part of a sentence that tells what the subject is or does

predicate noun   a noun in the predicate that tells about the subject. It is linked to the subject by a linking verb.

prefix   one or more letters added to the beginning of a root or base word that changes the word's meaning

preposition   a word that shows position or direction

prepositional phrase   a phrase that begins with a preposition and ends with a noun or pronoun

prewriting   the stage, or phase, of the writing process in which you think about what you want to write. You write down ideas, collect information, decide upon audience and purpose, and organize your ideas.

proofreading marks   a set of marks used by writers and editors to show changes that should be made in a written work

proper adjective   an adjective made from a proper noun that always starts with a capital letter

proper nouns   nouns that name a specific person, place, thing, or idea and always start with a capital letter

publishing   the stage, or phase, of the writing process in which the writer makes a final copy of the piece of writing in his or her best handwriting, (or keyboards it on a computer), add charts, diagrams, or illustrations, and presents it to the chosen audience

R

reflexive pronoun   a pronoun that ends with *-self* or *-selves* and refers to the subject of the sentence

revising   the stage, or phase, of the writing process in which the writer changes the piece of writing to make it better

rhyming poetry   poetry that uses rhyming words at the ends of the lines

rhythm   the beat or pattern in a song or poem

S

sensory details   details that tell how something looks, sounds, smells, tastes, and feels

sentence fluency   a quality of writing in which the sentence flows smoothly

sequential order   the order in which events happen or the steps of a process are to be performed

simile   a figure of speech that compares two things that are not alike by using the word *like* or *as*

simple sentence   a sentence that has one subject and one predicate

singular   one

state-of-being verb a verb that does not show action but shows a condition or state of being

story map a type of graphic organizer that is used to outline the events of a story

subject the part of a sentence that tells who or what the sentence is about

subject-verb agreement when the verb agrees with the subject of the sentence. The subject and verb must agree in number: they must both be singular or plural.

subordinating conjunction word that introduces an adverb clause

subtopic a subdivision of the main topic of a piece of writing

suffix one or more letters added to the end of a root or base word that changes the word's meaning

superlative form the form of an adjective or adverb that compares three or more of something

supporting sentences the sentences in a paragraph that tell more about the paragraph's main idea

V

Venn diagram a type of graphic organizer used to compare and contrast two items

verb word that shows action or expresses a state of being

voice the tone or sound of your writing. The voice of a piece of writing changes as the audience changes.

W

web a type of graphic organizer that can be used to show how ideas are related

writing portfolio a type of folder or notebook in which a writer keeps pieces of writing

writing process a process to develop and improve writing. The stages, or phases, of the writing process are prewriting, drafting, revising, editing/proofreading, and publishing.

Index

The **index** is a list of words and page numbers. It lists the different things that are in the Handbook. The words are in alphabetical order. You look in the list for the word you want to find. Then you look at the page number of the Handbook where it can be found. The index is a good tool. Learn to use it. It can save you a lot of time.

M

main idea, 234–235
main topic, 239
mechanics, 394–411. See also,
    apostrophes, 405
    capitalization, 407–411
    colons, 404
    commas, 400–403
    exclamation points, 399
    hyphens, 406
    parentheses, 406
    periods, 396–398
    question marks, 399
    quotation marks, 405
    semicolons, 404
    underlining, 405
memorable moment, 300–301
metaphor, 223
modifiers, 360
mood, 12

N

narrative writing, 114–161, 378. See also,
    biography, 122–127
    fable, 144–149
    folktale, 138–143
    historical fiction, 134–137
    personal narrative, 116–121
    play, 156–161
    realistic fiction, 128–133
    tall tale, 150–155
news story, 106–109
nonfiction, 90–93, 96–97, 99
nonrhyming poetry, 198–199
note cards, 113, 232–233
notes (taking), 232–233
nouns, 165, 198, 348–349

O

object of preposition, 356–361
observation report, 170–173
observations, 219
onomatopoeia, 228
opinion, 94, 96, 176–177, 182–183, 185–187, 262
order of importance, 25, 27, 262
order of impression, 272–273
order words, 101, 268, 274, 276–277
organization, 11, 30–31, 34, 77, 88–89, 93, 98–99, 104–105, 109, 113, 121, 127, 133, 137, 143, 149, 161–169, 173, 181, 185, 197

P

paragraph, 27–29, 80, 374–381
paraphrase, 233
parentheses, 406
participle, 361
participial phrase, 361, 402
pattern poetry, 200–201
peer conferencing, 33
period, 373, 396–398
personal journal, 58
personal narrative, 116–121
personal writing, 56–77. See also,
    birthday cards, 65
    business letters, 72–77
    dialogue journal, 60
    e–mail, 67
    friendly letters, 68–71
    get–well cards, 65
    invitations, 62–63
    journals, 58–61
    learning log, 59
    literature response journal, 59
    notes and cards, 62–67
    personal journal, 58
    telephone messages, 66
    thank–you notes, 64
personification, 223–224
persuasive writing, 174–191, 262–265, 273, 381. See also,

▶ Photo Credits: